Always A Countryman

by

LORD TWEEDSMUIR

London
ROBERT HALE & COMPANY.
63 Old Brompton Road S.W.7

Printed in Great Britain by
Lowe & Brydone (Printers) Ltd., London

CONTENTS——

		Page
	Prologue	9
1	Elsfield	15
2	Growing Up	25
3	A Young Fisherman	37
4	Lowland Pleasure Ground	46
5	A Highland Memory	55
6	Adventures With the Salmon	62
7	Return to Tweedsmuir and Some Yorkshire Fishing	68
8	Shetland Journey	74
9	Learning to Shoot	81
10	The Magic of Otmoor	88
11	Deer Stalking	95
12	Island of Mull	101
13	Up to Oxford	110
14	Oxfordshire Fishing	117
15	Hawking	125
16	St. Kilda Sanctuary	135
17	To the Faeroes	143
18	Appointment in Africa	161
19	District Officer	173
20	On Safari	180
21	Bigger Game	192
22	Convalescence in Kenya	208
23	In Search of Health	213
24	The Canadian West	219
25	The Turn of the Maple Leaf	229
26	Winter Expedition	234
27	Logging Camp	246

5

		Page
28	Fur Trading Post	254
29	The Hudson's Bay Company	261
30	Baffin Land Winter	270
31	Northern Spring	283
32	Active Service	291
33	Mediterranean War	301
34	Year of Reckoning	306
	Epilogue	318

Illustrations

facing page

Elsfield in the eighteenth century   32

Elsfield in the nineteenth century   32

Elsfield in 1929   33

Elsfield in the 1950s   33

Jack Allam, with behind him the pond and Dr. Johnson's summer house   48

With Jezebel, 1934   48

The day of the six-pound trout. Aged nine   49

Fishing for salmon on the Dee. Thirty years later   128

Avocet, Texel Island   128

Whale hunt in the Faeroes   129

As deckhand on a Hull trawler   144

Fellow trawler-men   145

Altercation in Africa, over a goat   208

Dan and I in Africa, 1935   209

First crocodile, 1934   209

Typical Teso country with Mount Kamalinga in the background. Uganda, 1935   209

Sally, my cheetah   224

Rapids on the Grand Peribonca   225

Alastair and I in British Columbia. Summer, 1936   225

At Teapot Lake, Ontario. Winter, 1936–37   256

Montreal Lake post, Saskatchewan   256

A trapper trading his furs in a Hudson's Bay Company post   257 *facing page*

Montreal Lake post. *Left to right*—Myself, Phil Hughes,
    Cecil Lockhart-Smith   257

Chesley Russell and myself, 1938   272

Our schooner   272

Hudson's Bay Company post, Cape Dorset, Baffinland   273

Our dog-team resting, while a snow-house is built   273

Eskimo encampment   273

Prologue

THIS book will not teach anybody anything new about sport, or nature, or travel. But these things are its theme. It is a record of the enjoyment of them all. If any of this enjoyment is imparted to a reader who has had the wish, but has lacked the chance, to do the same things, it will have been well worth the writing.

It is the sporting record of an indifferent shot and a very incomplete angler. It is a catalogue of travels which, though they could be called pioneering, never achieved the dignity of exploration.

In Britain we are a nation of countrymen. We are probably countrymen in a more real sense than the people of any other nation: though the French come near us in this. For, in most other countries, if a man becomes prosperous he moves into the city: in Britain he moves into the country. It is no inconsiderable part of the strength of the British people that they love sport and the countryside. The true countryman is perfectly happy to be by himself, and to think his own thoughts. Dictators are fully alive to this. They herd their citizens into nauseating community activities. It is too dangerous to let their people have their own thoughts to themselves.

In less than a century Britain has changed from a country where the majority made their living from the land, to a highly industrial nation, where by far the greatest number of its inhabitants live in the towns. But if the homes of its citizens be in the towns their hearts are in the land. For how many a city dweller, his hands stained by a day's work at the mill or the bench, or smudged with carbon paper or ink at the office desk, will delve till darkness in his garden for the love of feeling honest earth. On Saturdays and Sundays and holidays, in due season, men move in their millions to the countryside. The vast brotherhood of fishermen is made up of all sorts and conditions of men. The man with the rod, whether he be beside the canal, the chalk stream or the salmon pool is

9

the brother of every other man with a rod. They feel the same joys and suffer the same sorrows. How foolish are those who think that fox hunting is only the sport of the wealthy. Look at the Boxing Day meet of most packs of hounds. You will find that the vast proportion of those who follow the hunt do so on foot or wheeling bicycles. From the factory bench or the desk, they have looked forward for months to their day's hunting, and enjoy it every bit as much as a man on horseback. Love of sport and the countryside is a far more enduring bond between men than any political ideology can hope to weave around them.

If the way of life of the countryman is ingrained in you, whatever your immediate environment, it will always rule you. When I see a flight of mallard coming up the London river, slanting athwart a wintry wind close to the windows of the Palace of Westminster, no other preoccupation can hold my mind until they have passed. Multitudes beside myself will pause to listen to the murmuration of starlings in Trafalgar Square, as night falls, which can be heard above the noise of the busiest traffic, or watch for the blossom to come to the London parks when there is hardly a bud in all the land.

Fondness for sport and wild life and the things of the countryside can give you a lifetime of happiness in the environment in which you were born. But it may lead to a longing for a wilder life, amidst wilder men and wilder beasts in wilder countries. And so it was in my case, as it had been in the case of my father. For the Scots are naturally a far wandering folk, and Buchan is an occupational name: it is of the same derivation as the word buccaneer. Though men as huge as mice may extol the virtues of a life of drab and graceless uniformity, shorn alike of risks and rewards, nothing can alter the fact that we are ever a nation of adventurers.

My father had an ideally happy life. He had seen much of the world and much of adventure. Few men have been happier, because he could find happiness in small things. Those who do not value small things are unlikely ever to be happy. He was an adept sportsman and could take up rod or rifle, for a few weeks in the year, and use them as if they had never been out of his hands, because he knew the whole science of their use. He was a first-class field naturalist though he probably did not know the Latin name of any bird or any flower. He always deplored the way that naturalists and sportsmen would bicker and fight over their conflicting theories, because birds and beasts and flowers are things of pleasure, and sport ceases to be fun if you get angry about it.

This book is a record of a wonderfully happy childhood in a changing Britain; of a sojourn in an Africa which has changed almost out of recognition in the decade and a half which has elapsed since I left it. It is a record of that which is changeless, in the magical wilderness of Canada, and of the far north in the days when the Eskimo had seen only a handful of white men and never an aeroplane.

It is not customary for a man to recollect his past on paper unti he reaches the evening of his life. This book covers a life exactly half of the Bible's allotted span of years, but there is surely nothing wrong in looking back when you still have reason to look forward, in the pause between the end of one innings and the beginning of the next.

There is, in these days, much talk of unearned or undeserved privilege. The greatest possible privilege, that a young man can enjoy, is to have a really understanding father. Because I possessed this privilege, in the fullest measure, I was able to enjoy these happy, rambling years of youth which I have ventured to describe in these pages.

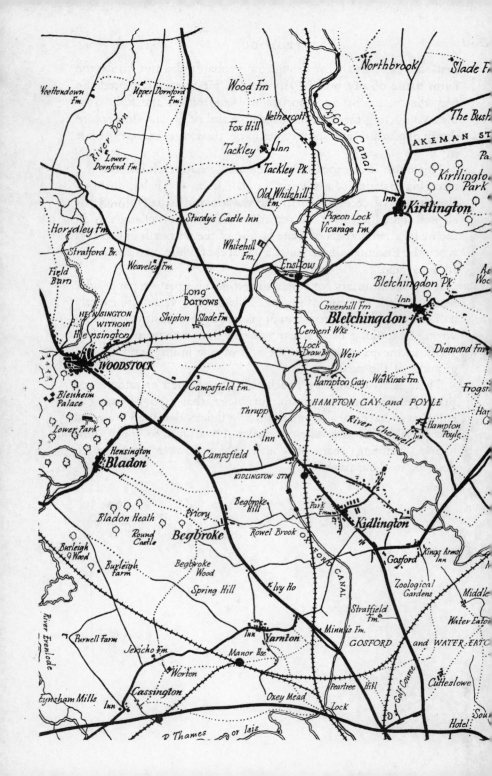

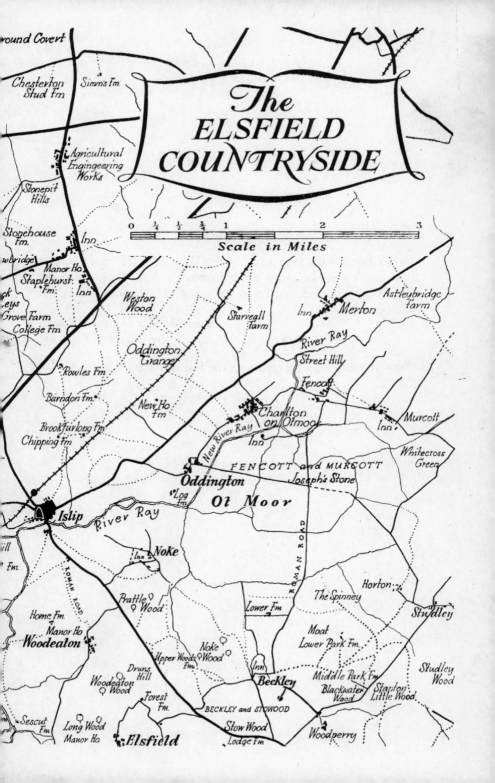

DEDICATION

"Beyond the Wild Wood comes the Wide World," said the Rat, "And that's something that doesn't matter, either to you or to me. I've never been there, and I'm never going, nor you either, if you've got any sense at all."

From *The Wind in the Willows*
by KENNETH GRAHAM.

To all those who disagree with the Rat this book is dedicated.

I

Elsfield

SPORT, my father was wont to say, is not a pastime but a way of life. Into this way of life we grew when we came to Elsfield, from London, just after the 1914 war was over. The eldest of us, my sister Alice, was eleven; I was seven, and my brother Billy was three. Alastair was a baby.

To Alice and myself London was a vague memory, but to Billy and Alastair life began at Elsfield. My father's family lived in Scotland, in the house in Peebles which my great-great-grand-father had been the first John Buchan to occupy. My grandfather, a Presbyterian minister, died the week before I was born. One of my father's brothers, Willie, had died young at the beginning of what had promised to be an extremely distinguished career in the Indian Civil Service. Another brother, Alastair, had fallen at Arras in 1917. Alice and I remember him as a slim, laughing figure in khaki, who had nursery tea with us in our house in Portland Place on his leave from France. Walter, the only sur-viving brother, was a lawyer and banker in Peebles. He kept house with his sister Anna, who was then launching on a success-ful career as a writer under the name of O. Douglas. Last, but by no means least of that household, was their mother. Each year in April they came to visit us at Elsfield. Each summer in August we spent our holidays with them at Broughton, twenty odd miles from Peebles, and some five miles from where Biggar Water joins the Tweed at the foot of Tweedsmuir.

My mother's father, Norman Grosvenor, had died many years earlier, but her mother lived in London and she too visited us regularly in the summer.

Such was the extent of our immediate family. The April visit of my Scots kin was a great event. It was more predictable than the coming of the swallows, or even of the May fly, for it occurred

between precisely the same dates each year. My father and my
Uncle Walter would take long striding walks together. My
grandmother and my Aunt Anna would be led by us to peer into
such nests that we had found in the garden as could be inspected
without climbing.

My father's mother was tiny in size and massive in determination. She had been engaged to my grandfather at sixteen. Her
beliefs were inflexible, her energy unbounded, but her kindness
was very real. I wish I had known my grandfather. He was a
scholar as well as a clergyman, and a man of infinite tolerance
and humour. He was only once known to use bad language, and
that was against the Government, when the relieving force failed
to reach Khartoum and General Gordon was slain. I inherited
from him the finest greenheart trout rod that I have ever seen.
The sporting tradition of this side of the family was one of
fishing and, for generations, each of the men of the family had
been noted catchers of trout. My Aunt Anna had fished hard
in her youth, and had been a skilful rock climber almost a
generation before that sport was invaded by her sex.

My Grandmother Grosvenor was tall and erect, in sharp con-
tradistinction to the Buchans, who were short. At Elsfield she
undertook long walks at a slow measured pace, and spent much
time painting, when it was warm enough to sit outside. She had
been brought up in the atmosphere of sport, and was a valued
companion. Her brother, Archie Stuart-Wortley, had been the
finest partridge shot in England, perhaps the finest that ever will
be. She loved the company of children, and whatever she was
doing was always glad to see us.

My mother had no brother. Her only sister and her husband
settled down in Buckinghamshire to farm, at the same time as we
came to Elsfield, and we visited them several times in a year.

My father had sold his house in London because he had decided
upon a country life. He had bought the Manor of Elsfield, which
lies five miles north of Oxford. Many changes have come to the
face of this countryside, in the course of the slightly more than
thirty years that my family has spent there. In those days the
country roads were still unmetalled. Farm labourers earned
between twenty-five shillings and thirty shillings a week. Pony

traps were still the common equipage of the farmer, who kept a saddle-horse as well to ride round his fields and follow the hounds on an occasional Saturday.

Those were hard days for the farmer, after the short-lived boom of the war years. But there were men alive then whose recollection went back to the days when the farming community rested on a balanced and sure foundation. There were those who remembered the years before the Black Harvest of 1879, and the gradual decline of British agriculture that followed it. Some of the old men still wore beards and sidewhiskers, for they saw no good reason for departing from the ways of their fathers. Our gamekeeper's father, a sturdy, erect figure for all his eighty years, had a long white beard.

Our old gardener, Tom Basson, owned, and occasionally wore, a beaver hat. Born in 1840, he could recollect as a small boy listening to the conversation of the village elders who could recall the England of the eighteenth century. He had hearkened to men who related their own personal reminiscences of Haynes and many other highwaymen, no doubt suitably embellished for his benefit. Another old man, his exact contemporary, worked in his allotment, when the weather was mild, wearing a smock.

That was only thirty years ago, but these men, and their way of life, seem as remote from the present day as Jethro Tull and his England. They seem almost of the vintage of the yeomen and the verderers grouped on the faded paper of old sporting prints. The change is not as deep as it appears. The present-day clothes may be different, but the man who drops his spade and perches precariously on the top of a stile to get a glimpse of the hounds running, is the same typical English yeoman. " 'Tain't no good, I can't do no work when 'ounds be running," said one to me in all sincerity.

The village of Elsfield straggles for nearly a mile. The manor opens straight on to the village street, which is not unusual in that part of the world. The village lies on high ground looking over the valley of the Cherwell towards the huddle of the Cotswold hills. It is not on the top of the upland, but sufficiently far below for the line of high ground to be seen above it, when you look up from the flat fields below. It commands a view of nearly forty miles on a clear day, when the hump of Cleeve Hill, above Cheltenham, shows as a dim outline. It is a view of which Dr. Johnson was very fond. No great walker, he would yet cover the five miles from Oxford on foot, to spend a day at the manor with his friend, Francis Wise. The tall stand of elms and beeches where the rooks nest, were seedlings then. The summer house in the garden, built like a Greek temple, beside the stone coping of the little pond, was his favourite resting place.

At the top of the village, above Woodeaton Wood, a great oak tree reaches its branches across the road. It must have seen five centuries of Oxford scholars, variously garbed, taking their Sunday walk in the country. It stands, slowly dying, one of the last survivors of the days when the Forest of Stow covered a huge tract of the countryside.

The road winds on along the upland edge towards Beckley till it meets the old coach road, at the crossing between Fox Cover and Stow Wood. The well there, mentioned in Domesday Book, never dries up even in the hottest summers. A few yards away stands a single elm tree, lacking its top. It still possesses an indefinable air of purpose. Ten years ago, when it was a tall tree, a loop of rusted chain swayed and creaked from the lowest branch. From it had hung the body of Haynes, the last highwayman in these parts. His final foray had been the hold-up of the Oxford coach where the road runs beside Stow Wood. He had ridden from the shelter of the oaks into the roadway and shot the driver dead. He was taken soon after. I remember an old man at Horton-cum-Studley, who occasionally came out beating when I shot there as a small boy. That old man was the grandson of the murdered stage-coach driver.

This old coach road has a Roman foundation, and a mile away, hidden among the brambles and hawthorns, there is a culvert of stone blocks that has stood for many centuries, and is believed to be the work of Roman hands.

Beyond the crossroads the Beckley road winds along the edge of Stow Wood, up a steep hill. At the top of the hill the ground falls steeply, and the traveller then beholds one of the most perfect views in all southern England. It is a great sweep of horizon untarnished by the crude works of economic man. From here you look down over the great marshy saucer of Otmoor, ringed by its seven towns, as its seven surrounding villages are called.

The peoples of these villages have been long on the soil. Thus it is the more remarkable that, at Elsfield, the parish records of a hundred years ago show only one name that can be found in the village to-day. But in the seven towns of Otmoor men change their habitat less frequently. In Islip there are several yeomen families who have lived beside the River Ray for many centuries. The Beckley family of Islip made a modest entry into seventeenth-century history. Mr. Beckley ferried Cromwell across the River Cherwell before the battle of Oxford, and received a grant of the fishing rights from him that survives to this day.

In the village of Beckley nearly every man of middle-age has a Biblical Christian name; Josiah, Amos, Jesse, Esau, even Shadrach. The ancient Oxford surnames are still to be found in the seven towns; Drinkwater, Beckley, Womersley, Gomm, Collet, Sumner and many others.

There can be no country as diverse as England. Within a day's travel on foot, the countryside and the people can change out of recognition. The aspect of the countryside differs, but its heart remains the same.

We owned less than 100 acres of land, but, for the first few years after we came to Elsfield, my father leased the shooting over another 400.

We did not rear any birds, but often had a fair stock of wild ones. Hares were much more common in those days, and certain winters brought in a good number of woodcock. We shot three or four times over in the season, with a great deal of strolling round with the keeper and his dog in between times.

My father was a keen and expert deer stalker, and a magnificent fisherman. But he was never really keen with the shotgun; after a few years he gave it up altogether, and relinquished the shoot to a syndicate of farmers. But such was the enthusiasm that he put into everything that he did, that the paucity of the bag was no index to the excitement of the day. Lord Edward Gleichen came out one day, with a loader carrying his second gun and hung round with bags containing hundreds of spare cartridges. The total pheasant population of the shoot was about forty, in that particular year.

But such was my father's enthusiasm that our visitor plainly enjoyed his day, and was as excited as we were about the only three pheasants that came over him. My father's real love was for the environment of the chase, and the particular form of contact into which it brought him with Nature. You see the countryside in the finest detail when you see it with the eyes of a hunter. But the actual shooting never really satisfied him, and after a time ceased to amuse him, for he regarded a cover shoot as a test of hand and eye, like billiards, where you had nothing of the excitement of outwitting your quarry.

As for walking round with a gun under the arm, to me one of the pleasantest forms of shooting, he found that he got as much pleasure from carrying only a walking stick. As far as Oxfordshire fishing went, he was not tempted to cast a dry fly for the big chub that lie under the overhanging willows of the Cherwell. It was very rarely that he made an expedition to the Cotswold trout streams; he would rather reflect deliciously on an August in Scotland where he would be fishing steadily for six days in the week.

He was a slim and wiry figure, always in tweeds or riding breeches. On his walks he carried a shepherd's crook and strode like a Border shepherd, stiff-legged from the hips. Most pictures of him make him look dour and solemn. His photographs give him a look of frozen gloom, a travesty of his good-humoured self. When he was working, his brow was furrowed with concentration, but out of doors he sniffed the air like a hound, and his face was that of a happy boy. His concentration on his work was complete, but never gloomy. It was the concentration of the pointer whose senses tell him of the proximity of a covey, and tense and excited he seeks to discover their exact position.

He had a simple, sensible régime of life. We had breakfast at half past eight in the morning, with short family prayers. He began work at nine and worked steadily and purposefully until one o'clock. In all his life he never worked in the afternoon, or after dinner, but he worked between tea and dinner which gave him a total of six vigorous working hours in every day, during which he steadily demolished each of the tasks that he had set himself. The afternoon was devoted to the open air, on foot or on horseback, and after dinner he read either to himself or aloud to us, or else we would talk or play games until, one by one, our bedtimes came round.

Let no one say that walking is not a sport in its own right. No one would presumably deny the title of sportsman to those vigorous young people, clad in hob-nail boots and with huge packs upon their backs, who match themselves against the Grampians or the Welsh Mountains every summer. It is equally a degree of the same sport to plan, as he did, a different walk for every afternoon, with a keen eye for the whole pattern of Nature, never following quite the same path each time.

You can cover quite a lot of country in more than two hours walking with a steady stride, with which we found it so difficult to keep up when we were children. It was a respite to our short legs when he would stop to chat with a ploughman turning his horses at the end of a long furrow, or to look at the view from the upland across that great sweep of England, or follow the flight of some distant bird. He made up many of the plots for his books on these afternoons, and would often tell them to us as they gradually unwound themselves in his mind. But whatever creation he may have been at work on, he had an eye for his surroundings as keen as any Canadian backwoodsman. Thus there was always something to report when we sat down to tea beside the fire at home.

In the great marshy saucer of Otmoor my father once saw a hoopoe; while a white stork and Manchurian cranes were seen there by several. On more than one occasion a golden oriole was seen in the woods, and that great rarity, the lizard orchis was discovered by the famous Oxford botanist, Sir Claridge Druce. We counted eighty-two different varieties of birds at various times. So our walks did not lack excitement. But, if that may seem tame, let me say that it was exciting enough to a man who had been one of the finest rock climbers of his time, and had survived five shots from General Smuts' own rifle. He loved walking, and in his youth had been famous for his feats of endurance. He once walked from Cambridge to Oxford as an undergraduate, and in the Galloway Hills covered round about eighty miles without sleeping. When I was myself an Oxford

undergraduate I once walked, for a bet, from Magdalen Bridge
at Oxford to the middle of London, in the course of a night. It
gave me some inkling of just what a walker my father must have
been. But that would have been very small beer to my father,
when he was at the height of his powers. General Smuts' lifelong
pleasure was walking, in the very different surroundings of the
Drakensberg. Together with fishing, it forms the ideal relaxation
for the thinker.

A countryside need not lack adventure merely because you
know every inch of it; its variety is immense. For here was a
wood full of badgers and there another, in a deep ravine from
which gnarled oaks reached skywards, which once had been a
lake and a king of England's duck decoy. In one field, above
Woodeaton, ploughmen still turn up Roman pottery when they
lay the furrows each year. A mile away stands a tiny spinney on a
green sugar loaf hill. Where the spinney stands was once a Roman
factory for the manufacture of the brooches that held the toga in
position.

My mother had grown up in the atmosphere of sport. She did
not care for shooting but most unselfishly accompanied me into
the woods on many an occasion, when I was too young to be
allowed out shooting without a chaperone. As a fishing companion she was a heroine, and forewent many a tea and caught
many a chill rather than cut my pleasure short. Her outlook on
the countryside has always been a blend of the appreciation of the
artist for the scene as a whole, and the intimate observation of a
lover of nature.

As a companion in the countryside, by wood in winter and
stream in summer, she has taught me much that I value of its
appreciation.

In his later life my father never followed the hounds, but he
kept an old hunter called Alan Breck, and we had sundry small
ponies. Until he became a Member of Parliament he rarely slept a
night in London, but would travel up and down from Oxford
in a day. He never wrote in the train, as many people believed
that he did, but the travelling time passed quickly as he lost himself in reading. On fine mornings he used to ride before breakfast.
His punctuality was precise and the sound of Alan Breck's hoofs

coming down the village street, and turning into the yard, meant that there was five minutes to go before breakfast.

Alan Breck had seen service in the 1914 war and was by no means in the first flower of his youth. He crossed his legs in a canter when my father was riding him on the upland, one blowy afternoon, and threw him on his head. Of the two, the horse was by far the more shaken and picked himself up and trotted back to his stable with the reins trailing, where he encountered a group of villagers who were attending the obsequies of a pig. The spirit of the pig had already departed to the shades and, as one man, the villagers proceeded to back-track the hoof prints, in search of my father.

He was unhurt, because his head was almost impervious to blows, and he had survived at the age of nine a carriage wheel going over his skull. He was negotiating a hedge, covered with mud from his gaiters to his face, when he found himself surrounded by a gathering of countrymen, variously armed, led by a stalwart stranger, grasping a long knife dripping with blood, who was the slayer of the pig. For a moment he was tempted to imagine that the Jacquerie had risen. My father died in Canada in the early February of 1940. Alan Breck survived him by a matter of days. He died a week later in his stable at Elsfield.

The length and the pace of those walks were not varied by the seasons or by the weather. They always started in the same way, with our wire-haired terrier pirouetting in paroxysms of excitement in the hall, while we decided just where we should go. Sometimes it was a stride in a sodden mackintosh, head down against the squalls of rain; sometimes the nails of our boots ground on earth hardened to iron by the glistening frost of an orange winter sunset. In summer there were sweltering walks amidst lush grass up to a small boy's waist, drugged with the scent of deep summer and dripping with exertion. Teatime was the great meal of the day. At breakfast, when the newspapers had come, you knew what was afoot in the world. By teatime you knew, what seemed vastly more important, what was afoot in the countryside.

One of the most distinctive characteristics of the Scot is his ability to get his roots down in other parts of the world, however foreign to his native land. As a young man at Oxford my father had been used to rising early, in the summer time, and bicycling out into the country. He had always stopped his bicycle on the road to Woodeaton, where the little Bayswater brook goes bubbling under its miniature bridge, and looked up a slowly rising slope of that upland to Elsfield and its surrounding huddle of roofs, and the line of high ground above it. It had taken a powerful hold on his imagination, and then it became part and parcel of a golden recollection of his Oxford life, in the last days of the last century. Now it had become his home and he could savour it as one who belonged there, with August every year in Scotland to take seisin once again of the land of his birth.

2

Growing Up

WHEN we came to Elsfield, we took over one or two employees who had been at the manor with our predecessors. One of them, Jack Allam, survives to this day. His gnarled, kindly, even beautiful face is little changed, and in his presence there is ever the homely whiff of country clothes and strong tobacco.

All his life he has been a gamekeeper. He came to this part of Oxfordshire to replace an under-keeper on the next-door estate, who had left for the South African War. He looks little different to-day from my boyhood recollection of him, in the days when the lives of my sister and my brothers revolved round him to such an extent. Though well into his seventies he is still a good shot, a noted fisherman, and a first-class field naturalist—a countryman with the habit of life of a simpler, sturdier England; above all a kindly man who has always rejoiced with us in our triumphs, and sorrowed with us in our distress.

In the course of more than thirty years there has been little change in his purposeful, shambling gait, or the angle of the gun in the crook of his left arm, both hammers cocked. In that span of years there has always been a dog at his heels and several generations of their kind have served him and loved him. He will always be to me an embodiment of the land that bred him. A land of oak and ash and thorn, of slow running rivers, slow speech and high human quality. A lover of children, he has always been denied them. His well-loved stepson Frank lost his life in the Second World War, so he has given his heart to all children, and they to him.

His other love is dogs. His first dog was a clumber spaniel. He was a first-class gun dog, but he had other talents; in the late spring he would go with his master on his walks and was adept at finding the nests of pheasant and partridge, bringing an egg in his mouth to show what he had found.

One night Jack was out for a stroll, stick in hand, puffing at his pipe, and Gyp was ranging round him in the gloaming. A man with a gun and a grievance saw the dog, but not his master, and wantonly shot him. It was providential that Jack had not his own gun with him, or he might well have shot his beloved dog's assassin. But Gyp did not die. Though badly wounded, he re-covered, and accompanied Jack for several years to come, albeit somewhat wheezy from a pellet in the lungs. After that it was black dogs up to the present day. Now it is a strange, whiskered black clown, half cocker and half wire-haired terrier.

Jack's cottage is a long low one with a high-pitched roof of thatch. Some years ago my father had the ivy taken off one of the walls, as it was threatening to damage the stone work. When the ivy was removed there was revealed a plaque with the date 1702 cut on a plaster medallion. Within the little living-room, which is also the kitchen, a fire burns briskly all the year round, heating it in summer to the likeness of a furnace. Almost every square inch of wall is covered by a picture or a photograph. There is a ticking clock and a row of tea caddies on the mantelpiece. In the corner leans his gun, and on the window-sill stand his cartridges, in lines, like soldiers. Beside the hearth his dog slumbers. He used his original hammer gun until it was worn to the thickness of brown paper, and even he came to regard it as unsafe. I replaced it by another hammer gun, of Belgian make, that I got from an Italian partisan outside Ravenna.

Jack has always been thought to be illiterate but, to use his own words, "he can read reading but he can't read writing". This cryptic definition means that he can read the printed word if he takes plenty of time to it, but not handwriting. He has retained in his speech certain words and expressions that have long dropped from the language of all but a few Oxfordshire countrymen. One is the Saxon word "gor", meaning a carrion crow, others are "jaypie" as a companion to magpie, the word "tiggle" meaning to move along slowly and quietly, and the word "puggle" to describe the action of prodding down a squirrel's dray with a long pole. Sometimes his speech is merely expressive without relation to language. Once, when we were shooting in Noke Wood, a rabbit eluded Jack by dodging into a pile of brushwood. "He dobbed into a chump" was his comment.

Almost all that we learnt about birds and beasts, as children, we learnt from him; and not a little of my father's knowledge of natural history came from the same source. We would quarter the hedges in his company. It was Jack who taught us the real art of finding birds' nests. We used to have a glorious nesting expedition to Noke Wood every spring. Grouped round the bottom of a tall oak tree we would watch Jack climb to a magpie's or a carrion crow's nest, moving up the trunk by the pressure of his strong knees and elbows.

Many and strange were the fragments of incidental knowledge that we collected from Jack; such as how to flush an owl from its nest in a hollow tree, not by beating the foot of the tree with a stick but by rubbing the stick on the bark; and how to attract jays and magpies within shot by simulating the screams of a rabbit in the grip of a weasel, which draws these inquisitive birds.

Many of his beliefs are not susceptible of absolute proof, but they are part of the lore of his kind and have come down to him from an earlier England, and I have always believed them. He has always asserted that a pheasant flushed from its roost on a moonlight night will fly a tremendous distance, and probably never return to its original wood. With all his immense experience of shooting he has always harboured the belief that if you saw a long line of birds perched along the ridge of a haystack, and took aim at the left-hand bird and, on pulling the trigger, drew your gun sharply down the line, from left to right, you would bag them all. It was under his tuition that I learnt to shoot.

His beliefs on other subjects outside his immediate sphere are somewhat strange. In spite of over a century of peace between Britain and France he has never lost the belief, which he inherited from his forebears, that if the world is threatened with war, the French are at the bottom of it. His mental picture of France, on which he has often dilated, is of a country peopled by a swarthy race with short, pointed beards, subsisting largely on frogs.

The Elsfield of our childhood was a completely self-contained village. The disintegrating pull of a big city, only five miles away, had not begun to make itself felt. There was then no bus service to Oxford, and goods were ordered by the Beckley carrier as he passed through Elsfield, on alternate days, on his way to the city, his old horse nodding at a foot pace. He delivered the goods on his return journeys in the late afternoon. The village had a small shop which stocked most immediate necessities such as tobacco and matches, and odds and ends of household requirements. The smithy, with its cheerful clangour, could be heard half a mile away, when the wind was in the right direction.

Jack's brother ran the carpenter's shop which was part of the manor out-buildings. We used to watch him, for he was a clever carpenter, marvelling as his plane smoothed the rough plank, and the shavings curled up like serpents. The village ran a football team and a cricket team, and even on occasions fielded a boys' cricket team as well. The proximity of the great city then brought little influence to bear on the lives of the little community.

Gradually, over the years, Oxford has exerted a greater and greater power on the surrounding villages. There has been no village shop for many years. The carrier went out of business when the multiple stores delivered goods in motor vans to the country folk round about. Jack's brother has long been in his grave, and there is now no village carpenter. The smithy is deserted and there are nettles up to its windows. To-day the young men of Elsfield hie themselves to Oxford for their diversions on a Saturday afternoon. Many a coffin has bumped down the narrow stairways of these cottages since we came to Elsfield, and the young have forgotten many of the ways of their fathers.

In the long period of boyhood, which is spent in being educated, one sees one's home in three seasons of the year. Home wears three aspects—winter and Christmas-time, Easter and the spring, and, last of all, summer.

I was sent to a preparatory school in Oxford in the year 1921, whither my brothers followed me in due course. But they were then in the nursery, and Alice, who never went to school, had a governess. I was a weekly boarder and came back to Elsfield for week-ends, in time for lunch on Saturdays, leaving early on Monday morning.

Although we possessed an early phase of the motor car at that time, my journeys were frequently in a pony trap behind a fat piebald pony driven by Jack. It could be bitterly cold at a quarter past eight on a frosty Monday morning, and a week seemed an awfully long time to wait before I saw home again.

One Saturday, when we were returning, Jack was leading the pony up Elsfield hill, and I was walking beside the trap. Quite suddenly the pony halted firmly, reared up and backed violently twenty yards downhill, towing Jack as it went. This was so unlike its normal, well-fed lethargy that we stared at this creature wondering whether it had gone mad. A moment later, with a slow and awful grace, the limb of a tall elm tree beside the road bent, with the movement of a man executing a bow, and crashed across the road where the pony had been.

That summer of 1921 saw the worst drought that anyone remembered. The lawn at the manor turned to the colour of the Montana prairie. Great cracks opened in the soil of the fields; these took a heavy toll of the baby partridges, scuttling in procession behind their mothers. The long yew hedge on one side of the lawn at the manor, planted that year, died almost to a tree. My father re-planted it the following year, and it is now so large and looks so venerable as to seem of the generation of the great trunks that go back to Dr. Johnson's day.

A small boy's life is an endless adventure, and never does time hang heavily upon his hands. One of the tragedies of being grown up is that one never has anything which is quite so precious as the first day of the holidays—that wonderful, frenzied day of continual rush, in seeing everyone and everything again. When everybody in the house had been seen, there was a rush to Jack's cottage to tell him everything, and ask a myriad of questions while his dog wagged, and he beamed, a welcome.

One of the first things that my eyes sought were the tall trees. In winter they soared bare and gaunt, but graceful. Sometimes in the evening the rooks would congregate in one tree, all facing the same way and perched close together as if the tree was carrying a rich crop of black fruit. That was a sign it was going to be a cold night, so Jack said.

We used to long for snow at Christmas but I do not remember that we ever had it. We had our measure of it at other times, however, and we would then build a table on the lawn outside the dining-room windows, and heap it with food for the birds.

Hungry, piratical jackdaws, their consciences too loaded with guilt to approach the windows, would lurk a little way off and pounce on a chaffinch or blackbird which was carrying a piece of bread away in his bill, and force him to drop it.

We had a myriad ploys of childhood. One of them was making bonfires in the crow wood. The fingered leaves of five tall and ancient chestnut trees bestrewed the ground, and these made a capital fire when they were dry.

I once asked my father if he could give me something with which to start a bonfire. He was writing busily at the time at his desk and must, on that occasion, have treated my question absent-mindedly, for he handed me a sheaf of papers, inches thick, written in his hand-writing. It made a splendid bonfire and the few scraps of paper that escaped the burning, blew about the crow wood.

The following spring I was climbing to a jackdaw's nest with Jack and found, among the many odds and ends with which jackdaws like to line their nests, some of these same scraps of paper. That bird had a better sense of values than I. It was the manuscript of my father's history of the First World War. No less than a million hand-written words in length.

There was the supreme climax of Christmas Eve and Christmas Day. On Christmas Eve, according to family custom, my brother Billy and I went round the length of the village and to the outlying cottages, with a donkey harnessed to a cart containing a Christmas pudding for every family. We always went for a long walk on Christmas afternoon to offset our Christmas dinner, to say nothing of the pink sugar pigs in our stockings, and other delicacies of that day.

My brothers never cared much for shooting, although they enjoyed being part of a shooting expedition. Riding shaggy little ponies was more to their taste, and they enjoyed fishing in Scotland in the summer. Alice was a fearless rider and rode with my father regularly, until her horse bolted on the road one day and by a miracle escaped colliding with a lorry; she never really regained her enjoyment of it again.

When Alastair reached the age of twelve he rode regularly with my father, his shaggy black pony pounding in the wake of Alan Breck's long stride. After much parental discussion he was allowed to attend a meet of the South Oxfordshire hounds alone. He came trotting back down the village street that evening, blooded, and with the brush. There was great rejoicing.

Many a winter afternoon and evening we spent in the woods, with Jack. One December afternoon, when I was ten, I shot a hen pheasant and threw open the door of the library, gun in one hand and pheasant in the other. My father was talking to a small man who was sitting beside him on a sofa. I held up the pheasant. My father acclaimed the achievement, bade me get ready for tea, and take the pheasant to the cook. He introduced me to the visitor with whom I shook hands, and who made some courteous comment on the pheasant. The face of the visitor was something I have never forgotten. It was the face of a man who has made and unmade kings.

With the pheasant in the hands of the cook, my face clean, my hands washed, and my hair brushed, I presented myself for tea. The visitor had gone. My father asked me every detail of the afternoon. Then I asked about the visitor.

"Remember that man, that was Lawrence of Arabia," my father said.

Years later I learned that the Arabs used to call him the "Man with a wolf's eyes". I understood why.

How pleasant was teatime, with the events of the day to talk over, for a small boy's day does not go on for very long after tea. In winter the shutters were drawn and we had tea beside the fire and the flames danced in reflection on the tea cups. In summer the muslin curtains were drawn against the glare of the westering sun. The rooks amidst the foliage of the tall trees cawed languorously and contentedly, and without cease, as the sun sank lower and lower towards the Cotswolds.

Sunday was the day which was difficult for a boy to approach with proper reverence, as it meant the curtailment of so much activity. The village church of Elsfield is small, and of great charm, but the cawing of the rooks would drift in through the window and distract my wavering concentration.

Undergraduates made a regular practice of walking out on Sunday afternoons to have tea at Elsfield. They arrived completely unannounced, and thus it was impossible to say whether there would be one visitor or thirty; on one occasion we sat down forty strong.

This Sunday afternoon tea custom began with the post-war batch of undergraduates of the First World War. David Maxwell Fyffe and Charles Petrie, Ralph Assheton and Evelyn Baring were among the earliest. They would engage my father in earnest conversation. He loved the company of young men. I would watch my opportunity to creep quietly from the room, for I understood little of their talk, and my rabbit had to be fed at five o'clock.

Until he went to Canada in 1935 my father kept this close touch with the rising generation, which is one of the charms of living near Oxford. Many are famous now, not only in Britain, but in other lands as well. After that post-war generation, of the early 1920's, the later generations came by in procession; Roger Makins and John Foster, and later Frank Pakenham and Alan Lennox Boyd, until the wheel had come full circle and the generation was that of my own Oxford contemporaries. We would more often appear on a weekday, after an afternoon of splashing through the rushes on Otmoor after snipe, or in the mud of Noke Wood launching fusillades at the few pheasants Jack's dog was able to flush, and burning much powder on rabbits half seen in the jungle of blackthorn.

The spring holidays were a different world. There was the annual visit of my Scottish kin. It was a migration like that of the birds. Snowdrops and aconites had appeared in the crow wood, and the catkins and the pussy willows in the woods; the dun background of the woods was seen through a mist of buds, and the green was returning to the grass in the fields.

Birds'-nesting was the great activity of that short span of leisure. There were expeditions to the Noke Wood, with Jack to climb for us to the magpies' and the crows' nests. There was a minute inspection of every bush, creeper and hollow tree in the garden for what nests they might hold. Then there was the excitement of looking for plovers' nests, in the pasture fields that had once been ploughed and now ran in neat ridges of grass.

Elsfield in the eighteenth century.

Elsfield in the nineteenth century.

Elsfield in 1929.

Elsfield in the 1950s.

We used to walk the ridges watching our feet, for it is easy to tread on those mottled, pear-shaped eggs. The cry of the tumbling plover was the true sound of spring, and it is thus all the sadder that this beautiful bird has now become so rare.

Our expeditions to Otmoor were spent hunting in the marshy pasture amidst the pipe of red shank, and the drumming of snipe, and wading out in the little patches of standing water to the big clumps of reeds where the coots nested, and the moor hens, and sometimes a mallard. The rooks by now had built up their colony in the crow wood and their sound was not the harsh cry of winter but a mellower note of domesticity. There were certain holes in the old trees where the jackdaws always nested, which could be reached by a ladder. But the great rooks' nests, on the swaying branches more than 100 feet above the ground, were beyond the reach of any man.

I only once had a chance of seeing the full cycle of spring, when the toils of school closed round me. In 1922 I was suddenly taken violently ill with an acute appendicitis, and was operated on by a surgeon whom my father summoned by wire from London.

I lay for nearly three weeks in bed at Elsfield, looking out at the rooks' nests. Jack fixed up a coconut outside the window, and I could watch tits at work on it. Sometimes, when the windows were open, a little wren would come into the room and carefully search the window sashes for flies, and then take himself off as humbly as he had come.

I could lie in bed and watch the rooks build their nests stick by stick. The rook flying with a twig in his beak is, above all others, the sign that the spring is really on its way. The great tragedy of the Easter holidays was that one might find nests of certain birds in abundance, but the holidays ended before the late nesters began. Thus one could not hope to find a blackcap's nest, which seemed a terribly harsh dispensation of providence. One spring the roof of the cowshed started to fall in. Builders were summoned to mend it. Meanwhile, we children discovered a blackbird had a nest in it, which she would undoubtedly desert if the work went forward. We presented a petition to my father for stay of execution. It was granted, and work ceased until the blackbird had hatched off.

c

When we returned for the summer holidays we had only a day or two before leaving for Scotland. There was a great packing up of rods and reels and belongings, for a six weeks' absence. The Oxfordshire countryside, at that time, is as lush and green as the jungle. The woodland paths are almost impassable because of the growth of flowers and herbage. The rooks' nests have disappeared from sight behind the billows of leaves. The cuckoo has long gone, and the last egg is hatched. The whole world seems drowsy and heavy with scent, and expresses itself in the sleepy murmuring of the wood pigeons.

We used to come back from Scotland only just in time to set off for school, but by then autumn had unmistakably come. Days might be hot in mid-September, but one could smell autumn in the air, and there was a chill in the night sky, and the mist of the early morning.

My brothers followed in order through the preparatory school at Oxford. The years between us meant that two brothers would overlap briefly, at the same school, for a time.

Going to Eton involved a drive of about two hours. Although I enjoyed it well enough when I got there, that journey was not a cheerful one. The car was like a ship bearing me on a long voyage to a distant land for a lengthy period of exile.

Long Leave from Eton was a whirl of excitement. It divided the term and it meant three nights at Elsfield. Every moment of it was planned, and, in the summer half, my father, mother and I went out of an evening to a Cotswold trout stream where I fished until dark, always unsuccessfully.

In Long Leave in the Christmas term we had an afternoon's shooting. In my second year at Eton my father, who had long laid aside his gun, decided to shoot with us in Noke Wood. All he shot was my brother Billy, who was well peppered from forty yards' range, but happily not much hurt. The total bag, exclusive of Billy, was two rabbits caught by Jack's dog.

Looking back over that pleasant vista of a country childhood there are certain happenings which stand out like irregularly spaced stones. Perhaps the most significant was the great storm of 1929 which laid low thirteen tall trees in the crow wood. One could go down to the Bayswater brook, look up towards the rising ground of Elsfield, and see that the storm had cut a swathe of some quarter of a mile in width, and had even clawed from the ground oaks which had resisted the storms of centuries. Four elms fell across the road on Elsfield hill. In spite of them the postman battled his way through with the mail. I admired his devotion to duty, but the single letter that he had brought for me I could well have done without. It was to inform me that, not greatly to my surprise, I had failed in School Certificate.

When one looks from the windows of Elsfield the lawn slopes away below to a sloping field. The bottom of the field is one with the flat land. Field after field goes away beyond, the lines of the furrows running along the line of one's gaze. When it has been raining they fill with water. They look like silver fishes when the sun is on them.

When we first came to Elsfield there was no view. For, in the midst of the lawn stood a gigantic Wellingtonia, and beside it an ilex whose branches reached down to the ground. The latter had the silhouette of a tea-cosy, and must have been of great age. The Wellingtonia may look well enough in the great forests of California, but its existence could not be justified when it withheld one of the finest views in England. The ilex, which did not cloak so much of the view, was allowed to stand, but became one of the casualties of the 1929 storm.

In those days the view was one of green pastures. As one looked farther and farther, so the fields with the hedgerow trees seemed to get narrower until in the distance these trees blended to form an irregular forest, with the Cotswolds lost in the haze beyond. To the right one looked down over the top of two little woods of oaks. Now, most of those fields are ploughed, and the green of pasture looks the greener for the surrounding squa of stubble or bare earth. Storms chase each other across this great sweep of landscape making the windows rattle and bringing the rooks slanting, against their force, close to the panes. Rain showers march across the vista. Sometimes a curtain of grey mist advances right to the bottom of the lawn itself.

The view is at its best on days of rain and sunshine when, from the grey clouds, breaks a shaft of golden light which transfigures the tract of country at which the finger points, and turns the green of the pastures to gold. Sometimes the cloud shadows chase each other across the expanse. and never does the view look the same for two days together. But sometimes all is still and one looks out, as if from a watch tower, on a great tract of England serene in the sunlight.

The sun sinks behind the rim of the world, and the trees lose their outline in a blue haze. I have thought often of that view, when in far-off countries, and been vastly refreshed to return it.

3

A Young Fisherman

PEEBLESSHIRE was our other world. In the summer my father's family migrated to Broughton, to a house on Biggar Water a few miles above its junction with the Tweed. It was a small house and we filled it to its capacity.

To a boy of eight learning to fish, the little burns were an ideal hunting-ground. The windings of the Tweed to boyish imagination held great hook-jawed trout of superhuman subtlety.

But this paradise lay beyond walking range of short legs, for mealtimes in my grandmother's house were inflexible. It was indeed a year before I graduated to even a direct tributary of the river, confining myself to the small burns that flowed into Biggar Water. Under an arch of rowans, overhanging a tiny pool in Kilbucho Burn, I landed my first trout. It crowned a long afternoon of patient endeavour, under my father's tuition. I had dropped the worm into pool after pool, only to retrieve it as it was caught by the tiny rapid at the foot of each. But this pool, shaded by trees, was a little darker and a little deeper. The cattle, sheltering from the golden August sun, moved away unwillingly to make room for us, swishing their tails to keep off the flies.

The worm dropped with an inviting plop at the top of the pool and curled with the current under the bank on which I stood. The line, sailing with the current, faltered and stopped. An exploratory pull set the rod jerking wildly; a two-handed heave and up came a small trout, it landed on the grass behind me. Taking no risks I picked it up and, after dropping it twice, carried it ten yards farther from the burn.

That evening I sat with it on a plate in front of me, not wholly convinced of its reality. Of the several thousand that have fallen to me since, none has given me quite the same thrill. From that day on I have never missed an opportunity to go fishing, however bleak the prospects.

There was a good range of burns within walking distance. In Broughton Place glen a tiny stream, so overhung with heather that it was difficult to land the worm in the water, flowed past the site of Murray of Broughton's fine house. Nothing but the avenue remains. Murray of Broughton, once high in the councils of Prince Charlie, alone of all his followers turned King's Evidence after his capture. Hunted by the Dragoons, he had not dared to return to Broughton Place, but had snatched a hasty meal at Kilbucho and fled on up to Tweedsmuir, to be captured at Polmood. Faced with trial he turned his coat, and his evidence sent several leading Jacobites to the scaffold. Branded with the name of Mr. "Evidence" Murray he cannot have gained much joy from the few years of life that he had bought so dearly.

From where the Tweed rises, to the old stone bridge at Tweedsmuir, is a distance of fifteen miles of moorland valley. It is some twelve miles on to Broughton. It is a glen of heathery pasture, where the sheep graze down to the water's edge. Just above Tweedsmuir Village, Fruid Water joins it, and, thus augmented by a tributary as big as itself, the river pours under the humped stone bridge into a deep black pot, the first sizeable pool in its course.

The glen, and the road that runs along the left bank of the river, are rich in history. Below the bridge on the right lies the old churchyard on a wooded hillock. On the left a great square of trees hangs on the face of the hill, framing the House of Oliver—still in the hands of the Tweedies. Below Oliver and beside the road stands The Bield, for centuries an inn, where Claverhouse stayed when he hunted the Covenanters. To the persecution of "Bloody Clavers" and his men, the many headstones in the old kirkyard bear witness. Some of the Records of the Kirk tell their own story: "No public sermon; soldiers being sent to apprehend the Minister, but he receiving notification of their design, went away and retired." And another entry: "The collection this day to be given to a man for acting as watch, during the time of the sermon."

As one goes down the valley, its character changes. On tall, rounded hills the greens of grass, and of bracken, change to the darker hues of heather and scree. Smoke rises among trees from the chimneys of the Crook Inn, which has been a hostelry since before the year 1600. From there on, the river has heather hills on both sides.

Where big burns tumble down to the glens, heavy baskets can still be made in times of spate. Where each one joins the river is a dwelling, whether shooting-box, farm or shepherd's cottage, surrounded by trees to break the force of the winter winds. They bear the names of the Peel Towers which once stood there, and are now no more than a ragged ruin of stones or a small green mound topped by a few Scots firs, gaunt and wind-blown. That chain of Peel Towers ran along the length of the Tweed, each one in sight of its neighbour above, and in sight of its neighbour below.

The Tweedies and the Veitchs might carry on their feuds, and their neighbours be spurred to action by the cattle thieving of Porteous of Hawkshaw, or Scott of Mossfennan, but they stood shoulder to shoulder against the foe from the south. The beacons blazed on every Peel Tower, and a fiery warning ran through the valley from Kingledoors to Stanhope, over to Mossfennan and the Wrae, past Drumelzier to Tinnies, across to Drever, down the Tweed and up the glens for all to know that the English were riding. Great was the hardihood of those Border riders in the "Killing Times".

> "*They rade in the rain in the days that are gane*
>   *In the rain and the wind and the lave.*
> *They shoutit in the ha' and they routit on the hill*
>   *But they're a' quietit noo in the grave.*"

Gone now are the Porteouses of Hawkshaw, and the Frasers of Fruid and Oliver have moved farther north. Simon Fraser of Oliver, stout supporter of Wallace and Bruce, was executed in London. There his noble appearance and gallant bearing provoked expressions of sympathy even from the rough London crowd. The waters of Talla, now a reservoir, have closed for ever over the Peel Tower of young Hay of Talla, executed for the murder of Darnley. Gone are the Hunters of Polmood and the Scotts of Mossfennan, and only the Tweedies remain. The ragged ruins of three castles straddling the lower end of the glen still serve as reminders of the reiving families who dwelt there. Clumps of gaunt Scots firs grow beside the ruins of the Peel Towers, planted by the hand of later generations.

In the valley bottom, stone walls keep back the moorland from the small fields along the water's edge. Here a field climbs up the hillside, and there the moorland reaches down to the river bank itself.

The Tweed winds its way over a bed of smooth stones, its course bestrewn with boulders. The current runs clear and fast, and in low water one can see every detail of the stones that it has rounded and fashioned, showing grey, blue and brown in the weaving current. Pools are few, but here and there the stream, washing against the far bank, has dug out a basin and scooped away the shingle to form a deep hole. The Upper Tweed seems to have no mean between spate and low water. The improved hill drainage means a clearer runaway of spate, and the increasing demand of the citizens of Edinburgh on the water supply has robbed it of one of its largest tributaries.

It is not until one gets almost to Peebles that one sees the pools whose amber depths reach too far down for the eye to follow, where imagination pictures great fish lurking. Below the long glen of Tweedsmuir the hills roll back from the broad flat fields in the valley bottom. Big tributaries cut across the width of the glen. Biggar Water, Lyne and many another sizeable stream joins its winding course. It is a Tweed, several times the size of the moorland stream that passes Tweedsmuir Bridge, that rushes through the rift in the hills above Peebles and washes the rock below Neidpath Castle.

Tweed has now the dignity of a great river, which will float a rowing boat, and hold a salmon. Below Peebles the famous fishing beats begin. Here are the long, open pools overhung by beeches which must be fished by boat or deep wading.

The Tweed is a difficult river for trout, in that it takes a great deal of knowing. There are big fish there, even in the stony reaches at Tweedsmuir. But they lie in unexpected places. Clyde fishing is at its best on a rising water. The Tweed and its tributaries are finest as the flood abates, and the river falls. Tweed fishers say, a little slightingly, that Clyde trout are easy to catch, but be that as it may, the characters of the two rivers present an absolutely different study. If Tweed trout are clever, so also are the fishers. The trout taken in one year would show that, in the vast majority of cases, they were caught on a dry fly by men with years of experience of fishing at dusk, or in the hours of summer darkness. These anglers who catch big trout, year after year, will probably not use more than half a dozen patterns of fly during the season. They will deny that the river is any less good than it was in their youth, and records confirm this.

Ever since the laying of the railway in the last century the Tweed has been accessible to thousands of anglers other than those who live on its banks, who come regularly to fish certain stretches that they know well, and go home with varying baskets. Motor car travel has brought many more. But it has made little difference, as casual fishermen do not know the river, though many of the tributary-burns have suffered disastrously.

There are times when big baskets may be made, fishing on a falling flood with a minnow or worm. The biggest fish have most easily been caught by a device known as parr-tail (which has since become illegal), consisting of a salmon-parr cut diagonally across the middle and hooked in a special way; when drawn through the water it has some of the same action as a wobbling bait. There are also times in the beginning of the season when trout are hungry after the winter floods, and will gobble a March Brown. But at all times and seasons they take a great deal of catching.

You may take good fish after the Lammas floods in August, when the heavy rain of days and nights has brought the river down in a smooth brown torrent, level with the top of its banks, with only eddies to mark where the big boulders stand. The valley is full of the roar of the river, and the noise of the swollen burns pounding down the hillsides. Then the river is sinister, and the flotsam of broken hurdles, corn stooks, and the half-submerged bodies of drowned sheep, whisked so swiftly down the brown flood, bring home its power to you. But as the water falls, leaving the grass on the banks smoothed down by its force, the river changes from brown to black, and you can see the bottom once again at the tail of the pools. Then is the time for a wet fly, and you may make a basket in daylight.

To see a really heavy rise on a stretch of river is an instructive sight, because only then can one estimate where the big fish feed. It varies as the season progresses. Trout worn out by winter storms are lean and hungry in April, and they prefer the slower runs and the slack of the pools. But by August and September they are full-fed and strong, and lie in the neck of the pools, and the broken water between the boulders, revelling in the rush of the water.

But all this was far beyond the range of a small boy with a short rod, a Stuart tackle, a strong cast, a tin of worms, and two short legs. Broughton Place Glen was the scene of most of my earliest expeditions. It was a kindly glen. Now and then a grouse, drinking at the burn, would burst from the heather beside it, his protests growing faint as his silhouette grew smaller. A friendly herd of highland cattle used to look on, tousled and interested.

There were two bigger pools, in one of which my uncle had once caught a half-pound trout, many years before. The lower of these was just above the junction with Broughton Burn, another tributary of Biggar Water.

One afternoon after fishing the lower one unsuccessfully, my sister and I were seated on the bank, watching the cloud shadows chasing across the far hillside, when a small ragged boy appeared. He had an unmistakable air of purpose and absolute confidence, as he sat down on the bank and removed his boots. He wore no stockings. He was joined by a small, ragged girl who carried a short barbed stick.

Then followed a masterly demonstration of skill. Crouching low the small boy picked his way along the bed of the pool. He seemed to pass his hands under each stone on the bottom, and into every hollow under the bank. In five minutes he had plucked three trout from the shallow water. At the end of twenty minutes the barbed stick was threaded with trout to the top and the small girl had produced a piece of string to thread the others. We watched for nearly an hour, fascinated. Then the small boy donned his boots again, and, wearing his string of trout like a necklace and carrying his stickful, trotted off with his companion to his cottage home, and supper. It seemed magical the way the groping hands so deftly removed the trout, killed them, and tossed them ashore. Like fly-fishing, it was one of the Black Arts—far beyond us.

A small mill-lade flows out of that burn, and hard by the site of the old house. Near it was a deep well with a stone coping with a wooden cover. In my father's youth an enormous trout had lived there. He had long passed beyond, and the present incumbent was a thin hungry half-pounder, lurking among the stones at the bottom, who seemed grateful for the worms that were thrown to him. Many a time I was tempted to lower a baited line to him, but managed to resist the temptation. A fishing conscience was gradually forming.

The mill-lade led into a large shallow mill-pond, whence it poured down a narrow course to turn the mill wheel and then, found its way into Broughton Burn. At first inspection the mill pond seemed shallow and devoid of fish. It was several years later that I discovered that it held not only trout, but big ones. Broughton Burn into which it flowed was a fair-sized water. But it was very clear, and, except for the foot of Broughton Place where overhanging trees darkened the pools, such trout as there were, were very dour.

Occasionally one could see a village boy, bare-legged, in mid-stream, purposeful as a heron, guddling trout. At old Broughton village, half a mile below, the burn broadened with a wide ford for carts, with an old wooden footbridge beside it.

The smithy stood beside the ford, and many a sunny morning was whiled away listening to the cling-clang of the smithy mingled with the subdued roaring of the furnace, while the quivering shapes of tiny trout darted hither and thither in the shallows of the ford. The smithy and the old footbridge have been gone many years. and the ford is now spanned by a squat stone bridge of no beauty. The burn meanders on through green fields for a mile or so, ending in a large circular artificial pool like a small pond, before tumbling over a concrete slab into Biggar Water four feet below.

When Broughton Burn was in spate that waterfall seemed to have all the terror and majesty of Niagara. The pool below this fall is the first sizeable pool in Biggar Water. Biggar Water rises at Biggar, and follows a broad valley of fields and crops. Before the laying of the railway in 1864, it had been a marshy stream meandering through boggy flats. The builders of the railway had to straighten it. They made it flow straight as a canal from Biggar to Broughton Station, beside the two lines of steel. It was now without pools in the early part of its course, and of even depth, but good trout lived in holes in the banks. It was an ideal place for learning to throw a fly, as the banks were the edges of green fields, devoid of trees. That long flat is still a haunt of wild geese, which come from Cobbinshaw or the distant Solway, circling high over the valley and leisurely descending to the fields, to take wing again if a human approaches within a quarter of a mile.

The long flat ends at Broughton Station, and, turning at the road bridge and augmented by the waters of Broughton Burn, it shakes off the man-made lines, and bubbles and winds its way to the Tweed. It travels in a succession of deep flats and small rapids, sometimes overhung by trees and bushes, sometimes through open meadows, over a bottom of gravel or mud, with hardly a boulder or a stretch of shingle.

A mile above its junction with the Tweed it is joined by Holmes Water, which flows crystal clear from the slopes of Cardon. It holds bigger fish for its size than any burn that I ever saw. Seldom more than eight feet wide, it has pools over five feet deep, and, in each of its innumerable twists and turns, it burrows deep under the curves of its banks to make those shelters that trout love so well. Like Stanhope, its head waters fall in a succession of tiny falls and potholes, with a good fish in each one. A four-and-a-half pound trout was taken from a deep pool in its lower reaches, narrow enough to jump across, and clear enough to see a sixpence on the bottom. A gated moorland road runs up the valley beside it; broad fields which climb the hillsides at the glen foot shrink as you ascend the glen, and the heather moorland presses closer and closer to the burn.

My first fishing expedition there ended in disaster. Deciding to fish from the far bank I took off my boots, and, holding them tightly under my left arm, I started to pick my way across a rapid. One boot fell from my grasp and was whisked away, and as I gained the far bank was sailing bravely down the rapid below. Dropping everything else, I gave chase down the bank in bare feet and lost precious seconds picking my way through some thistles. For three-quarters of an hour I searched every pool and rapid, but could find no trace. After a three-mile walk in bare feet I reached Broughton, with no fish, only one boot, and deeply humbled in pride.

4

Lowland Pleasure Ground

BIGGAR WATER, from Broughton Station to the junction with Tweed, became my pleasure ground for ten years of summer holidays. Visits to the other burns merely gave variety to it. It was said that I wore a path along the bank. It was with wild excitement that I rushed down each summer, fresh from school in England, and it was heartrending to say good-bye to it each September. In the war years, going back to the Army, at the end of a week's leave, produced much the same feeling, but was never quite as bad. There was a remote possibility that the Germans might surrender, or be smitten by pestilence, like the Assyrians of old, or destroyed by act of God. But there was no chance that the school authorities would surrender. They seemed invincible, and beyond the reach even of the Almighty. Neither the General Strike of 1926 nor the heavy Thames floods of 1929, could wring a day's respite from them.

The six weeks of summer holidays we spent at Broughton were during that most perfect season—the last of the summer and the first of the autumn. There is rarely fine, settled weather at any season in Scotland; a still, sunny day in August, and another in September, are perfect in their own way, with fine shades of difference.

A hot afternoon beside a burn in August has all the languorous charm of summer. When it is so bright that fishing is hopeless, you sit on the bank and drowse among cushions of heather. The warmth brings out the honey smell of the heather bloom, and ponderous bees fly buzzing back and forward. The noise of the burn beside you changes as you listen; first comes the sound of the rapid below, then of the rapid above, and every now and then a faint murmur from a more distant cataract. The burn seems to chuckle to itself as the water hurries along, and in its merriment is perfect peace.

Sound carries far, bringing the contented clucks of hens sunning themselves in a farmyard; and the slow baa-ing of sheep on the far hillside, looking like a string of irregular pearls as they progress along a tiny path, itself invisible from where you are. The heather patches stand out in richest hues against the dark oblongs of the burnt ground, and the green of grass and bracken. Here and there the sheep have nibbled patches which show pale emerald against the dark opaque of the bracken and white thatches of bent. A covey of grouse, dropping down to the burn to drink, see a recumbent human, and swing away calling angrily. There is nothing to do but drowse and look up at the blue sky. You will catch no fish until dusk.

As September comes, the nights grow chillier, but the mornings are brilliant. Here and there a beech tree shows a spray of leaves turning yellow; the rowans are bowed with berries, and the birches, hanging over the water, begin to fade. Bracken starts its cycle from green to yellow, to golden, and a dry faded brown.

The September morning sun, taking on the hazy quality of autumn, turns the dewy grass to silver; and the fresh-cut corn stooks throw their pyramid shadows on the lower slopes.

Nature seems to wake later. The sun is not warm on one's face until nine in the morning, and in the heather an old cock-grouse calls and talks to himself crossly, as if he had just awakened and was out of temper. A hill partridge in the corner of the stook-field gives his rasping cry to call his large family together.

A shade of gold has crept into everything, the hazy sunlight, the bracken, the leaves of the birches, and the light on the fresh stubble. The cutting of the corn has made a harvest for the wild creatures. You may sometimes see grouse in the stubble, and a great black-cock trenchantly perched on a stook, just far enough away from the nearest dyke to be out of shot. Pigeons go back and forward among the fields all day, and at night the ducks glide down in search of spilled grain. Pheasants, too, who will always walk rather than fly, hop on to the stone walls, perch for a moment to scan the fields, and drop down the far side, intent on their share. White mist lies in the haughs and gives way slowly to the morning sun.

The trout are changing their habits; a big fish may take a fly in the daytime, and they lie now in the fast water and not in the slack pools.

This was the Scotland to which we looked forward in the summer, and indeed the whole year round; doing the same things in the same changeless glens that my father and grandfather had done as children. I did much of my early fishing with the same rods that they had used at my age. My grandfather's wicker creel, though lending a great air of importance, was more trouble than it was worth, and quite unnecessary, for my own jacket pocket held my worm tin and the few other tools of my trade. I had little use for a landing net, but carried one to give myself more prestige. As for the few fish that any one day yielded, they were carried proudly on a forked stick for all the world to see. The net had too wide a mesh, and they were apt to slip through it.

Subject to the limitations of meal-times, and bed-time, the world was mine. Being allowed to go fishing alone conferred a delightful feeling of emancipation. On the whole, I would rather fish alone to this day. If there is one fisherman accompanying you it is generally all right, but if there be more than one they are apt to conspire together to return home, taking you with them. Their approach is by insidious argument that the fishing is no good; that it is nearly tea-time, and that everybody is wet. All these arguments are probably sound, but to me they are not valid.

It was during my first year of fishing that some visitors asked me how I was spending my holiday. I replied that I spent my whole time fishing. The guest then said in all sincerity: "But you can't fish every day and all day." With equal sincerity I replied that I could and did, and have proved it over thirty years in three different continents.

During my first year I was not allowed to fish alone. My mother, or my aunt, nobly endured the rigours of the weather to look after me. The next year the ban was lifted and I felt vastly important. In those days the practice of official calls upon neighbours still persisted. As every house stood in a valley, and therefore beside a burn, I always took my rod. On one occasion we went to tea at a house, beside which was a burn famous for the size of its trout. After tea our host suggested that we should all visit the rose garden, myself included. Stunned by this diabolical suggestion I

Jack Allam, with behind him the pond and Dr. Johnson's summer house.

With Jezebel, 1934.

The day of the six-pound trout. Aged nine.

caught my father's eye. My case was made. Five minutes later my worm landed with a musical plop into the largest pool.

If you practise a sport alone you learn the basic rules of it more quickly than if you rely on the advice of a mentor. A rudimentary understanding of the trout's faculties and reactions was born in on me. For instance, it soon became apparent that for some reason the trout might refuse my worm in a pool where they normally took it.

Gradually a chain of ideas formed. To lean over the pool and stare into it; to stand silhouetted against the sky above it, or to let one's shadow lie athwart the water, seemed to be connected with this umbrageous attitude. If you could see the fish you couldn't catch them, because they could see you, and outguess you.

When the water fell to a certain state of clearness, catching fish seemed impossible, except by chance, and no dweller in drought-ridden prairies ever prayed for rain with greater fervour. But one conviction grew and has been strengthened by years of experience, namely, that, however bad conditions are, there is always one fish who is fool enough to take, if you can only find him.

Another fruit of experience was connoisseurship in the different types and conditions of worms. The banded worm of the midden-heap, and the small red garden worm seemed to prove the most alluring, though the sturdy and intriguing lob worm had its merits. The others were accorded a cold reception, except in brown flood water where the trout would take anything.

But as experience brought some rudimentary skill, so also became clear the limitations of my art. The great trout of the lochs and of Tweed, were demonstrably beyond my reach. A big trout sucking down a fly was for others than me. I could merely mark the spot and hope that some day my worm wriggling past him might tempt him in a weak moment. I watched my father fishing with a fly with absolute fascination, but it seemed to be a method practised by, and reserved for, grown-up people.

In 1921, we spent a part of our summer at the Crook Inn at Tweedsmuir. After a winter of anticipation to find myself a few minutes' walk from the Tweed was breathlessly exciting. The monsters of Tweed, which in my scale of values were any trout of over a quarter of a pound, were no easier come by than in the burns.

It was the year of the great drought at Elsfield, which extended to Peeblesshire. The river was low, and only the ubiquitous salmon parr saved me from many a blank day. In England, that drought was considered the worst of the century, and the Oxfordshire fields were burned brown as the prairie, by day after day of torrid sun.

But the Lammas floods came in August, and, overnight, Tweed rose to the top of its banks, covering the shingle beaches and the grey boulders in brown flood. We woke to the muffled roar of it each morning. The floods lasted long enough for salmon and sea-trout to thread its long course and reach Fruid Water. It took some days to run down.

During this period of suspense my father took my sister and me on a gruelling walk to the top of Broad Law, the second highest hill in the south of Scotland. To our short legs it seemed the highest in the world. Just after midday the mist came down and turned to heavy rain. In the late afternoon, aching in every joint, we reached the shepherd's cottage at the head of Talla, drenched to the skin. No people exceed, and few equal, the hospitality of the Borderers. The shepherd's wife took us in and we sat in front of a fire of glowing peat, wrapped in blankets while our clothes dried, eating scones and cloudberry jam.

Talla Reservoir, in spite of its artificial nature, still possesses the rugged wildness of a hill glen. High hills of bent and screes rise steeply from the water's edge, and seem to hang over it. A road runs beside the loch from Tweedsmuir village, then crosses Talla and Gameshope Burns at the top, and climbs steeply on to the plateau above. The trout in Talla Burn, like those in Stanhope, have that prettiest of all markings, black backs and yellow bellies. One may catch them, too, in the reservoir, with the same markings, near the mouth of the burn. What factors condition the colouring of trout I have never discovered, but like people their appearance gives them a pleasing individuality.

Three hundred yards back from the head of the reservoir, Talla Burn falls from its high plateau in that wonderful series of cascades known as Talla Linns. This was a favourite rendezvous for the conventicle of the Covenanters, and one such is recorded when the singing of the faithful drowned the noise of the Linns, while a few miles away the prowling Dragoons followed a false trail.

There is always a pair of ravens at the head of Talla, and my father saw a golden eagle there in 1920. Duck are fairly plentiful, but the fishing has never been good, as the fish are thin and underfed.

The loch can be dangerous at times, when the wind, contained between the two high walls of hills, sweeps down with concentrated force and whips the waves to the likeness of a sea gale. My father and I came near to drowning in such a storm, which took only half an hour to get up. With the speed of a racehorse, it swept us down four miles of loch, hurling our boat far up the slope of the dam at the bottom end.

The year 1921 yielded us no monsters from the Tweed, though a few baskets of small trout when the floods had run down. But it yielded one of the biggest baskets that I have ever made in Scotland. We had moved back to Broughton from the Crook Inn, preparatory to returning to England. It was well on into September. As a last treat my father proposed an expedition to Hopecarton Burn, which joins the Tweed just opposite Mossfennan. Our car was laid up, and we used the only available means of transport, which was to ride with the postman. He was an elderly man who took the mail from the railway station at Broughton up the valley of the Tweed. His conveyance was a pony trap, with a steady-going old pony who knew every halt on the road. It was an unsettled day with blinks of sunlight, and Tweed was running shallow as we crossed at the sheep-bridge below Hopecarton Glen.

The burn is a small one, and looked unpromising. When we foregathered to eat our sandwiches at midday, we had not a single fish. Then the weather broke. Rain hissed down in torrents, and the burn—before our eyes—slowly swelled and took on a tinge of amber.

As the postman and his trap would not be at the rendezvous for two hours, we decided to get wet where we were. The rain slackened to a drizzle, and stopped. The mist rose clear of the hilltops, and suddenly the trout began to take. We had two worm tins, but mine fell in and was carried over a waterfall and disappeared. At every cast we had a bite. The worm shortage grew so acute that we fished our hooks as long as a shred of worm remained on them, and still the trout took them. At the end of an hour we had no worms left, and were turning over stones to find them.

Time sped by on wings, and at last my father dragged me away. We crossed the Tweed, swirling down in smooth brown flood, and jogged back to Broughton behind the postman's pony. We tumbled our catch on to the kitchen table, two bags full and the contents of four mackintosh pockets—over fifty trout in all. Every detail of that day is as clear in my memory now as if it had all happened yesterday.

On our way back to England we spent a night with the Olivers at Edgerston. Fred Oliver[1] was then at the height of his powers, and was one of my parents' closest friends. There was an hour to spare before tea-time, a small loch, and a boat. Our rods and tackle were packed, but a rod, reel, and cast of flies were lent by our host.

My father rowed, ducking low at the oars, while I made wild sweeps with the rod, hitting the water behind me as well as in front, as often as not immersing the top joint of the rod with each ponderous swing.

Our time was almost up when, in heaving back my rod to cast, I encountered unexpected resistance. Reft from the water by the force of the heave, a half-pound trout bounded across the wavelets in a series of laboured leaps. Frantically collecting the slack line, I drew him by main force to the boat's side, and as my father whisked him up in the net the fly came out of his mouth. I appeared in the drawing-room carrying him. He weighed a full half-pound.

Charles Whibley, the author, was holding forth in front of the fire. He admitted that my feat was more important than his anecdote.

During that winter I pondered many times on this miracle. To catch a trout on a fly was to be an angler of stature, however hazy one might be as to how it all happened.

[1] F. S. Oliver, author of *The Endless Adventure* and other books.

Winter in England had its compensations, but as summer of the next year came, and with it the glorious thought of Scotland and fishing, excitement became tumultuous. We spent only a short time in the Lowlands before moving north to Ross-shire. Long enough, though, to spend a good many hours on the bank of Biggar Water industriously casting a fly.

The grandeur of being a fly fisherman was immensely agreeable at whatever cost this status was bought. There were heavy casualties. One rod broken, and every thornbush on the far bank decorated with flies from which forlorn wisps of gut depended. One complete fly cast, lost on a thorn bush overhanging a deep hole, remained to mock me every time I passed.

Two valuable lessons came with growing experience. The first was the necessity of curbing excitement long enough to take all reasonable precautions. To roll up a cast sloppily, after a day's fishing, often meant harrowing delay next morning. It meant feverish work with fingers that got clumsier, and more inept, as frustration mounted. Hard experience taught the danger of using an unsoaked cast which skimmed along the surface in dry loops, opening and closing like a spring. From this unnatural phenomenon, even the guileless and hungry parr recoiled in horror.

To this day I cannot trust myself to soak a cast properly by the river bank, if a big trout is rising. Experience has taught that the only safe *modus operandi* is to approach the river with rod up, cast well steeped and fly mounted, all ready for immediate action.

The second lesson was the realization of that striking reality—the malignancy of inanimate objects. The rowan tree behind you which catches your cast and causes the fly, in a twinkling, to wind round the branch half a dozen times in several different and complex knots. Tall reeds that catch a low back cast, and in which the fly hides so effectively that you have to trace it by running your fingers along the gut, until you prick yourself on the hook. The hawthorn tree, whose topmost branch catches the fly, and, in your effort to disentangle it, your cast catches one thorny sprig after another until, stretched tight, it outlines a strange geometrical pattern. These catastrophies make a fisherman feel that the greater part of creation is put there to plague him.

But the mood does not last, and the flash of a passing kingfisher, or the sight of a dipper bobbing on a stone in midstream, puts you in temper with the world once more.

Leaving Scotland, to go south to school, was to know the nadir of sadness. But there were two places on the journey south which were exciting enough to lift ones thoughts from this *via dolorosa*. At Berwick-on-Tweed there was often a flock of wild swans on the estuary. Just south of Penrith the railway crosses an iron bridge over a deep wooded ravine. The tops of the tall trees growing up from the foot of the ravine are still below the level of the bridge. There is a rookery in them and, as you rumble over the bridge, you look down into the nests and on to the backs of rooks cawing from the branches. Used, as we were at Elsfield, to look up at the rooks' nests swaying more than a hundred feet above us this vista fascinated us. After that there was nothing to think about except what a very long time it was to next summer.

CHAPTER 5

A Highland Memory

OUR visit to the Highlands was a memorable one for, on one magic day, within the space of an hour, I caught two trout far bigger than have ever fallen to my lot before or since; and that in the space of more than three decades of fishing. It took place when I was ten years old. My father, my mother, my sister and I formed the party. We were the guests of Alec and Rosalind Maitland.

We stayed at Letter-ewe, looking out over Loch Maree, in Ross-shire. It was reached by motorboat across the stormy breadth of the loch; in itself a fitting prelude to adventure. In an atmosphere of pleasant drowsiness that first evening, I overheard the morrow's plans being discussed. The party was to visit some distant lochs the next day, if it were not too rough. If it was rough I was to be allowed to try with a worm on a nearby burn, which I had already seen and marked with approval, as it was dark and deep. Otherwise I was to accompany the party and be permitted to troll. Just what that meant I wasn't sure.

As the following day was one of the highlights of my existence, it is not surprising that I remember it in vivid detail.

We set off like an African safari some eight strong, including ghillies, mounted on plodding, good-natured ponies, and loaded with all possible accoutrements for fishing. Our slow cavalcade wound up a long, stony glen with the burn below us getting smaller and smaller until we reached its point of origin, a patch of wet green moss.

A fresh wind in our faces met us on the watershed. We sat back on our ponies as they picked their way down the far side, hooves slipping on the shale of the path. A dampness on the hillside became a trickle, and then a burn. What appeared to be a large crow, high overhead, was certified by my elders as being a raven.

We turned a corner in the steep defile, and there below us was water. Two lochs separated by a causeway, wrinkled by the breeze, and expanding as each plodding step of the ponies took us further into view. They were aptly named Dubh and Fionn—the black and white lochs. Looked at from the causeway that separated them, where our little cavalcade halted, Dubh Loch lay girt by steep slopes with a long crag of dark rock down one side. Fionn was a sea of sparkling, dancing ripples, as far as the eye could reach.

A vast, heavy rod was assembled for my use. It had a permanent bend in it from much trolling, and in its youth had been a salmon rod. I was entrusted to the charge of a dour and silent ghillie called Kenneth. He appeared to have no other name. Rosalind Maitland made a third to the party. We bailed our boat down to the last irreducible half-inch of bilge, and pushed out into the dark waters. We spent the hour before lunch fishing wet fly at the mouth of a sandy burn. Our object was to catch some small trout to use as bait. This was achieved at the expense of my hooking Kenneth twice, once in the collar, and once in the cap, but with no other mishap. We landed for luncheon, and the smallest, worthiest trout was encased in a harness of hooks and attached to the trolling rod.

The happenings of that afternoon are as clear in retrospect as if they had happened yesterday. A sombre pall of mist hid the mountain tops. We passed close enough to the dark cliff to see the tiny rock plants along the damp ledges. The regular creak of the row-locks, and the regular splash of oars, blended with a faint sizzle of rain; the rod point bowing slightly at every stroke.

Above us in the mist an unseen raven croaked. With the suddenness of a bursting bomb the heavy rod kicked and plunged, then leaped like a live thing, the heavy-checked reel screeching in sympathy. I hauled it erect with all my might and main, and it took all the strength of my ten years to hold it up, with the plunging weight at the end of the long line. There were long periods of reeling in slack, varied in exact proportion with steady pulls that stripped the reel again. Kenneth, muttering and grim, kept the line taut by prodigies of watermanship. I was ten, the fish was probably about the same age; we tired at the same rate.

As his runs became shorter so my arms became feebler, and my breath shorter. He didn't break the surface until the last minute when he showed for a moment as an indistinct bar of glimmering gold in the dark water. Then, with a majestic swirl, there was a great shiny black back and the fluke of a strong tail, and Kenneth thrust a wide net, with a haft like a broomstick, under him and tumbled him into the boat. We laid him out full length on the floor boards. Order was restored, the tackle disentangled, rebaited and thrown over the stern once again. He was black and gold, with spots that seemed as big as coloured threepenny bits. He weighed five and a half pounds.

From then onwards I was in a trance, paying little attention to the rod because it did not seem possible that the law of averages could countenance more than one such happening on the same day, or even the same year, or perhaps in the lifetime of the same person; but it did, half an hour later.

The rod kicked once, then leapt and jerked while the noise of the reel rose to a screech. Kenneth again performed prodigies at the oars, but like a tired boxer, who can raise his weary arms only with difficulty to keep up his guard, it was with the greatest difficulty that I kept the rod and myself erect.

My hostess had finally to hang on to me to hold me up, and enable me to fight the battle out to a finish. This fish tired quicker. He came slowly to the surface twenty feet from the boat, and allowed himself to be drawn along the top of the water.

He was even bigger than the first one, and beside me, Kenneth, abandoning the oars, snapped open a telescopic gaff. The great fish faltered, turned away a yard from the boat, and seemed to gather himself for a final run, but Kenneth's gaff shot out and lifted him in one sweep into the boat. He was lighter in colour than his fellow, and weighed 6 lb. 1 oz.

The drizzle had stopped when we landed. The mist rose, and blue sky appeared. The two great fish were laid under a piece of sacking, and I waited for my father and the others. He came at last. I approached him with all the composure that I could muster, and asked how he had fared. He had been fly-fishing, and had caught a dozen or so—the biggest over a pound. He described the capture. I pitied him. Manoeuvring him forward, avoiding his questions with evasive replies, I knelt, twitched away the sacking, and revealed my fish in all their dignity. It was the only time in my life that I ever saw my father completely nonplussed.

Trolling ranks low as sport. There is no skill except perhaps the handling of the boat. Your tackle is, of necessity, too strong to give the fish a fair chance. Yet *Salmo ferox* is a great and splendid fish, and he will look at no lure but a spinning bait. Perhaps a sporting compromise could be reached with a light spinning tackle, and a bait cast instead of trolled.

Days succeeded each other in supremely pleasant routine. Breakfast and the outward journey on the ponies; arrival at the loch and the putting up of rods and unravelling of casts, while the ghillie bailed dirty water over the side until that last half inch was reached that always laughs at you. Then pushing off and watching the water change colour as it deepened, while the cast was trailed over the stern; halting at the appointed spot, turning broadside and beginning to drift.

The halt, when we rowed ashore for lunch, made one aware for the first time of the surroundings. Eyes, which had been concentrated on the path of each cast, saw the shape of the hills. For the first time one became aware of the rich, sweet smell of wet moorland, and saw other life stirring beside fish. It might be a pair of divers on the far end of the loch, or a raven croaking among the crags, or a ring-ousel stopping to perch on a stunted rowan tree. Very occasionally an eagle or a buzzard wheeled or floated across the sky above. These were birds that had been mere illustrations in a bird book before, and for whose very existence one had to take the word of others. Now they were invested with glorious reality.

After lunch there was the afternoon's fishing and the hauling up of the boat; washing fishy slime from one's hands; taking down the rods, and then the plodding ponies to bring us home.

Education came with experience. Casting from one end of a boat, without endangering one's companions, required a great deal of concentration. A rising fish which gave a wallop and escaped, argued that one had struck too hard. With experience came the feel of how much pressure could be safely exerted in playing a fish, and the technique of the give and take of the reel. As time passed, the taciturn man at the oars appeared to wince a little less when my line was drawn in to cast, and would occasionally bestow a few words of approval.

Sundays were days when one lived over again the previous week, in thoughts, and longed fiercely for the next to begin. Monday was a blessed day; and it was hard to believe that one had ever dreaded it. Sunday, in spite of the enforced truce with fish, had its compensations. There was the Sunday when all four of us climbed Ben Slioch, and a great herd of deer, deceived by an eddying wind, clattered past us through a stony pass, the four stags in the lead and their hinds straggling after.

On another Sunday, hot and windless, my sister and I set about stalking a park stag, imported to better the breed, who lived in an enclosure of many acres, bounded by a deer fence. He was viewed with some suspicion as, another like him, in a distant part of Scotland, had recently killed the stalker who tended him. It was said that this stalker, who was on excellent terms with the stag, had been either drunk or wearing his Sunday clothes. No one could say exactly which. These two apparently divergent theories were based on the premise that, either by garb or condition, he must have been unrecognizable to his charge. This did not deter us. We scaled the deer fence and, after having walked hither and thither, sat down in the bracken beside a small burn.

We lay there drowsing in the buzzing of the flies and the smell of warm bracken and heather, when we looked up to see the figure of the great stag not ten feet distant. He was moving at little more than a walk, swinging his splendid antlered head slowly from side to side, every hair in his coat visible. He picked his way into the bed of the burn, and breaking into a trot clattered up the far slope and was gone. The story of the mishap to the stalker came unbidden to the mind, and Alice and I climbed the deer fence with speed and in silence.

In following every field sport you learn something new every day that you go out. I began to formulate simple theories about certain flies and certain ways of working flies.

Various incidents gave glimpses of what further experience proved to be patent truth. Fishing one day with Alec Maitland, it fell a dead calm. We had fared but poorly, and what little enthusiasm the fish had shown, up to that time, died away.

The mist was on the hilltop, and I had already begun to identify this as a bad augury. It rolled down the hills lower and lower until it seemed to gather at the far end of the loch and roll towards us. In a matter of minutes we were engulfed in a white fog so thick that we could see each other only indistinctly. We had kept on automatically casting, as one does, when Alec Maitland hooked a fish, and within a minute I had hooked one too. We caught one fish after another; then the mist lifted, the blue sky came through, and it settled down to be a fine day.

I have never since caught fish in a mist, though I have seen them take hysterically during a hailstorm. But the incident served to show that trout obey general rules only, and that they own to no laws of behaviour that they will not break occasionally.

On the day that we sorrowfully left Letter-ewe I contrived to catch three small sea-trout in Loch Maree, which set the seal on a perfect summer of sport.

The following year we went to Sutherland. We stayed at the inn at Rhiconnich, which was then the very back of beyond. The fishing was in a series of small, mossy lochs. General Stronach of Kinlochbervie, a friend of my father's, allowed us to extend our range to a hinterland which contained more than a hundred other lochs. To fish several of these lochs in a day required a good deal of walking. The rain fell quite steadily on almost every day. It fell pitiless and unhurried, and the midges defied description.

The salient recollection is of lochs in pockets of mossy moorland, dead calm and patterned with rain; our garments sodden, and the insistent, maddening whine of midges always in our ears. Sometimes we fished from the bank, so drenched that we waded in without caring how much wetter we got. Sometimes there was a leaking boat, so full of rainwater that bailing was futile, and the only way to empty it was to turn it over.

We fared indifferently with our catches, with only one red-letter day. That day we fished two lochs in even denser rain and darkening mist. We moved to a third just over the ridge, and launched a very leaky boat that was beached on its peaty margin. My mother and sister remained ashore, my father and I pushed off together. Slowly a change came about. The mist grew a little lighter and began to disperse; the rain slackened to thin strings of heavy drops, and stopped. A patch of blue sky appeared, and with it a light, warm breeze blew in our faces, bringing the sweet smell of sodden moorland. Then a big fish seized my tail fly, a butcher, and the fight was on. That fish played for more than fifteen minutes. I never saw him until my father scooped him out with the net, before he had once broken surface. At that psychological moment the fly came out of his mouth. He was as black as night and weighed just over two pounds. The sun was warm in our faces as we rowed ashore to find my mother and sister drying their shoes and stockings on a patch of sandy beach. Seated in front of a peat fire that evening, faces and fingers soaked to a soft pink by the rain, there was great joy.

6

Adventures with the Salmon

THE following year, 1923, we returned to that part of Scotland. We stayed with General Stronach at Kinlochbervie. It was my first encounter with the salmon. The prospect was dazzling; the performance sometimes heartbreaking, but always thrilling. Ghabhaig Beg was rated very high among the salmon lochs of Scotland. Its outlet to the sea was a small rocky river.

This little river derived from a loch farther inland, Ghabhaig More, and entered Ghabhaig Beg just above the narrows. From the rocky south shore of the narrows, salmon could be caught from the shore.

For the great adventure of catching a salmon I was lent a strong sea-trout rod, which was considered the heaviest weapon that a boy of eleven could reasonably wield. On this was mounted a reel, a cast, and a fly, all of which seemed of quite phenomenal calibre. The fly was a silver Doctor, of medium size. I have it to this day.

My father gave me detailed advice. He warned me to keep the fly as long in the water as possible; above all not to strike, as one would at a trout, but to let the salmon take the fly and tighten on him as he bore it downwards. The first I observed, the second was entirely beyond my powers of self-control. My response to a rising fish was then an involuntary snatch of the rod. It was often too vigorous and tore the fly away. But it was all I could do. A calculated strike was absolutely beyond me. There was sad proof of that to come.

Conditions during that first day's fishing were ideal. Our host took station on the south shore of the narrows, at the upper end. My father set out in the boat. I was placed on a rocky promontory. I fished all the morning to no purpose, except for one very small trout that took my fly in the shallows. Far out I saw a salmon leap into the air and fall back with a mighty splash. Nearer to me I saw a great swirl in the water, from which spread a widening ring that was almost a ripple. My own efforts seemed pointless. Nothing happened at all.

It was about midday that I saw the boat heading for me, probably to call me to lunch. My father hailed me. The salmon were moving well on the far side, and he had caught a good one. He wanted me to take advantage of the conditions, and to fish that same drift while the conditions lasted. We sped across the loch, dropped my father on the far side and started the drift.

At the third cast, with the smooth liquid motion of a rolling porpoise, a salmon turned over at my fly. A smooth, shining, black back, a great fin, and it was gone. My fly, snatched from the fish by a reaction beyond my power to curb, flipped through the air and landed in the boat beside me. The swirl subsided. The monster had gone for ever.

I started to cast automatically and without purpose, convinced that my chance of a salmon had likewise gone for ever. A dozen casts farther on, it happened again. This time there was a great swirl that boiled round the fly; again nothing. The ghillie besought me in a few, fierce, significant words not to wrench at the fly. I couldn't explain. I was a prisoner of my own excitement. There was no question of being able to watch unmoved one of the monsters taking their leisurely time over my fly. Flesh and blood were too strong. The wind was falling now, but a gentle breeze still puffed at the ripples that reflected the blue of the sky.

We were almost at the end of the drift when my fly encountered solid resistance. It was the resistance of hooking a submerged log, instantaneously distinguishable from the resilience of a trout. Then the sea-trout rod bent, the reel rose to the note of a whistle, and at incredible distance from the boat a salmon jumped, and jumped again, and I realized that it was mine. It took fifteen minutes to land it, during the latter part of which shattering period we went ashore. I was up to my knees in the loch, shaking like an aspen, when he turned on his side and allowed himself to be drawn within reach of the gaff. He weighed exactly eleven pounds.

That morning fortified me against endless days of failure that were to follow. We fished Ghabhaig Beg on a good many other occasions, but I never caught another salmon. Many were the salmon we saw, some leaping two feet clear of the water on a thundery day; great boils in the water in the path of one's cast, of salmon unseen and intangible.

Once a great fish rolled over at my fly, took and held it long enough to double up the rod, then carelessly released it. Once, after a small boiling rise disturbed the ripples, I found that the fish was still on, but my reel and my rod did not react in a normal way. The ghillie laid aside the gaff and, with a snort, dug a landing net into the water, bringing out a sea-trout just over a pound.

My host and my father caught their salmon skilfully and methodically. My father, for all his slight figure, could throw a salmon fly thirty yards, and use a heavy greenheart rod all day. He was one of the finest salmon fishers that I have ever watched. The rod appeared to do his work for him. The perfect curve of his back cast seemed to follow forward with the fly drawing out the long, straight line ahead, independent of his agency. It is the hallmark of all experts that the instrument appears to do its own work.

My lack of further success began to worry our kind-hearted host, General Stronach. He became afraid that despair and despondency might bear down on me. A strictly ethical fisherman himself, he consented to my breaking an ethical rule—in fact, he suggested it.

There was a very small river nearby. In the course of its short and headlong career to the sea it tumbled over a high fall, into a rocky cleft. At certain heights of water the salmon could ascend the fall, getting leverage for a second leap from a ledge half-way up. In time of spate they could not do this, but assembled in the dark narrow pool below, hurling themselves upwards into the glittering thunder of the fall, to be washed back struggling into the pool below. The pool was virtually unfishable by any means other than worm or prawn, and that from the containing walls of black rock, fully twelve feet above the pool itself. To gaff a fish hooked in those swirling depths the ghillie must climb down a gully in the rock wall, or else the angler draw the fish downstream to an accessible point below. My host, anxious that I should get a second fish, volunteered to take upon his own soul the crime of fishing with a worm. He dispatched me with a ghillie, a short, broomstick-like rod, and a can of worms.

The pool seemed to be heaving with salmon. Every few minutes, with the suddenness of a bomb, a salmon would hurl itself into the air, strike the falls half-way up, and be borne downwards by thunderous rush of water, kicking mightily. The water was high, and rushing over a spur of rock close to the far wall, it sent a spray of water into the air which pattered on to the leaves of a tiny rowan bush, which clung to a cleft just above the level of the water. After this short, and inspiring, reconnaissance I hove my worm into the dark depths computing, as I had done since the previous evening, the great number of salmon that I must inevitably catch. In spite of the weights on the cast, it traversed the length of the short pool in a trice, and I hove it in once more at the top. All the morning and all the afternoon I did this until, haggard with frustration, we left as darkness descended. Not only had we not caught a fish, but we had not even hooked one.

Again and again the worm came back half eaten. Sometimes there was the feel of a gentle, insistent pressure that ceased when an attempt was made to strike. The ghillie replaced the worms methodically as they were removed by the fish. On his advice I tried striking fast and striking slow, every time there came that subtle pull. I tried not striking at all, in the hope that the fish might swallow it whole.

Nothing availed. Rain fell steadily. Great salmon leapt regularly at the falls to accentuate my disappointment. The rowan bush continued to nod like a mandarin as the rill of water played on its leaves. I begged the ghillie to explain what was wrong. He would have, poor man, had he been able to do so. He professed himself utterly puzzled. It was a sodden, dispirited pair that left that pool at evening. Salmon will often take the flat of a worm-hook between their jaws and release it when they have got most of the worm, or any pressure is put upon the line. But the laws of probability should have been overwhelming, during that long wet day, on the side of my hooking at least one of them.

There was yet another place of mystery and romance in that wild and delectable place. It was a loch noted for the size of its

E

brown trout, where one might expect to catch a great fish, or nothing. All its senior inhabitants were reputed to be cannibals and vulnerable only to trolling. We were not to visit it until evening.

In the morning we fished with wet fly in a nearby loch, to catch suitable small trout as bait. We filled a bucket with water to receive the fish as we caught them, as the longer they stayed alive the fresher they would be. It was a warm morning. My father and I fished in a dead calm, slapping at horseflies that attacked us. What few unwary little fish we caught were dropped alive into the bucket. My father, in a reverie, talked spasmodically with the ghillie as he fished. The ghillie answered slowly, and there would be another long pause. My father broached a new topic.

"Have you any children, Colin?" he asked, over his shoulder.

Colin's eyes were on the bucket of fish. His thoughts were concentrated on them.

"Eight," he replied, counting the inmates of the bucket.

"How are they getting on?" continued my father.

"All dead," said Colin, ruminating on the eight small fish who had now begun to float belly upwards in the turgid waters of their prison.

"Really·" said my father, deeply shocked at the thought of the awful tragedy that must have befallen the sturdy Colin and his wife. "What did they die of?"

Silence, while Colin peered into the bucket. "Bad water and rough handling," he observed in that measured West Highland speech which does not vary in intonation in triumph or disaster.

My father laid down his rod, absolutely appalled, and riveted his eyes on Colin; and not till then did he realize at what cross-purposes their trends of thought had been.

That evening we circled the big trout loch many times, clutching stiff rods with our bait traversing the depths behind us. No trout came anywhere near us. The rods nodded slightly at every stroke of the oars. It was one of those West Highland evenings when the colour pink predominates, and turns the water and the moorland hues to coral.

A single big fish rose in the middle of the loch, with a swirl and a circle of bubbles to mark the spot. On a nearby hilltop two dots appeared that were not deer, but wild goats. The light started to fade; the midges began, and we withdrew without touching a single fish. I am never depressed by a blank day on water where one catches a big fish or nothing. It is far more disheartening to catch nothing where fish are plentiful, mediocre, and usually hungry.

How remote and how fascinating was that wild part of Sutherland in those days, and no doubt still is. We were more than two score miles from a railway station or a telegraph office. The only habitations were at the head of those long rocky arms of the sea, where little puffs of smoke rose from turf-roofed cottages in the still evening air. The motor-car was not so universal then, and many other present-day commonplaces were still absent. The crofters' economy was based on in-shore fishing, and tilling the little squares of cultivation on the hillside above their cottages. Many spoke English with difficulty, some not at all. There you saw the West Highlander, little changed since the '45.

7

Return to Tweedsmuir and Some Yorkshire Fishing

THE next summer we spent on Tweedsmuir again. It had been prophesied that my experience among the salmon, the sea-trout, and the *Salmo ferox* would make me discontented with the small trout of Peeblesshire. It was happily not so. After all, Gulliver, when his travels were at an end, saw nothing strange about the folk of his own country. The giants and the midgets, that he had encountered on his travels, he had always managed to see in their proper proportion.

The giant fish of the Highlands belonged to a separate existence. The trout of Peeblesshire and Tweed were reality and the pursuit and capture of a quarter-pounder, in Biggar Water, had lost none of its charm. To a Lowlander no hills are like his own. The grandeur of Highland scenery and great torrents, brown with peat, are unforgettable. But so are the Border hills, and like no others, in the world. They have so many moods; in outline they are like the shoulders of sleeping giants. They have a myriad hues. There are the days when an east wind drains them of all colour, and the patches of heather are opaque brown smears, and the glens are a flat lifeless green; and the rare days of sunshine, when the distant heather is a bloom of dark purple, and the rich green of the bracken contrasts with the lighter green of the hilltop, while cloud shadows chase each other across the slopes, and bees buzz among the heather.

Then there are days of warm haze which brings out strange tints on the green hills, suggestions of pink and mauve; and sunlight will touch with gold a distant ridge, like a shaft of light through the stained glass window of a cathedral. High up on the hillside move those figures, timeless and ageless—the shepherd and his dog.

At the bottom of the valley the burn chuckles and gurgles over its bed of mottled stones, and explores under overhanging banks of turf. A dipper bobs on a stone, pert and contented, occasionally darting upstream with an air of great purpose, to find another stone to sit on, or a shallow to explore for water spiders. Sometimes a heron flying high, with great drooping wings, gives his outlandish call, and sometimes a curlew pipes. Golden evening light touches the glen and fills the hollows with shadow, and sheep cry from the grassy slopes. And again there are days when grey mist creeps down the hills and shrouds the valley. Then the grey outcrops of rock darken almost to black, the rivers run dim and slate-coloured, while the rain marches down the valleys in tall strings, and everywhere is the sweet smell of wet moorland. There are hills in plenty the world over, but none for a Lowlander but these. They seem beyond age and beyond time. They were the same when Porteous of Hawkshaw and Wat Scott of Harden saw them at daybreak, while dropping with fatigue they urged on the stolen herds, with the country raised behind them.

They were no different when Prince Charlie led the half of his army down Tweedsmuir, on his way to Derby, and found that the Tweedside folk, worn out by the "killing times", had no inclination for a war that was not in defence of their own hearthstones. All except Hunter of Polmood, who went up to his bedroom to change into his fighting clothes, to offer his services to the Prince. But his servants locked him in his bedroom until the column was passed. They did not want the laird to make a fool of himself, in a cause that they did not understand.

Returning to old haunts was none the less pleasant for the wonders of the Highlands. It seemed strange, at first, to use such tiny flies again. They were bought at the village shop in Broughton, selected from a wooden box on the counter, after grave thought, in an atmosphere blended of cheese, tobacco and biscuits.

Someone gave me an artificial minnow, as a birthday present, and I caught some fish on it before I lost it in a snag. A minnow fished in a spate is probably the best method of attracting the cannibal trout. But a trout that is pricked by a minnow is badly pricked, and in normal water to fish a stretch with the minnow puts the trout down badly, whereas it often stirs up salmon to take a fly. It gives a glimpse of the precarious existence a live minnow must lead, when little fish hardly bigger than itself considers it fair game.

I arranged, too, a clumsy attempt at dry fly fishing. But my robust reaction to the rise of a good fish was generally too much for a tapered cast, and I would end the day furious with my own lack of self-control, while an aggrieved half-pounder, down at the bottom of the pool, rubbed an olive quill, and an inch of gut, out of his jaw. Occasionally we made an expedition to the few small lochs in the vicinity, such as Stobo and the Glen. The fish ran about three to the pound, and a half-pounder was a big fish. In the Glen Loch there was a curious racial mixture of Loch Leven, rainbow and brown trout. Both lochs owed their existence to artificial dams built at the top of steep glens of great beauty, and these expeditions were full of excitement. Then there were some expeditions up to the small hill burns, preceded by a careful digging of worms to select the small ones with pink heads. Even the tiniest burns have one or two deep pools where a big fish may dwell. Lean and hungry, the small burn trout is so excited by the plop of a worm into his pool that he is not disposed to be over-critical, even in low water. Sometimes we would fish several of these burns in a day, and cover a good many miles, rod in hand. Hill-climbing with a rod was tiresome, but it seemed an unwarrantable amount of trouble to take it to pieces.

One great discovery was the mill pond at Broughton Place. I often passed it on my way up the tiny burn. It had seemed to be one of those waste spaces of creation—a sheet of water that did not contain trout. Even when I was told that there were trout there it did not seem credible. It was about fifty yards in length and half as broad. Like all waters that have even bottoms of sandy mud, and no pebbles or weeds, it seemed to be only a few inches deep. It was worth taking time to explore it. I took all my flies, and landing net, which was a sign of an important emergency. It was quite a long walk on a hot morning, and the mill-lade that tinkled over a miniature fall sounded very cool and refreshing. The hens from the farmhouse clucked and scratched in the dust. There was no sign of fish at all. By the time the cast was soaked and the rod essembled a cloud had stolen over the sun, and a warm breeze puffed a tiny ripple across the pond. At the third cast a fish took the tail fly under water. Looking for a quarter-pounder at the best, I realized that this was something far beyond my expectations. But he played lazily and without much spirit, and was on the bank in a few minutes. He was just over a pound; a monster. His fellows took warning by his example, and I landed nothing else. I did that journey to the mill pond many times afterwards, and though I rose fish, hooked fish, and on one occasion played one for several minutes, yet I never caught another.

Sport is a great equalizer. Those who catch big trout regularly on the Tweed are masters of their craft and of their water. They are tolerant of Clyde fishermen, but are careful to add that "Clyde trout are far easier caught." Some of the greatest masters of dry fly that I have ever watched have been miners from Wishaw and Motherwell, and weavers from Paisley. You may be unable to touch anything, and look upstream to see a burly figure fishing the tail of the run above, and prospering exceedingly. He is worth watching. He casts with effortless precision. Every now and then you will see the top of his rod kicking, and a fish drawn into the shallows, netted, and dropped into the long wicker creel on his back. At the end of the run he will splash slowly ashore; all his movements are unhurried. He seats himself deliberately on the bank and opens his creel. From beneath the slippery mound of fish inside, he detaches his "piece", generally a huge cheese sandwich wrapped in newspaper. You fall into conversation and he tips out his catch on the bank, and allows that he has not done too badly.

Now look at his tackle. He has an old greenheart rod, tied with tape at the joints. Instead of a shining gun-metal reel, with a chaste little knob for your finger and thumb to grip, his is of brass, with a note like a corncrake, and a handle like a coffee-grinder. His cast may conform to type, but may as easily be a series of strands of horse-hair, culminating in a fly of his own tying. His home-made landing net has a stout four-foot shaft, and does duty as a wading staff or a walking stick. He probably cannot remember when he last had a blank day. Listen well to what this man says. You are in the presence of an expert.

Night fishing began to exert a powerful hold on my imagination at this time. Cabined and confined by a regular bedtime, it was galling to see the night fishers setting out at the time when I had to reel in for the day. They always seemed to make the biggest baskets. I bitterly envied them their freedom to move in this sphere, which was denied to me. I have had many opportunities since. There is nothing more fascinating in all the many forms of trout fishing than the evening rise as the sun sets, and fishing on into the warm summer darkness.

As the warm evening sun sinks lower it draws with it the hues of daylight. The pool turns to a sheet of orange glass, etched with a weaving pattern of ripples. The hatch begins. Against the slanting rays of the sun, the hovering flies above the water, flit as transparent dots. Dusk comes on apace as the sun dips behind the hillside, and the stream turns to ebony. The nailed boots of a countryman, going home to his supper, crunch on the gravel of the hill road. Without halting he lights his pipe and his match makes a little star of winking light in the dusk. A partridge begins to call insistently close at hand; then the whirr of wings, and silence except for the sound of the river. You strain your eyes at the rings of rising fish on the dark pattern of the waters. Sometimes a big trout rises with a great noisy swirl, and having announced his presence settles down to make ring after ring with the regularity of a clock. It is too dark now to see a dry fly. Though there is a faint glimmering streak where your line falls, soon both will be invisible.

The river has no longer any features beyond the dark banks and the patch of foam in the rapids. On the bank you stumble over stones and tufts of grass. A wedge of ducks, flying low overhead with a whistle of wings, are faintly discernible in outline. Lights appear in the windows of the shepherd's cottage half-way up the hillside. You cast a now invisible line which falls without sound into a pool of darkness. You hook and play a fish by sense of touch alone. It is hard to say how big he is. You see nothing of him until his light underside shows in the net. However well you know your water in daytime you are fishing in a world of touch, not of vision, and you can make many mistakes. It is a form of fishing where knowledge of the water is essential. You will lose enough fish and enough tackle even then.

The following season was my first summer holiday from Eton. It was a holiday packed with travel and happenings; a visit to Shetland, some fishing in Yorkshire, and a short time spent in the sporting paradise of Argyllshire.

In Yorkshire we stayed at a fishing inn at Chapel-le-dale. It is a strange and beautiful part of the world, lying just inside that triangle formed by the three big hills of Ingleborough, Whernside and Penygent. It has many strange features. The trout stream in the valley, which is of substantial size, disappears without warning underground, and reappears further down the valley. It is the country of potholes, and close to those two terrifying black chasms, Gaping Ghyll and Alum Pot. On the hillsides are outcrops of weirdly-shaped stone encrustations called "clints". It is a pleasant country and abounds in sport, as well as these wonders.

We fished the trout stream at the bottom of the valley. It had good looking pools, but we achieved virtually nothing. We continued to achieve nothing until by chance we stumbled on the secret. Fish in different waters harbour their own special prejudices. These fish were unbending in theirs. They would not look at a wet fly fished across the stream and allowed to swing round with the current. Seeing a big fish upstream one day, and being rather precariously perched on a stone, I cast upstream at him. I caught him. He was just over a pound. From then onwards we fished out wet flies upstream at the steepest possible angle, and prospered mightily. What the explanation of this is I have no idea at all, though there are parts of the Tweed where the trout will go at wet fly while it is being drawn across only, and will not touch it when it tacks round with the current.

We varied our fishing with expeditions, mostly on foot, and left the valley with regret. But we had a great adventure in front of us. An expedition to the Shetlands.

8

Shetland Journey

THE more hazardous the journey the more exciting is the arrival. Any journey by sea seems a vast undertaking to a small boy, and to take ship from Aberdeen to Ultima Thule seemed the crest of all adventures. The party was comprised of my father, my mother and myself. Even the disquieting roll of the ship and the creaking of its woodwork and the unpleasantly blended smell of dining-room and engine room, could be forgotten. The gulls keeping effortlessly abreast, and the waves ruffling under the growing dusk were absorbing enough to drive out these uncomfortable phenomena.

The Pentland Firth was as quiet as its tide race ever allows, and it was without casualty that we entered Lerwick harbour in bright sunshine, with its white wreath of gulls screaming above the fishing boats.

The port of Lerwick gives one a feeling of being not so much in a foreign country, but on the soil of a different origin. The names over the shops have a Scandinavian tang. The cut of the fishing craft, and a hundred other small differences, stem from a different stock from that of Britain.

Shetlanders they call themselves, not Scotsmen. "Bad meal and bad ministers are all we get from Scotland," was a current saying.

Our destination was Unst, the most northerly of these islands. This time in a smaller ship, the *Earl of Zetland*, which now lies on the bottom. After a long and useful career she ran aground in a fog, a year or so afterwards. Lerwick, with its paving stones climbing up the hill, and the gulls screaming round its various assortment of small craft, grew smaller. A fresh salt wind tumbled the blue waves as we stood out into the sea.

Many were the ports of call. Sometimes there was a wooden

pier to go alongside. More often we lay just off-shore, and the varied cargo was transhipped into boats.

Everybody came down to see the ship. A great deal of shouting went on from our own deck to the small boats below. At one such place we took on board a Shetland pony which was slowly drawn up into the air by the ship's derrick, by means of a large waistband, from either side of which the protruding ends of the pony drooped disconsolately.

How attractive were those little ports in far northern sunshine, and the water in those miniature fiords was so clear that you could see the bottom in detail, where it shallowed towards the shore. As we threaded our way northwards skuas were added to the population of gulls. They were dark, piratical birds mostly in pairs. A gull flying close to the ship and carrying a small fish was hounded by a skua until he dropped it. The skua caught the fish deftly in mid-air.

We reached the island of our destination at evening. We were all rather weary. It was a long bay or a voe as they call it there. At the upper end a little burn came from a small loch, a few hundred yards inland, and channelled its way through the beach of white sand in a miniature delta. There were a few sea trout moving in the calm water at the burn mouth. We followed the shore road past it. On the hillside a little herd of Shetland ponies turned to gaze at us through shaggy forelocks; and then we were at our destination, the Manse.

Our host, the Reverend Charles Dick, was an expert fisherman and naturalist, and a friend of my father's from university days. He was a great experimenter and at that time used only two flies, both of the same pattern, but of widely different sizes. The theory was then becoming popular that it is not the fly that counts, but its size. On the whole he caught less than my father who believed in the colour and type of flies, and in changing them frequently.

The Manse was ideally situated. It was an easy walk to the little nearby loch at the head of the burn where there were brown trout and sea trout, when the water was big enough to let them run up. At the foot of the burn, when the tide was right, the sea trout would take a fly in the sea. Farther afield were other brown trout lochs, and other burn mouths to cast for sea trout in the salt water.

The country was low and rolling, and the wet hollows were full of snipe. Little bands of Shetland ponies moved hither and thither, as their larger brethren do on the plains of the American West. They peered doubtfully at us, and were disinclined to fraternize with strangers. With their coats half moulted, they looked half pony, half door-mat. In that clear northern light it is hard to judge distance, and a stone on the hillside may be 500 yards away, or it may be several miles. When you realize this, you find yourself making too much allowance rather than too little, and imagining that everything is farther away than it really is.

The impression is one of a land long lived in, as the upright Druid stones betoken. It is a country of no trees and an ever blowing salt sea wind. But clear northern sunlight is not the steady fare in the summer months. The weather goes through such a bewildering number of changes, in so short a space of time, that it must be regarded as a climate peculiar to the Shetlands.

The people of Unst were forthcoming folk. In those days there was much in their way of life that was picturesque to the point of the historical. There still may be, for aught that I know. There were the turf-roofed crofts, and the occasional spinning wheel in active and unselfconscious use. There was the unusual clothing, and indeed the whole distinctive manner of life of the islanders, going about their business of fishing, milking, and cultivating little squares of crops on the slopes above the sea.

They were deeply religious. A cattle boat, whose coming had been long awaited, arrived on a Sunday while we were there. It was vital to get the cattle on board with all speed, yet no man would so compromise his conscience as to load a boat on the Sabbath. For this they were commended from the pulpit, at a service which we attended.

Cars were still a novelty there. We had the use of a T model Ford for our expeditions farther afield. But we had fishing at our doorstep. It was only half a mile's walk along the edge of the sea to the head of this voe where the burn came in. Up the burn, a few hundred yards, was the little loch. We were not very successful here. It was difficult to fish it from the bank, as the shores were boggy and the bottom too soft for wading.

The brown trout that we caught seldom exceeded half a pound. They often had an unnatural silver hue, as if they now and then slipped down the burn into the brackish water. The burn itself yielded nothing. It ran through a miniature delta of sand into the clear waters of the voe. As we waded in, we could see the sand stretching out before our feet under that clear seawater. There appeared no sign of life at all, except an occasional flat fish disturbed by our feet, scurrying away with a trail of churned-up sand. Sometimes they would take our fly on the surface and give us the feeling of a very heavy fish. But in the gentle undulating wavelets a ring would appear now and then, and sometimes the suggestion of a fin or a tail. These were the sea-trout, for there are no salmon there.

Far and away the best fly was a three-hooked sea-trout lure with a long Eton-blue wing, silver-bodied and red-tailed. We touched a great many fish for the few that we landed. A sea-trout in his natural element fights magnificently, and those long straight runs out to sea bring one's heart to a standstill, wondering if he will stop in time, and, if not, whether the end of the line is really firmly knotted to the reel drum. Two pounds was our biggest at the burn mouth.

We fished when it was dead calm, which it rarely was, because in the smallest swell wading was impossible. Tackle had to be carefully cleaned after fishing in the salt water. It became an evening ritual.

We made many expeditions farther afield, to the small lochs that were dotted about. Our host, who never departed from his selection of two flies, was not in a position to advise us on what to use. My father and I had thus to run the gamut of experiment, changing flies until we found one that the fish would take. We fished these lochs from the shore, or waded when the bottom was hard enough. Much time had gone to reaching them, and a corresponding allowance had to be made for returning home. Consequently we had to fish hard and furiously in the short time at our disposal. The lochs stood on high ground and the ever-blowing sea breeze kept down any really strong hatch of fly. It was a rise here, a rise there, and two or three fish each for the day. On one occasion we caught only one fish between us. It was just under half a pound. As we walked to where we had deposited our rod cases and luncheon we saw a gull, flying with extreme difficulty, carrying a fish. We watched it as it mounted slowly. When we reached the rod cases we realized that the gull was flying away with our one and only fish that had been laid on the ground beside them.

We made many expeditions, some of them without our rods. On one we visited Muckle Flugga, the northernmost lighthouse in the British Isles, and saw the Great Skua Sanctuary. Another expedition was made to the little port of Balta-sound, where the ribs of derelict ships rotted on the tide line, and there was a so strangely strong Scandinavian flavour.

Expeditions meant an early start and a late return, and much walking. At least once in the day a rain storm would blow up, but the sun and wind would chase it away, and wet clothes could dry again.

All knowledge is compounded of experience. The lessons most truly learned in sport are those based on bitter mishaps. Something that was left to chance, and was never left to chance thereafter.

We had a long-standing project to visit a distant voe. It was far from a road, and its upper end was bordered by a beach of pure sand, through which a fair-sized burn cut a channel. Our host had caught good sea-trout there. I packed up my tackle and we started off for a day-long expedition. The others left their rods behind.

Before we left the road it occurred to me to put my hand in my fishing bag to reassure myself that all its contents were there. There was the familiar feel of fly books, the circular cast box, odds and ends such as scissors and spring balance, but no reel. In a frenzy of anxiety, I tipped the contents out on the ground. The reel was not there. We were miles from home. The opportunity to fish the voe could never be repeated. Crisis became chaos, and then victory was snatched from the jaws of defeat.

Our host knew of a minister whose manse was not far distant, who might lend us one. We made our way to the manse. The minister was delighted to help. He had not fished for years, but thought he had a reel somewhere. After much searching he found it. It was reminiscent of the pioneer days of the tackle-making industry. It was of brass. It turned with rusty protest. The line was solidified into what seemed to be a solid block. With great difficulty the free end was discovered, and the line wound off. It was not very long. On winding it back on to the drum its coils did not adhere quite so grimly. Anyhow, it was a reel, and that was what mattered.

When we reached the end of the voe we had little time at our disposal for fishing. But the conditions were perfect. The tide was right. A glassy surface undulated with a gentle murmur along the edge of the sand. The brass reel looked very curious occupying the place of the usual neat gunmetal one, with the purring note and the waterproof line.

Wading in as far as possible I sent the blue-winged lure as far out to sea as it would go. A hoarse, metallic croak from the reel drew attention to its precarious mechanism, every time the line was paid out. Nothing happened to ruffle the gently undulating mirror of sea, beyond the just perceptible wake of the lure. My father and our host, perched on the beach behind me, counselled moving position and casting farther out or farther in.

And then, in a matter of seconds, came crisis, triumph and utter disaster.

The line was half-way through its course, when it was arrested by what seemed dead weight. The mirror surface was broken by a smooth dark back and a fin that gave way to the unhurried swing of a great dark tail. The rod bent, and bent, and bent again. The reel set up a screech such as might be wrung from a vast choir of corncrakes in the depth of despair. The fish still on the surface, great tail weaving, headed straight for the open sea. In a trice the reel was almost empty, and then the gut snapped, unequal to the strain of that ancient mechanism. There is an awful finality about losing a big fish. Over seven pounds was my father's estimate.

No philosophy that one can summon to one's aid can bring a ray of comfort. The clear afternoon sunlight, the mirror sea surface, and the great stretch of sand at the head of the voe, became hideous. I returned the minister his reel by post; but not for some days. Ever since that day I have never set off to fish without first repeating a short incantation, "Rod, reel, flies, casts, and net", and patting each to assure myself that they are really there.

One day I hope to revisit that voe, and those other fascinating fishing grounds, traverse again those low moorland hills, with the sudden unexpected glimpses of that northern sea in that clear northern light. Then when the salt sea breeze is stilled, and the tide is right, try conclusions again with the descendants of that great sea-trout.

9

Learning to Shoot

A GREAT deal of a man's shooting life is conditioned by his introduction to it. My father had been taught, as a boy, to shoot with a muzzle loader, and this made him careful with each shot. He started me at Elsfield, at the age of nine in the year 1921, with a single barrel sixteen bore. It was light, but ill balanced, and kicked like a horse. It certainly had the effect of making me careful too.

To have fired it was a triumph. Every empty cartridge case was kept as a treasure. So much concentration went into gripping it tightly and estimating the area of safety, that there was little left for marksmanship. It was a long time before I could keep both eyes open at the moment that I pulled the trigger. Those who have been taught to shoot as small boys can be most easily taught to be safe shots. There is no shadow of excuse for the dangerous shot, and my father was an inflexible disciplinarian on this point. There seemed to me, as a novice, to be two theories of marksmanship, both of which produced expert shots, in spite of the fact that these theories were directly conflicting.

My father's friends who used to shoot with us at Elsfield, when questioned as to how far to shoot in front of a bird, would look rather puzzled; then they would say that they looked at the bird, and that the gun looked after itself. Two of those friends were eminent professors, as well as good shots, Sir Jack Egerton and Tommy Merton. But this answer seemed at once unsatisfactory and unscientific.

Jack Allam propounded a much more precise doctrine. It was the doctrine of taking the long swing, aiming down the bead, and laying the right distance ahead. He was prepared to give figures to prove it; a foot and a half ahead of a pigeon and three et ahead of a mallard. This seemed so much more practical that

I set myself to copy him, and at every miss would ponder on how I had miscalculated my distance. When I missed, cartridge after cartridge, I was urged to shoot farther in front of my target. nothing better resulted, for just as many shots are missed in front as behind, and there was still nothing to bring home.

But on my ninth birthday there was deep snow. In the grey snowlight of late afternoon we were in the woods—Jack, his dog Gyp, and myself. This was my second season's shooting and I had so far hit nothing. Suddenly, Jack stopped and pointed to an ivy-covered stump. In the snow was a single rabbit track leading to the screen of ivy, and no track went on. I pointed my cumbrous weapon at the stump, and with the crash of the discharge a rabbit rolled out dead.

We plodded home through the snowy woods, with the rabbit grasped firmly in my left hand, in a glorious haze of perfect content. Gun and rabbit weighed nothing. I breasted the slope to the house as fast as my short legs would carry me, and threw open the door of the room where my birthday tea was awaiting me; hat on, boots covered with snow, gun in one hand, rabbit held high in the other, to the cries of male approval and feminine dismay. After tea it was solemnly entered in the game book, and from then onwards I appeared at shooting parties as a gun, and not as a beater.

Such moments of achievement must always stand out clearly in the perspective of memory, for they were seen with unclouded eyes. But the steady exhilaration of sport, to most men, never dies. The satisfying clank of the closing breech, the smell of smokeless powder and gun oil, the crescendo outcry of the beaters as a cock pheasant rises, do not perhaps bring the same wild, choking excitement that they did once upon a time. But they provide a steady and unfailing exhilaration.

First achievements always group themselves together in the vista of memory. For they are undimmed by comparisons and have the force of a revelation. My first pheasant fell on a day of frosty December sunshine as we were driving a thin plantation of larch and Scotch fir, planted for the good Queen's jubilee, and named accordingly. There were a few cock pheasants there, and they flew down the line of the plantation. The few guns were divided between the two sides, keeping their distance ahead of the beaters. Three cocks got up together, and the two who were leading crashed into the plantation under fire from the far side. The third swung over, gathering powerful momentum, along the near edge of the trees where I was standing. My gun went off before I really intended to fire, and the great cock pheasant crashed into a larch tree, rebounded from the layer of branches in a cloud of copper-coloured feathers, and fell to the ground just outside the rabbit wire fence, not ten feet from where I stood. I tried to look nonchalant and indifferent when my father appeared as the guns converged at the end of the plantation. But it was impossible. My face was cloven by a grin of the purest delight.

Pigeons were a different matter. They were recognized by all the experts as being difficult. But shooting at them was not attended by the fearful publicity of driven pheasants. In Jack's company I burnt much powder, in the twilight, among the oak trees of the three little woods which stand on the flats below the manor.

Pigeons were birds of infinite romance; stream-lined shapes gliding and twisting among the oak branches, and seemingly invulnerable. To shoot further in front, or further above, to take a longer aim, or no aim at all, somehow seemed to make no difference. They steadily went on their way after the crash of the discharge, twisting into the evening sky. Thus it seemed nearly a miracle when a high pigeon, slanting athwart a westerly wind, checked at my shot, then crashed into the branches of an oak tree, nearly 100 yards farther on.

It was not for several years that I had accounted for a specimen of all the birds that were headings in the game book. But a rabbit, a pheasant and a pigeon were the basis upon which a boy of ten could build.

My father gave up shooting with a shotgun, and relinquished his double barrel twelve bore to me. It was a far more satisfactory weapon, for its heavier charge was more than offset by its better balance, and the bigger pattern of shot gave greater confidence, as did the possession of two barrels. It had belonged to my Uncle Willie, and had been made before the turn of the century. But as my father handed over the twelve bore, so he relinquished the 500-acre shoot, and my activities were limited to the forty-acre wood which we owned at Beckley, the marsh of Otmoor (which filled with snipe and duck at certain seasons), ferreting with the farmers, and the permission to shoot pigeons in the woods after they had had their annual pheasant shoot.

Cover shoots were rarer events, to be anticipated for weeks ahead and savoured for weeks afterwards.

But in the main, shooting came to mean the pursuit or the flighting of game with Jack. I was not allowed to go shooting by myself until I was sixteen. Sometimes, when Jack was not available, my mother would come with me; she has been my companion on many days of sport.

The quarry and the countryside have differed, but I have had a world of pleasure in three continents, in the course of thirty years, just walking with a gun. In place of the broad shoulders of Jack Allam, I have followed the taut and precise movements of African trackers, the silent, catlike tread of expressionless Cree Indians, the waddle of smiling Eskimoes, and the flamboyant strides of Italian partisans, against strange backgrounds of sunrise and sunset, amidst a wild medley of forests and plains, hills and streams. "Walking with a gun" is the only kind of shooting where one has the full fascination of hunting one's own quarry. Big cover shoots, where the pheasants are in hundreds, tropical duck flights, where the duck are in thousands, make magnificent and memorable days. But I will always prefer walking round with a gun, or a morning or an evening flight. I have never even possessed a shooting-stick.

Pigeon shooting is the sport, *par excellence*, for limited means. The pigeon is an outlaw, a destroyer of crops. He makes reasonable eating. He is difficult to outwit, and hard to bring down. He requires no keepering.

As winter deepens, the English ringdove is joined by millions of his cousins from Scandinavia.* He is a different problem at different months of the year. In the early autumn with the leaf still on the trees, he bursts from the shelter with a clapping of wings, screwing wildly in the air as he catches sight of you. When the flocks are eating the hips and haws, on the overgrown thorn hedges, they are often so tardy in breaking cover that a gun on either side of the hedge can walk up to within range. You may

* I am no longer convinced of this.

wait for them to fly into the corn stooks, and take them coming wickedly low, while you lurk cramped and confined with the heads of corn tickling your ears.

While the leaf is on the trees you have him at a disadvantage, for his weapon is his keen eyesight for movement and silhouette. But he will turn in his flight and go screwing away as you raise your gun to fire, as he sees the pale upturned blank of a human face. He is a bird with a lightning reflex, and that twist in the air too often lets your shot expend itself in space.

But when the oaks have turned to gold, and the leaves rain down with the November gales, you have to be more and more wary. It used to seem, as a small boy, that if I could find a place of ambush where pigeons could not see me then I in turn would not see to shoot, which posed an apparently insoluble problem.

Gradually, as time passed, I came to learn certain valuable tactical points. One was that when pigeons are coming in against a gale with rain, they are almost blind, and one can reveal oneself without much risk of being seen. Another point was that if a pigeon has fixed his eye on a branch, on which he intends to settle, he sees nothing else. There is also that time of year when they start to eat the ivy berries, and if you stand in early afternoon beside an ivy-covered tree you will nearly always get the chance of a good shot; otherwise the golden rule was laid down by Jack, "let 'em come while they will".

Towards the end of February they gather into bigger and bigger packs. At any time of the day, then, they must be stalked on the edge of the root fields, or a position be found behind a hedge when they are flying backwards and forwards from one field to another, or you may try your hand at decoys.

It is very seldom that there is a good acorn year at Elsfield. On the rare occasions when it happens, the pigeons feed in the woods all day, and rise up from the ground through the tree tops at one's shot, only to return when the alarm is forgotten. Then, in broad daylight—and particularly if there is a strong wind, which always confuses them as to the origin of the shot—it is possible to take up a position where they are flying backwards and forwards in search of their favourite food.

Only once in my life did I ever completely out-manoeuvre

them, and that was during a total eclipse of the sun. The eclipse was due to take place at two o'clock in the afternoon, and I planted myself at the edge of the wood where they roosted. As the sky darkened with the eclipse, the pigeons naturally assuming that night was falling, made for their roosting places. In a matter of half an hour or so the eclipse was on the wane. The afternoon sun was coming back into its own, and the pigeons, believing it to be another sunrise, set off once more to their feeding grounds.

At four o'clock in the afternoon dusk began to fall in earnest, and again the pigeons made for the oak trees for a night's rest. Thus I got three flights in the space of two hours. But I was small, my marksmanship uncertain, and so I had only one pigeon to show for this impeccable strategic planning.

The farmers were very kind to me and always asked me to come to their ferreting expeditions, along the hedgerows. There were so many people about, and so many dogs, that often, when the rabbit bolted and zigzagged along the side of the hedge, I would not dare to shoot. But my hosts had no such inhibitions about niceties of safety margins, and I would huddle amidst a ragged and ear-splitting discharge.

Often my hands would be so cold that, when it came to pushing up the safety catch as the gun went to my shoulder, there was not enough feeling left in my small thumb to move it. Sometimes, to get warm, I would lay my gun down and help handle the ferrets, just to get under the cover of the hedge and out of the biting winter wind.

Then there were the rare days of going to a grown-up shoot with lots of beaters, and a large cartridge bag that weighed down my shoulder. Ronald Henderson of Studley Priory invited me twice a year to his cover shoots. He was a great friend of my father, and they were several years in the House of Commons together. His son John was of an age with myself.

It was one of those many pleasures in which apprehension blends.

I took my place in a ride, always at the extreme end of the line of guns, watching grown-up experts settling themselves down on shooting sticks, holding their guns with confident relaxation, while I gripped mine tight with excitement. The distant sound of the beaters being marshalled came from the far side of the wood, and then a loud cry from the keepers, and the strange medley of tappings, whistlings, shouts and movements showed that they had started. Before they were close enough for their noise to obscure all other sound, I would hear the patter of a rabbit coming closer over the leaves, halting when he saw me, to turn and dash back towards the beaters. Then would come the staccato of those first few pheasants, which rise at the beginning of a drive and come soaring over singly, while the eyes of a whole gun-line are on the gun whose target they are.

I used to pray that those early ones would not come over me, and that nothing would happen until the other guns were too preoccupied to see how I was getting on.

During the day the bag of cartridges got lighter. Sometimes things went right for short periods; and with a sudden burst of confidence, three shots in succession would strike their target. Sometimes things went uniformly wrong and a fearful load of shame would bow me down coupled with a certainty that I would never be invited again. Then it was a nightmare of loading and firing, and loading and firing, at shapes that rocketed above, and all as hopeless as King Canute trying to keep back the waves. But always the doings of the day, hour by hour, would be a fascinating recollection to be related to my father at home and to Jack in his cottage, with no single detail omitted. Ronald Henderson was a kind host and a very good shot. He gave me better advice on shooting than anyone else. Even Jack deferred to his opinion.

I grew in to my father's twelve bore and then grew out of it. At the age of nine it was too long for me, but at thirteen it fitted me exactly. I then began to grow out of it and it was not until I was an undergraduate at Oxford that I had the stock properly lengthened, and achieved some kind of accuracy again. I have done a great deal of shooting since Oxford days with that gun but I cannot begin to claim that I am a good shot. But I will always be profoundly grateful that I was brought up by my father to be a safe one, and taught by Jack to know something of the ways of birds and beasts, and learned from both how to enjoy even the blankest of days.

10

The Magic of Otmoor

WE had come to Elsfield in 1919 as four small London children. We had grown into the Oxfordshire countryside, and will never grow out of it. As I have already said, it had become one hemisphere and Peeblesshire the other. Being half Scots and half English these two hemispheres made up the world, and a very happy world at that.

For children, romance is waiting at the door. Adventure is the imminence of the unexpected or the unknown and, to children, all the world is one or the other. In later life it must be sought farther afield, but they are most fortunate who can find it in simple things.

In our childhood a visit to Noke Wood, or to any of the surrounding spinneys, was as fraught with interest and excitement as great as that of an expedition to the forests of Northern Canada, or even to the green depths of the Congo. The flat vista of Otmoor was as thrilling, to us children, as the broad sweep of the Canadian prairie must have been to the early settlers driving their covered wagons. My father had a strong streak of romance in his character, which was one of the secrets of his deep enjoyment of life.

Noke Wood is exactly forty acres in extent. It has a long, thin appendage, like the tail of a dragon, of about another ten acres, which is not our property. The timber was cut to the ground in the last century, and the present oaks and ashes had to struggle their way up against the rabbits and the undergrowth.

Rides had been cut and some drainage carried out, but at certain times and seasons it was almost a swamp as well as a jungle. To us as children it was the most thrilling of all jungles. It starts on the slope beside Beckley village and runs to the flat land on the edge of Otmoor. I have since managed to drain the wood.

It was done by German prisoners, after the 1939-45 war. One of them carved a swastika, and the lightning sign of the S.S. on the bark of a silver birch. I value that birch tree, so I have not cut it down, and in time those symbols of cruelty and hatred will be effaced by Nature.

Although they have not been long growing, some of the oak trees are now of considerable stature. It is always sad to see an oak tree cut down, its branches lopped off and its sturdy trunk borne away, like the body of some stout old soldier who, after surviving many wars, has at last been laid low.

There are many foxes in this wood, and we greatly encourage them, for they keep the rabbits down which gives the self-seeded ashes and the little oaks a better chance of survival.

Sometimes foxes increase in numbers to the point of menace in this part of the world. The South Oxfordshire hounds drew Woodeaton Wood, when I was a small boy, and found no fewer than fourteen foxes. I stood with a crowd of villagers on the slope above and watched this extraordinary scene of confusion. The hounds went home leaving many couples behind, each happily enjoying a day's hunting by themselves.

The tropical jungle creeps in fast and will soon efface the works of man. But I do not think that it creeps in any faster than the jungle of an Oxfordshire wood. Cut back the hazel and the black-thorn, the hedge maple and the dogwood, and in two years' time it will be as high as your head again.

In summer the rides become almost impassable, with the lush growth which springs from what was bare ground in winter. Cut back the undergrowth in the winter and, with April, ane-mones and bluebells and primroses will be dotting the forest floor, with here and there an orchid.

I have always preferred the woods in winter, for then you can see every detail of the stems of the trees, the strange writhing branches of the oaks, and the slim wands of the ashes. When there is snow on the ground I can fancy myself back in the forests of Northern Canada, with a brooding snow sky darkening with the twilight, and the gentle thud of my feet on the white carpet beneath me. The branches of the oaks are picked out in thin etching of white, and the pigeons flock in from the fields of kale in a multitude, and the clapping of their wings is like thunder when a shot disturbs them from their roost.

Evenings in the wood in winter never lose their fascination. If the afternoon is very still, you can hear Beckley clock chiming the hour from the square tower of the old church and the roosters in Beckley crowing lethargically from half a mile away.

Alfred Sumner, who used to be my father's groom, is now our woodman. He lives beside a little valley which runs down from Beckley to Otmoor. He can see the clock on the church tower a quarter of a mile away. He tells the time by it in daylight, aiding his vision by the telescope sight of a German 88 mm. gun, which his son brought back from the war.

In the silence of the wood there come other sounds. Somewhere in the distance is the noise of a tractor. It is a noise which has become as much a part of the countryside as the sound of the reaper in summer. If it is frosty, one can hear pattering on the leaf-strewn earth. Maybe it is the measured tramp of a cock pheasant, or the noisy scuffling of a grey squirrel on the ground, or blackbirds turning aside the leaves to find some food in a chill, hungry world.

Gradually the sky takes on the deeper blue of evening. High up the rooks are making their way to their rookeries, plodding through the sky and looking as if they had done a good day's work and deserved their rest. A jangling flock of jackdaws passes just over the tops of the trees. In the field outside the wood, there is that strange, rasping call of a partridge.

And the wood becomes full of its own noises. There is the scolding of those pirates, the jay and the magpie; unbelievably wary birds, who have no honour, even among their own kind, for they rob nests and delight to reveal the presence of a hard-pressed fox by their screeching. A carrion crow on a dead tree gives his raucous caw.

There is only one animal in the world that I really hate, and that is the crocodile. But I am not far from hating the carrion crow. He is a symbol of decay, of birdless woods and untended land. You may see him in daylight and the long liquid sweep of his wings, flying warily high. As night falls in the woods, you may see him joined by his fellows, whirling in circles, in a strange witch's dance that lasts till darkness has fallen and he settles to roost.

It is at that moment, when the curtain of darkness is almost drawn, that crow, magpie and jay lose their wariness and may blunder past you within shot. The fieldfare and the redwing with their brisk chatter come over the tree tops; those slim, attractive birds who will return to nest whence they came, in the far distance of Siberia. Imperceptibly the twilight deepens, and the noises of scurrying feet on the woodland floor become fewer. The chink-chink of the blackbirds is ceasing, and one's ears are strained for the sound of pigeons' wings.

The crack of a gunshot wakes up the little world of varied life that the wood contains. There is a clapping of pigeons' wings, and a scurrying of feet on the leafy floor, then silence. The detail of the hazels and the tree trunks is getting dim, and the only clear field of vision is against the sky through the tracery of the branches. Over the horizon comes the moon, turning the water in the ruts to silver. Such few cock pheasants as there are, are settling down to roost after noisy bursts of pompous challenge. You stamp chilled feet. The pigeons' shapes are no longer things of grey and white but dark, slim outlines.

Then all is quiet, and it is time to splash home down the rides, along the dim avenues until you are clear of the ceiling of branches and under the open night sky. Here is a world of infinite romance. Time has not made it one whit less the happy hunting ground that it was to us as children.

The long thin dragon's tail of Noke Wood comes almost to the edge of Otmoor. That edge is a great circular ditch, once full of rushes and a great nesting place for the moorhens and the occasional mallard, but now cleansed and vastly enlarged by a dredger.

If you go to Otmoor in a dry summer you can cross the ditch and you will find yourself at the bottom of a great saucer of land, of reedy, rushy fields where your feet will slip on hard clods beneath. There are always broad ditches, which are full of pike, and one piece of permanent water, not above an acre in extent, where the water birds nest.

You can look back from the bottom of this saucer and see Beckley on the upland above you, the same upland which winds round to Elsfield. But Otmoor after heavy rains is one great sheet of water, hundreds of acres in extent, from which stick out lines of gnarled willows and straggling blackthorns to mark the boundaries of the fields. And the fields are big, one is 100 acres in extent and there are several others not much smaller. Those are the two extremes. From Beckley there runs down the hill, and right across the middle of the moor, passing along one side of the little patch of standing water, a Roman road. You cannot discover where it runs unless you know. On many a night there, in quest of duck, I have sought it with my feet, and felt the nails of my boots grind on the Roman stones.

Otmoor is full of snipe at certain times and seasons. Its absolute tranquillity is now shattered at intervals by the Royal Air Force using it as a bombing target. But this has not noticeably affected the birds.

Shooting snipe is surely one of the most exciting of all forms of shooting. There was a farmer who lived on the edge of the moor, below Beckley, who did a great deal of it, and on every frosty night in winter would stroll down from his farm to the boundary ditch, on the chance of a duck. He was the only man, that I have ever seen, who would get two snipe in three shots. He always shot at snipe at exactly the same distance away. He let them get to thirty yards, even if they got up at his feet.

There are few more exciting ways of spending a day than following snipe. For long periods you splash through soft green rushes and rank grass, then, quite suddenly, not one but four snipe will rise at your feet. They are fatally easy to lose, once they are shot, in ground like this. You mark one as he falls beside a tuft of rushes. You walk towards the tuft—another rises at your feet with a harsh squeak—you turn to shoot at it and then you look for the tuft of rushes, beside which your first snipe fell, and you find your bearings are completely lost.

From the broad ditches round the fields a mallard may rise, with a great quacking and splashing, when you least expect it. You will almost certainly miss him.

Once on a sunny, windy January day I was walking up snipe with Jack, who belongs to the school of thought which says, "Shoot at the snipe the moment he rises." We were going through some long rushes, breast high, and I heard his gun go off and saw a bird pitch out of sight. It turned out to be a spotted crake, a rarity which he would never have molested, had not his hair-trigger reflex been too much for him.

Among the villagers of the seven towns of Otmoor are several families who, for generations past, have been fowlers and gained a large part of their living from the pursuit of the wild fowl.

Many a night Jack and I, with Pat Heathcoat-Amory and other Oxford friends, have sallied across the flats to take a stand beside the open water for a duck. We would take up our positions at the last of daylight, muffled and booted for the cold of the vigil and, seemingly, completely alone.

Then darkness would fall. We searched blue-black sky and pricked our ears for the whistle of a mallard's wings. And gradually we would become conscious that we were not alone. A pin-point of light would illuminate the darkness, as somebody a quarter of a mile away lit a pipe. A snatch of conversation would come to us, that sounded in our ears, though it might have been anywhere in a half a mile radius.

Quite suddenly, a golden sword of flame would strike upwards in the darkness from an unseen gun, followed by another, and before the reverberations came back to us from the containing hills, there would be a great quacking as ducks, which had pitched undetected into the ditches and pools, shook the water from their sides and took to the night sky.

Shooting in the darkness is a trick which takes practice to acquire. With practice one gets the trick of adjudging degrees of darkness. There comes a point when any bird that one can see is necessarily in range, and probably in close range at that.

A shot in the dark would set all the birds on the moor piping and calling. There would be many minutes before quietness returned. When it was too dark we would hear Jack's shambling footsteps and his whistle, and we would rally round him and splash back along the line of the Roman road, until we crossed the boundary ditch and our feet were on firm ground once more.

Many is the happy winter afternoon and many the dusk and dark that I have spent on Otmoor with Jack; and with Pat Heath-coat-Amory, who was a close friend both at Eton and Oxford. I trust there will be many more days like them, but they will not be with Pat, for he lies where he fell—"slain in the desert by a wandering spear".

Otmoor in summer is a magic sight. The air is full of the piping of the redshank, and the drumming of the snipe. There are still a few plover there, though they have grown sadly uncommon in recent years. It is a paradise for the ornithologists. One wet spring there was much water lying, and the birds had raised their nests on little platforms of rushes. We found a mallard's nest on a great footstool of reeds, which was visible from 100 yards away. We found more plovers' nests than you would ever find now, each conspicuous on its little raised platform in the marshy water. We found the nests of a redshank, and of moorhens in abundance. It was not what we found that was so exciting, it was to be striding about in the sunshine among the rushes, amidst that wonderful chorus of birds, each raising his own wild cry of alarm, that was so deeply fascinating.

I never saw a rare bird's nest on Otmoor. I once flushed a pintail, which was at that time supposed to nest only on the coast, and searched for three days on end for its nest, without finding it. Malcolm MacDonald came out a week later, when I had gone back to school. Among his many other distinctions, he is a very fine field naturalist. He found the nest the first afternoon that he went down there.

But the rarest visitors to Otmoor were the winter ones. One of the greatest ornithologists of that time was the porter who stood at the door of the Clarendon Buildings in Oxford. Experts the world over deferred to his opinion. If we ever wanted confirmation of a bird, we could get it on the highest authority from him. He would whisper the names of great rarities that sometimes visited Otmoor, but under seal of secrecy. But it is not the rareties that give it its magic in the summer, but that wild free chorus of birds, and the wind blowing fresh and scented across this great marshy prairie. Otmoor, too, has not lost the romance it had in boyhood. Anything might happen on Otmoor.

It is from this world of Elsfield that we went sadly back to school three times a year. And as the years passed we moved from the nearby preparatory school, to the distant spires of Eton, for the wheel to come full circle and bring us back to the University at Oxford.

II

Deer Stalking

My first summer holiday from Eton finished with a glorious
ten days at Ardtornish in Morvern, then the home of
Gerard Craig-Sellar. He had been a friend of my father, since
South African days. His was a large domain. The house was huge,
ugly, and comfortable and lay at the end of Loch Aline.

To this day I regard any dwelling that has to be approached
by a boat as mysterious and exciting. It was said in those days that
the three best sea-trout lochs in Britain were Loch Stack, Loch
Na Shellaig in Ross-shire, and Areanas, which lies on the Ardtornish property. Without wishing to start any controversy I put
them advisedly in that order. Even then Areanas was considered
to be declining from its greatest days; but it was still wonderful
fishing. From Areanas, the little River Aline runs a short course
to the sea. It was a good, if highly temperamental, salmon river.
The stalking was excellent although the hills are not as high, nor
as rough as the best stalking country really should be.

Gerard Sellar was a wonderfully kind and thoughtful host.
A rich man, he had most of the things that money can buy, and
many of those more precious things which are beyond the power
of money to acquire. He made himself extremely happy by putting happiness in the reach of other people.

My father and I spent many happy days on Areanas. Consider-
ing the reputation that the loch held, we did not do unduly well.
We caught large numbers of sea-trout, a good many of which
were between two and three pounds in weight. My father caught
a rusty old sea-trout, long up from the sea, which weighed just
under four pounds. By classic precedent the biggest always seemed
to get away. My weapon was a nine-foot greenheart which was
too light for that calibre of fish. After a lost battle, which had
lasted twenty minutes, with a sea-trout estimated by the ghillie

at over seven pounds, my father decreed that I should have a sea-trout rod. His decision was strengthened two days later, after a short nerve-wracking battle with a salmon, which bent my little rod like a blade of grass, had ended in my discomfiture. The rod duly appeared at Christmas. We had no fortune with the salmon in the river, and when we were not on Areanas we were usually stalking.

The introduction to stalking was gruelling. On my father's estimate we rarely covered less than twenty miles in a day. My short legs ached abominably, and I fell asleep immediately after dinner. But it was worth it, a hundred times over. The ritual was thrilling. First the reconnaissance, from beside the road; lying on our backs searching the far hills; the stalker with his long tele-scope, supported by his crook; my father with a pair of German binoculars from the 1914 war, and myself with a humble instru-ment called a "monocular", like the eye of the Cyclops. Years later, in 1943, as the Commander of a Canadian Battalion, I searched the Sicilian hills for Germans, with these same German binoculars. I was holding them when I was wounded and, in falling, one of the eye pieces was smashed on a rock and they have never been quite the same since.

The stalker, trained in the Lovat Scouts, used to point out the distant stags by the clock system of target indication; "Reference the tall scree, four o'clock and just on the edge o' yon bracken."

Then came the stalk. Eyes on the ground as we climbed, as we always seemed to be climbing; breath coming faster, short legs getting feebler; red, yellow and grey sponges of moss; deep, dripping heather, black patches of almost liquid peat; sweltering in bursts of sunlight, drenched in rain, and always trying not to lag. I learned here the truth of a Canadian backwoods motto— "One good step is worth half a dozen bad ones." A stumble or slip back that broke the rhythm of the climb brought on fatigue in a wave. Somewhere, on the other side of a world of suffering was this being—the stag. As the mind tired with the body it be-came a creature of nightmare. "The stag at eve had drunk its fill" —had it really? It must have been very thirsty to take all that time. How long was it going to be, before my father could dispatch a winged crumb of lead to lay low this beast who was torturing us? How long, how long, how long?

It became a little less exhausting with experience. I learned what to step on, and what to avoid, until it became almost second nature. Unconsciously I copied the way that the stalker went up a hill, not on his toes like a man going upstairs, but laying his feet sideways to the slope. The crawling was easier, as it usually began when we were fairly close to the stag, and there were frequent halts where we froze in position. The stalker's telescope would wheeze as he opened it, and thud as he shut it. Then the shot, when I lay just behind my father, waiting for the crack of the rifle to set the echoes rolling round the hills; and then the look on his face which told whether or not it had gone true. But even before I saw his face I could guess from his back view whether or not the stag still lived.

After a good many expeditions as a non-combatant, it was decided that the time was ripe for me to try a shot. I went to bed the night before in a sober frame of mind, feeling what a great responsibility had settled on me. I awoke full of apprehension. I was seen off with many good wishes for my success.

To familiarize me with the rifle we visited what was known as the "Iron Stag". This was a silhouette, not of a stag but of a hind, executed in solid iron, and painted bright red. It was half as big again as life-size, and lacked one ear which had been carried away by a bullet. The sacred rifle was drawn from its case. I was given brief instructions about the safety catch, advice about squeezing, and not pulling, the trigger. After aligning the sights and squeezing the trigger, through what appeared to be an arc of at least ninety degrees, the rifle went off with a roar. The bullet hit the huge rufus beast with the noise of a blow struck on a gong. My father and stalker applauded, and we set off to do real battle.

The feeling of responsibility was heavy and thrust fatigue into insignificance. As we concluded a long stalk, with occasional view of our quarry, instead of dropping discreetly back I was thrust forward.

With hideous suddenness the moment came.

The little herd of deer fed serenely on a ridge, and we lay concealed across the valley of a little burn behind the next ridge, some 150 yards distant. The ghillie gingerly extracted the rifle from its case, unable to conceal his apprehension, and handed it to me. The stag was pointed out and, slipping off the safety catch, I ground myself into the heathery bed to take aim. How different had been the neat joinder of the sights against the huge red background of the "iron stag". The sights seemed to cover this beast completely. By magic it seemed suddenly to have shrunk to the size of a goat, and to be hiding behind the foresight. From the moment that I started on the first squeeze of pressure I realized that the sights were gently rocking backwards and forwards. Releasing the pressure I re-sighted, but the sights would not stay still, and they began to swing through a wider and wider arc.

Desperate now, I grabbed at the trigger. The muzzle jumped as the shot boomed out. There was a hurrying and a scurrying of frightened beasts, and the ridge ahead was empty.

We followed them until nearly dark, and quite suddenly came on a stag and two hinds, huddled at the foot of a bluff of grey rock. Dark mist was curling down, and I had my last chance at nearly 200 yards. This time I really thought that I fastened my sight correctly on the dun-coloured outline against the dark rock, for fatigue had dulled my nerves.

As the rifle kicked, a spurt of rock dust leapt from the dark wall a foot above the stag's shoulder, and in a second they were in the mist. My father then decided that it would be as well to let some time elapse before I tried my hand again. It was not until four years later that I got my first stag.

Stalking in Scotland has no exact parallel anywhere else. Like all real sport it calls for enterprise as well as skill, but it is hedged by artificial difficulties which make it far more exacting than the pursuit of deer or antelope in any other part of the world where I have ever hunted. The red deer has better eyesight to detect movement than any of his tribe that I have ever encountered elsewhere, and every bit as good a sense of smell. Scope of manoeuvre in the stalk is limited by the consideration that frightened deer must stampede back to your own ground, and not over the march.

But the real difficulty is the stalker. He insists on carrying your rifle so that you have grown unfamiliar with its touch when you take your shot. He withdraws it from its case, and thrusts it into your hand, with nervousness so ill-concealed that it communicates itself to you, and destroys what confidence you may have had. He is not to blame. He is as anxious as you are that you should be successful, but he is tormentd by apprehensions; apprehensions not only that you may miss and the deer be frightened to no purpose, but that you may wound and, bound by the etiquette of the sport, have to follow the beast, if necessary, across another forest until you get him; or that through some ill luck the deer may cross the march. Lastly, he is rightly proud of his reputation and, if his marksman misses, he feels that a stigma attaches to himself.

Four seasons after my first unsuccessful attempt I got a stag on Sal Mor, overlooking Little Loch Broom. A good deal of practice with a rifle in the intervening years had given me new confidence. After a day of rain and sun and changing wind, we were winding our way round the path above the lochside when, not seventy yards away, a stag leapt to its feet higher up the hill and stared at us.

That was its undoing. Quick as lightning the stalker whipped the rifle from its case, and thrust it into my hand. No time to kneel, a free shot with no rest, and the stag rolled head over heels down the screes towards us, almost before I knew that I had fired.

The walk home down the mountain-side was one of the pleasantest I ever remember. A misty blue Ross-shire evening, the stag swinging athwart the plodding pony, and the little plumes of smoke rising from the chimneys of the crofts by the lochside below us.

We had one day's fishing for sea-trout on the fabulous Loch Na Shellaig. I mentioned it earlier as being reputed one of the best lochs in Scotland. It was a long walk from the roadside, following the whole course of the Gruniard river. Mist was on the high hilltops when we got there, and there was a glimmer on the ripples, which were both bad signs. We caught two sea-trout, just over three pounds each. A triumph so far as I was concerned, but we were told virtually a blank day for that fabulous sheet of water.

In 1930, my last season of Highland sport before I set out on travels that did not end until 1945, my father and I had a wonderful feast of Highland sport. In achievement its results were small, except for the catching of a two-pound trout at Loch Choire, in a loch where one pound was the previous record. This was in itself a strange fluke, as I had merely put up a rod to fish for half an hour before dinner. For the rest it was a record of salmon struck at too soon, and disappearing with a farewell jag at the reel, and stags missed in four forests.

But it could not have been pleasanter or more exciting. Of the stags I missed I can claim in several cases to be the victim of bad advice. Each of them was a downhill shot. Each time the stalker besought me to shoot low. If a high velocity rifle is accurately sighted, the bullets will hit the point on which the sights are aligned. If one shoots low, one will hit low; to shoot too low results in a complete miss, and I did. By a great stroke of luck I got a stag on the move with a second shot, which I had wounded with my first. The fear of wounding now transcended all my other apprehensions.

It was a wonderful season, in spite of the paucity of its results; stalking in sunlight above the Tay at Bolfrax; the views from Ben Armine and sight of a hummel, a great hornless beast, leading a little band of hinds; watching in pouring rain a fourteen-point stag at Langwell, with the old Duke of Portland who stalked every day, hale and hearty, at seventy. There was a stalk under the clear sub-Arctic light on the rolling heathery Caithness horizon at Dalnawhillan. There were unsuccessful days on the Thurso, and the fascination of watching a gigantic ghillie, nearly twenty stone of muscle, cast a double handed fifteen-foot green-heart rod with one hand.

And last of all, a day's stalking at Dunrobin, with a stalker who had originally come from Tweedsmuir, and dropping down through the pinewoods on our way homewards, startled by the clatter of a capercailzie among the pines.

12

Island of Mull

As a family we spent two delightful summer holidays in the Island of Mull. It is a paradise of sport, if you like your sport rough. Rain and mist, mackintoshes and midges predominate in recollection, varied by days of August sunshine which turned the whole country into a paradise of warmth and colour and delectable scent.

It was sufficiently remote for us to have to take with us everything that we were likely to want, as it was impossible to get anything there. That problem called for a good deal of thought and resulted in setting off heavily loaded. It is quite fatal in such circumstances to have one of anything, whether it be fly or spinner, unless one wants to risk grave disappointment. This was brought home to us with brutal suddenness when my brother Billy, aged eleven, with his tiny trout rod tossed our only blue minnow into the brown water and lost it in a big fish. At not one of the other spinners, that we had, would the sea-trout give a second look.

Our first visit was in 1927. We took a small shooting lodge called Ardura, which stands on the shores of Loch Spelvie, a sizeable arm of the sea. We had to charter a small craft to reach it from Oban, and we were well soaked with spray by the time we got into its quiet waters. It was contained by high hills covered with an ungainly forest of scrubby birch, which held woodcock in the winter and nothing else but rabbits at any other time of the year. A long, shingly beach bordered its landward end. At one side of the beach the little River Lussa entered the sea loch through a natural delta of shingle banks. At the opposite side was a tiny stone jetty and the path which led to the shooting lodge. Then the valley narrowed where the river was spanned by an old stone bridge, crossed by a road which looked like a gravelled garden path. It was the main artery of communication in the island, but to see a car was as much an incident as seeing the smoke of another vessel in mid-Atlantic.

The little house was perfect for its purpose—small, comfortable, warm, and had a surprisingly good library of books. It was set on one slope of the valley, and looked down on the narrow flat below to the best pool in the Lussa set at the far side of the valley bottom. Just beside it, in a pocket in the hillside, was a boggy loch, of perhaps an acre, which winked with rising trout every evening.

After one attempt we gave up trying to catch them. The bank was a quaking bog. We could not reach the verge. We could cast out into the loch with fourteen feet of line lying in a bed of bog cotton, and to get any fish ashore of any size was entirely beyond our skill. Our sporting rights were one bank of the River Lussa from the sea, up three and a half miles of valley. Above that was a waterfall, Tor Ness, where we used to go on Sunday afternoons and watch the salmon jumping, but on which we had no rights. A few miles above that was a reedy loch, in which the river rose. Here we had, on every other day, the use of the boat. We rarely exercised this right, as no one will fish from a boat when he can fish a river on his own two feet. I have always found it hard to adjust myself to the concept of big silver salmon lurking among reeds and rushes, but there were undoubtedly a great many there, for we saw them jumping, although we never caught one.

There was a vast area of ground included, that could be measured in thousands of acres, to describe which the term "rough shooting" might have been coined. It swarmed with rabbits and big blue mountain hares. It held a certain number of grouse which we occasionally pursued, more as a ritual than as a serious day's shooting. On hot days we sat down to rest with a great deal of circumspection, for the countryside was full of adders. I have seen, in a two-mile stretch of road, no fewer than twelve which had been out sunning themselves on the unfrequented highway, and which had the misfortune to be run over by one of the very few cars which traversed it.

My father at that time had ceased to care for shooting with a gun, though he remained a desperately keen fisherman and deer stalker. My brothers, who were aged respectively eleven and eight, and I used to go after rabbits, sometimes of an evening, on the green slopes among the birches. Our armaments were a single barrel sixteen bore, a single barrel .410 with a bolt action; and a small air gun.

But to all of us the river was the real magnet, and in five weeks we wore paths along the edge of every fishable stretch. There were plenty of salmon in it, at times, but they ran up fast to the pool below Tor Ness falls. The sea-trout were the real quarry, and there were good brown trout as well. The river was so small that with a brown trout rod we could not only reach any part that we wanted, but could also fairly hope to play a big fish by running up and down the bank.

My father wrote many books in his life but never one that he did not write for the pure pleasure of the thing. Because it gave him so much pleasure he used to write on his holidays— although he refused to see a newspaper or consider anything that, in his view, might correspond to work. He sat in a little study on the ground floor and wrote till twelve o'clock. Nothing ever distracted his steady concentration, but as he paused to re-light his pipe he would gaze down the slope, across the little valley, at the bend in the river between the bridge and the sea pool.

As we got to know it, we could gauge by looking at the number of stones that were showing exactly how ripe the water was for fishing.

My father's rod was up and his cast had been soaking since breakfast. At twelve o'clock he dropped his pen and was down the winding path to the boat pool, rod and net in hand, with a fly box in one pocket and a cast box in the other. At one o'clock he was back in the house again. I do not remember him failing to bring home a sea-trout. My younger brothers and I used to leave the sea pool undisturbed for him in the mornings.

We walked a mile up the river to the Pedlar's Pool, nearly fifty yards of still deep water, overshadowed by birches on the far bank. It was a rough walk through a ragged forest. The ground was boggy and full of hard tussocks. My brothers wore black Wellington boots, black mackintoshes and black sou'-wester hats. Each grasped a trout rod and a can of worms. They looked rather like small black seals.

Above the Pedlar's Pool the valley steepened, and the river fell in a series of small cataracts into deep potholes. The incidence of the fish we lost seemed amazingly high for those that we captured. I fished with a fly, as befitted a fifteen-year-old fisherman of some seven years' angling experience. My brothers fished with a worm with a small cork as a float. The best fish they ever brought to the net was one and a quarter pounds.

It was a consolation prize for a tragedy of an hour before. Billy had made his first cast of the day. A fine fat worm had disappeared into a dark pothole. The cork had hardly started to move when it disappeared, only to reappear a second later with a four pound sea-trout leaping clear of the water, and then to disappear like an arrow over the cataract into a pothole below, snapping the cast at the knot. When adults lose a fish they seek to summon up some philosophy to mitigate the sting. They are always unsuccessful. When boys lose a big fish they give themselves up to ten minutes of unashamed lamentation, and feel the better for it.

That kind of small river does not seem to have a normal level. It is either high or it is low, rising or falling. Fishing the first three inches of the spate on the rise was a great moment. Every fish caught had sea lice on him, and had been in the sea perhaps half an hour before. When a spate came, we dropped everything and rushed to the river.

During our third week at Ardura the worst school report that I have ever had—and that is putting it pretty high—arrived by the somewhat erratic post. It was a terrible indictment of wayward idleness. My father was horrified by it. It was a close thundery day when the post arrived. Then the clouds broke and the whole valley was a smoking deluge of thundery rain. Within fifteen minutes it was reported that the river was rising.

My father was a fisherman first. We grabbed our rods and all four of us tumbled down to the sea pool, where there was only room for two to fish at once with any kind of elbow-room. My father went to the bottom of the pool, and I went to the neck at the top. On the bank between us my brothers watched their two corks gyrating side by side in the rising water. We lost several fish but, when we came back—soaked to the skin—we were carrying a heavy basket up the steep slope to the house. Practically nothing was said about my report after that. It was talked over briefly, but without rancour, as one might discuss an unpleasant happening, reported in the newspapers, in some part of the world where Britain had no responsibilities.

It was a very happy holiday. Indeed we were fortunate to have many such, as children. My father's book *John McNab* had not long been published. He received a letter, just as we were leaving, signed "Three Labour M.P.s", wagering that they would kill a salmon, a sea-trout and a brown trout on our stretch of water without our being able to catch them.

Among the small Parliamentary Labour Party, then in the House of Commons, there were one or two extremely expert fishermen, most of whom did their fishing on the difficult reaches of the Upper Clyde. It was always a great source of regret that we did not have time to take this wager. I do not think they could have caught a salmon, as we only caught one in the whole of our tenancy, but it would have been very hard to watch three and a half miles of river and stop three determined men from catching a sea-trout and a brown trout.

Ardura laid a powerful spell on us, so the following year we planned another holiday in Mull. I arrived a week later with my Scots kin, who were to be our guests for several weeks as they had been at Ardura. My own tardy appearance was due to having to attend an Officers' Training Corps Camp, which held most of the horrors of war without any of its compensations.

This time we took ship from Oban on *The Lochinvar* to Tobermory. It took two T model Fords to accommodate our family and our belongings and convey us to a little fishing lodge that overlooked Loch Baa. Loch Baa is a long loch some three-quarters of a mile in breadth. Tall rugged mountains enclose it, covered on their lower slopes by a forest of birches. At the near end of the loch there is a shore line of green grassy hillocks on which the fishing lodge stands. At one end of this shore line, where the mountains run down to the lochside, the River Baa sets off on its short and turbulent course to the sea, which it enters at the end of a long arm of inlet called Loch Na Kiel.

Loch Na Kiel is deep and sheltered. In the 1914 war it was often used by units of the Royal Navy. As a reminder of those days there lay, at high tidemark, a rusty globe of steel—a mine that had long been harmless. It looked like a huge rufous sea-urchin.

Ben More Lodge is approached along the shores of Loch Na Kiel passing under the lee of Ben More, the highest mountain in Mull. Then the road traverses the neck of land beside the little river, and this comfortable, if somewhat austere, dwelling is reached. And there is the loch running away between its high mountain walls that frame the narrow horizon.

At the upper end of the loch two large burns come in. In both of these we tried the worm with varying success. A busy family of otters made it difficult for any big fish to survive long in these little pools.

A crofter and his family lived in this mountain-girt remoteness, a mile beyond the upper end of the loch. We knew of his existence but we did not see him. Ten days after our arrival, his small freckle-faced son came riding down the valley, at the best pace that he could knock out of a hill pony. He told us that his father had been terribly injured by a bull. Crofting families have to be self-reliant, and in an incredibly short time the boy had covered the long distance to the nearest doctor, and the doctor was making haste up the valley. In spite of terrible injuries the crofter made a complete recovery.

The walls in the main living-room of the fishing lodge were decorated by pictures of the larger salmon that had been caught in the loch. They were portrayed vertically, standing on their tails. The date of their capture, and their weight, were inscribed beside them. As murals, they would probably be considered rather more curious than beautiful. My brothers and I would eye them for hours at a time. They could not have fascinated us more had they been the works of Giotto or Ghirlandaio. The largest room was a billiard room in which my father worked and kept his papers. It had a full-sized billiard table, furrowed by much playing of billiards fives. After a day's fishing, our wet clothes steamed in the drying-room and, after basking in the comfort of a hot bath, and rendered torpid by a great feast of scones and jelly, my father and I had many a game on that table. The record break was fifteen.

It is a fascinating thing to live in a house looking down on a loch and see all its changing moods. There were many salmon in it but we caught only one. In parts there were a good many brown trout, though we never landed any of size, but the sea-trout are plentiful.

There was only one place we could fish the loch from the shore. When the wind was right my father used to get out on this sandy point with his big greenheart salmon rod. We watched his line cut a straight path through the ripples, crowned by the plop of the fly at what seemed to us an incredible distance from the shore. But nearly all our fishing was done from a boat. It was a big, heavy boat and we had a bearded ghillie, Ronald MacDonald, who used to row us to the fishing grounds. He was steeped in West Highland legend and history of the fighting times. When we asked for the name of a mountain or a point of land in the loch, he always had some tale to tell of it—some legend of fairies, or fragment of the battles. He was famous for his keen eyesight, and could see as much with the naked eye as most men with binoculars.

Two other fishing lodges had rights on this loch, but they kept to one shore while we kept to the other. One party used to go down the loch almost every morning with an outboard motor. The hum of the motor growing more distant was part of the morning scene. They used to troll behind the boat, and on one occasion hooked a salmon on a spinner, with the motor going full speed. It is almost incredible that a salmon should take under those conditions, for the noise of the outboard motor, at that range, must be devastating to the sensitive organs of a fish. It is hardly less amazing that a salmon should take a bait moving at such a pace, but there is no rule that you can make about the behaviour of fish which they are not prepared to break at least once.

For the most part the skies were grey and the wind came down the loch towards us, driving the ripples on to the shore below the lodge. Our best drift was along the edge of the green links below the house. Salmon we saw, as occasional disturbances of the ripples by a swirl of a shiny back and fin, or leaping clear when there was thunder in the air. No loch fishing compares with fishing in a river, but it has its own fascination. As one gets to know a loch it ceases to be a single great stretch of water, but rather a series of places where one knows fish may be caught, as distinct as separate pools in a river and as different in character.

Working one's line through the indigo of the dark ripples has its own particular fascination. No fish in the world, for its size, takes the fly with the dash and force of a sea-trout. The wrench at the rod seems to come even before the eye catches the swirling disturbance on the surface, and almost before you are aware that you have hooked a fish, he is in the air.

When the mist wreathed the high mountains above us, we might catch fish. When it started to press down the hillside our chances got fewer and fewer. It was on the dark days, when the outline of the mountain walls was clear and a fresh warm western wind blew down the dark loch setting the ripples running in little waves, that excitement rose to fever pitch.

It was on one of these days that my brother Billy and I caught, in the space of thirty-five minutes, a salmon, and a three pound sea-trout, and five other sea-trout over one pound. The salmon and the big sea-trout did not come to a fly. As we finished the drift, and rowed back to begin it again, we put out two minnows.

Trolling is not accounted much sport, but there is something curiously exciting about the arc of the rod swaying gently with each stroke of the oars, and then beginning to leap like a wild thing with the reel screeching. Those dark waters we felt might yield a fish of any size—even water kelpies, in whose existence Ronald implicitly believed.

On this particular occasion I was trolling with a trout fly-rod, which I never should have been doing, but boys in their excitement are heedless. I had a trout reel, a light cast with a small Golden Devon. The salmon took it and, in one long steady run, stripped the line down to the drum. Frantic with excitement, I leaned over the stern holding the rod the full length of my arm to give him one more yard, and then quite unexpectedly he turned and swam towards the boat. Ten minutes later the gaff, which had come to be looked on as more for ornament than for any purpose, was extended to its full length and the salmon was on board.

There were sometimes days of calm. Sometimes the mist would press down almost to the water, and a sizzling drizzle made a myriad of pinpricks on the great smooth sheet of the surface. We could see the rising fish then, up to half a mile away. On one such day, finding ourselves at the far end of the loch, we tried the worm in the biggest pool in the larger of the two burns. I hooked a splendid trout of just over two pounds and landed him after a wild fight on very fine tackle. He had the dark back and yellow belly, which is the most attractive of all the colours brown trout may assume. He had survived the depredations of the otters only to fall victim to an infinitely less experienced enemy.

Sometimes there were days of blazing sunshine with hardly a cloud in the sky, those days when one absorbs the hot smell of rich moorland, to the accompaniment of the incessant drone of flies. The loch was one great limpid sheet, with here and there a salmon, or a sea-trout, rolling over lazily to a fly. My brother Alastair, who was then aged nine, was left behind to fish, while we went off to take advantage of the weather and climb a mountain. When we came back he had nearly always caught a fish. Ronald had rowed him round all day long, trolling a cast of three flies on a very long line.

What a wonderful month August is for the schoolboy! It is the holiday of all holidays in the year. When September comes he has entered the month which is going to see him back at school. It has never that fine, careless feeling that August has.

13

Up to Oxford

ETON came to an end for me in the spring of 1930. I had
been there exactly five years. My career had been an epic
of obscurity. My scholastic prowess was as meagre as my achievements in games. In the Officers' Training Corps I was second
senior private. But none of these shortcomings clouded my
enjoyment at the time, or my memories of it since.   One of the
many examinations that I failed to pass was Certificate "A". The
first question on the paper was to the effect that you had marched
your platoon for many miles across a desert to reach a water hole.
When you reached the water hole you discovered a dead horse in
it. What steps would you take? I still don't know the answer, and
I threw in my hand there and then. As we came out of the
examination room, I confided to a friend that this question
had floored me. He said, loftily, that it was easy. Years after,
when I was commanding a battalion in action, a Liaison Officer
reported to me from a neighbouring formation with a message.
He was a rather disillusioned-looking captain.   It was he who
had known what to do with the dead horse.

Eton is not situated in the most delectable part of the English
countryside, but there was a good deal of fun to be got out of
it, whether following the beagles in the winter, or watching
birds in the spring. It is a remarkable place for birds. Bitterns
are sometimes seen on Windsor Racecourse. The only time that
I have seen a Great Grey shrike was on a summer evening, when
I was bathing at Cuckoo Weir.

The summer was always the pleasantest time. I ended up
playing cricket in what is known as Fourth Middle Club. It was
composed of those who were senior in years and completely
unteachable duffers. We were left to ourselves and played on a
triangle of greensward enclosed by lines of ancient trees, along

one side of which ran the Thames. We passed the hat round
whenever anyone hit the ball into the river, and usually drew
stumps about mid-afternoon and went off to bathe. In the
Thames at Eton were some mighty trout of almost supernatural
cleverness. Only one was taken in my time. It was captured, after
years of siege, by Penrose Tennyson.

Eton can be enjoyed wildly while one is there, but it cannot
really be appreciated until one has left it and can look back on it
in retrospect. Pat Heathcoat-Amory and I had been friends since
the day that we arrived as new boys. Together, in our last year,
we sat for the entrance examination to Oxford. He passed and
I failed. So it came about that I spent the spring and summer
of 1930 working at Elsfield for my second attempt to get into
Oxford.

The interim between Eton and Oxford gave me the first
spring and summer that I had had at Elsfield since before I went
to my preparatory school. It was a delectable time. I worked in
my father's room that he had built. When he was there, we sat,
each at his own table, opposite the windows which looked over
the view. He wrote steadily, his pen scratching its way over
page after page. I laboriously translated *Herodotus* on to sheets
of foolscap paper. He had been a Member of Parliament since
1926, and was in London for the middle days of each week.
Alice was in London, too, having a season of gaiety. Billy was
at Eton. Alastair was a day-boy at the preparatory school at
Oxford and returned each evening.

My hours of work did not prevent expeditions with Jack down
to the banks of the Cherwell, in the early morning, after chub.
The afternoons allowed intensive exploration of Otmoor in the
nesting season. And so spring became summer and the examination time came. I dressed carefully on the morning of the examination, and got into my little car filled with the awe of the
coming contest. The car flatly refused to start. In terror I ran to
the only farmer who had a car. His farmhouse was about a
quarter of a mile away. He was not there, but was believed to be
on the upland somewhere. Sweating and panting in my examination clothes, white bow tie and dark suit, I dashed uphill. He
was some way off, walking his big horse and surveying his

fields. He heard my hail and trotted towards me. I poured out my story and we made our best pace to the farm, and his car. I got into the examination five minutes after it had started, hot and dishevelled, with my wits sadly scattered. *Mirabile dictu: I* passed.

Life must be uneventful for those who find examinations easy. Perhaps it is this absence of struggle that results in so many of these talented beings going to seed in later life, and disappearing from the scene without even a bubble to mark the spot. But in their heyday how much they are envied.

That autumn I went to my father's old college, Brasenose. He had gone there from Scotland, as a young man, making his first foray to the south. He had greatly distinguished himself, as had his brother Willie who had followed him and then set off to make his career in India. Both are commemorated to-day by memorials in the college chapel.

Going to the University at Oxford was merely an extension of life at Elsfield. Had I not treated it as such I might have got a better degree.

For me, unlike most freshmen, the place had no real novelty. I had lived near it since I was seven years old, and been to school there. The beautiful old walled city with its appendages of the dreariest nineteenth-century suburb, and the most hideous twentieth-century manufacturing town, in all the world, were familiar from childhood. The difference lay in being part of the University instead of merely looking at it from outside.

My days there were happy as could be. My achievements were meagre in the extreme. Having no facility or fondness for any ball game, I took to rowing. I rowed in twenty-eight different races, the highlight of which was rowing in the Brasenose boat at Henley in the year 1932. Of all the twenty-eight races, in which I rowed, we only succeeded in winning one.

To row at Henley is an experience all of its own. You can turn round as you wait for the start, and see the long white booms converging in perspective to the winning post, in a riot of colour, with Henley Bridge and the church tower beyond. It is only 1 mile and 550 yards away, but before you see the flag pole, at Fawley, which is just half-way, you feel that you have swallowed a steam engine and your arms and legs are not limbs but facsimiles of limbs made of cotton wool. The last 300 yards is a delirium of noise and exhaustion and a topsy turvy vision of ladies with parasols, and gentlemen in spotless white trousers, comfortably reclining in punts beside the booms, and enjoying this Roman holiday.

I read for an Honours degree in history, with very little confidence. There were falcons to be fed, and exercised, at Elsfield. There were snipe on Otmoor, and for the expenditure of £12 a year I acquired an admirable little syndicate shoot in the Cotswolds, near the village of Chadlington. In the summer there were trout streams in the Cotswolds. All these distractions, added to the demands of rowing, seemed to leave little time for work. The memory of them forms a happy picture of undergraduate life as we lived it in the early '30's.

I have no regrets that I did no work, for I have done a great deal since. It was the time to be young and to enjoy life. General Smuts was old when he was young, but more than made up for it by being young when he became old. So many of my serious-minded Oxford acquaintances, whose talk was of White Papers, Blue Books and Three Line Whips were never young at all, and now never will be.

Britain was settling into the deepest pit of the economic depression. Friends were suddenly not there, when a new Term started. It was discreetly whispered that their family had "come a cropper". There was the talk of the possibility of war. It did not seem convincing, because we had all been taught to believe that the 1914–18 war had ruled out the possibility of another world conflict. Those who talked of such a thing seemed on a par with the scientists who predicted an earthquake, at some time in the near future, because there had not been one for some time past. These were academic speculations, that might be interesting, but were not convincing. And, anyhow, why should we have marred our days by fretting about wars? If war came the burden would only too plainly fall on us, and there was no use in meeting trouble half way.

The Oxford Union passed its notorious resolution declaring its unwillingness to fight for king and country. This reverberated

H

round the world, for the world quite mistakenly believed that the Union represented Oxford's real views.

Nothing can represent Oxford. It is not a world of different peoples, but a universe of different worlds.

A country upbringing had ingrained a love of sport and wild life and wild places. Gradually, a desire was beginning to burn to go further afield in search of wilder life in wilder places. The study of maps became more and more absorbing. Maps of the Arctic were particularly so, especially where the shores of the Arctic islands were not bordered by neat black lines, but by dotted ones which denoted mere conjecture. Gradually, this feeling grew from a spark to a glowing flame. It was not just the wish to visit wild places, but to live among wild men and drink adventure.

My first summer vacation was in 1931. I had been asked to go with the University Exploration Club's Expedition to Akpatok Island in Hudson's Strait. Two great friends, Christopher D'aeth and Nicholas Polunin, were moving spirits in it. My father considered that I was as yet too young, and would not let me go.

The expedition was marred by tragedy. Christopher and Nicholas got caught in a storm some way from their base. Christopher succumbed to exposure. Nicholas survived: his Russian toughness pulled him through. He is now one of the world's leading botanists.

My father allowed me to go on a less ambitious expedition, to the St. Kilda group of islands, which I have described elsewhere.

I returned from the sortie to St. Kilda to find my family, and also my Scottish kin, at the place which my father had taken in Wales. Frwdgrech was the house, and Brecon the nearest town. It was a delightful, friendly house, with wild country behind it running up to that beautiful group of hills, the Brecon Beacons.

We had several miles of fishing on the Usk, and some rough shooting. My brothers rode ponies from morning to night, and I fished. My father did both, and the rest of the family took life easily in the company of a large number of dogs who belonged to the house, and roamed in and out of it during the hours of daylight.

St. Kilda set my father's mind running on islands, and the summer following he and I set off for the Faeroe Islands, where we greatly enjoyed ourselves.

That visit to the Faeroes was the only expedition of any distance that my father and I ever took alone together. I have described it in a separate chapter. When the next summer term came round, there was no rowing, and only a day or two could be spared for fishing. Three years of energetic idleness were exacting their retribution. My final Examinations were in June, and I had not yet been once through the subjects in which I was going to be examined.

All that term I slaved away in the sultry heat of an Oxford summer, reading, writing, cramming and getting deeper and deeper into a slough of bewilderment. The term drew to its close, the awful week came and dragged past. Then there was nothing to do but wait for my *viva*, which coincided very nearly with the date of my sister's wedding to Brian Fairfax-Lucy, and I filled in the time as a deck hand on a Hull trawler, fishing off the Faeroe Islands. I did not deserve to get a degree, but to my unbounded relief, the lists informed me that I could write B.A. after my name.

After Alice's wedding we went back to Frwdgrech, where I had to make several visits to London for interviews for the Colonial Service. Greatly to my surprise they accepted me. Colonial Government budgets were lean in the year 1933, and there were many more aspirants for the service than there were places. I could not help feeling that my acceptance, with such a humble degree, was on the principle of the intentional flaw in the Turkish carpet, that the makers of such things insert into their wares to prove that they are genuine.

That summer at Frwdgrech was the last holiday that we spent together as a family.

As a cadet of the Colonial service, I had another year at Oxford, at the Government's expense. Tony Richards of the same college had, like me, been accepted for service in Uganda. We shared digs in the quiet seclusion of Ship Street and puzzled over Swahili grammar and diagrams of how to build bridges or plans to prevent erosion.

Then in June of 1934, we set off on our adventure.

It was a sad leave-taking, and Africa seemed suddenly terribly distant, and Elsfield very dear. But my hand was to the plough of adventure, and if you want adventure, you must sacrifice all else to it.

In the pursuit of adventure it seemed worth while to let all else slide. My determination to avoid the careers of soldiering, politics or business was inflexible. I have since been heavily involved in all three, and by a curious irony found myself commanding a battalion and speaking from the Opposition Dispatch Box in the House of Lords for several years, as well as being deeply involved in various businesses. But to this day I am not quite clear how it all came about.

14

Oxfordshire Fishing

You cannot see the River Cherwell from the manor, although it is only six fields away across the valley. But you can see the line of willow trees along its margin. It is deep and slow-running, and usually some twenty yards in width. But there are one or two places where it flows over gravel shallows, where the slow, even surface becomes streaked with lines of current, and there is a faintly audible chuckle of moving water.

The stretch, that we fished, runs very nearly straight until it falls into a series of elbow bends at the lower limit. At these bends the current, with the passing of ages, has burrowed deep holes, and it was here the biggest fish were believed to lie. The water is dark with the depth, and one such bend, called the Owl Hole, still seems slightly forbidding.

In our minds fishing properly belonged to Scotland, but we need only be beside the Cherwell on a spring evening, when the big chub came nosing their way up from their haunts in the weed, to be reminded that there were big fish here, if not so noble. As children the only time we could fish this little river was the winter season. In the Easter holidays the fish were out of season, and for the most of the summer holidays we were in Scotland.

Jack and I spent many a grey, bleak winter afternoon beside the Cherwell, when leafless willows dabbled bare fingers in water the colour of lead. Our rods lay on the bank, each held in the cleft of a forked stick, while large floats slowly gyrated in the eddies in front of them. It was a sport for which we put on all our warmest clothes, thrust cold hands into our coat pockets and did a form of sentry-go up and down the bank, within sight of our float. Sometimes we would lift our gear, and move down the bank and cast it in beneath another over-hanging willow-tree, hoping for better luck. It is incredible, in retrospect, to remember how many hours were spent in this pursuit, and how little there was to show for it.

For four consecutive winter holidays we fished, for the total bag of one pike, perhaps half a pound in weight. I struck the luckless creature on the head, thinking to kill him as one kills a trout.

It must have been an hour before we reached home for luncheon, and I handed him over to our cook. As I did so, he gave a flap. We forthwith filled a basin with water, and put this remarkably vital creature into it. It lay for a moment on its side and then gradually turned to float right way up, and from the faint agitation of its tail was plainly alive.

An hour later, when lunch was finished, I brought my father down to inspect this phenomenon. He decided that it should be put in the pond, where there were no fish, and never had been any. At one end, the pond is about nine feet deep, and was then full of weed. We did not see the pike again, when we visited the pond to look.

The following two winters the pond was drained to allow some of the weed to be dug out. Ten years later, on a hot summer day, our gardener was cutting the nettles round the edge, and suddenly beheld the pike sunning himself, according to the manner of his kind, a few inches below the surface.

This hardy fish lived for thirteen years there and, as far as I know, had nothing to eat but newts. I do not think that when he died, he was five pounds in weight. He was alleged by Jack to have been responsible for the demise of a number of little moorhens for, small as it is, the pond has two moorhens' nests every year, and has had during all my recollection. The small black, fluffy chicks tumbling from the nest to take their first swim, could well have been a temptation to this lank, sharp-toothed creature.

It was only when I left Eton and had a summer of working for the entrance examination to Oxford that I realized the fun to be had on this river, so close to our door. Jack has told me many stories of big chub, and he had once caught one of over five pounds on that stretch. He fished by a process called "bobbing", and if anyone were to ask for further elucidation he would say "bobbing with a dumbledad". This translates into "dapping with a bumble bee".

Jack has always possessed a single general purpose rod, long and stiff and, with such curious joints, that when assembled it does not make a straight line but a series of angles. He has one reel, without a check, and a very short line. In the course of a lifetime's fishing he has accounted for a great number of coarse fish, with this simple armament.

His method with the chub was to approach them at high summer, preferably early in the morning or at the dusk. He would patrol the river, standing well back from the bank until he saw the telltale ring of a chub on the feed, or that very faint movement of the water that betokens a fish, close to the surface and in search of food.

The banks at that time of year are waist-high in a riot of scented herbage, and the old willow trees leaning over the water dip slim green fingers in it and make caverns of shade, under which big chub love to lie.

Jack would have a foot or so of gut, and a big hook on which was impaled a large and lively bumble bee; creeping forward, he would lean against a sloping trunk and very gradually thrust out his long rod like a long leafless branch of the same tree. He would let the bumble bee settle on the water, as near to the sign of the moving fish as he could get. Then he would make the old stiff rod vibrate until the bumble bee on the surface was the centre of tiny pulsating ripples, and the feeding fish was attracted to the scene to investigate.

Jack would watch his fish come up, with the big round mouth open, and take in the bee, drop his rod point as the fish turned away from him and then strike hard. His tackle was strong and he never believed in letting a fish have a longer chance to get off than was necessary. If one were near him one would hear the succession of splashes, and then a large, silver body would be bumping on the bank, and disappearing into the herbage at his feet.

During that summer, while I was working for my Oxford examination, we were often on the bank together. I was going through a rather tiresome phase of being a dry-fly purist. I have long since ceased to be that, or indeed any kind of purist. I now distrust all absolute creeds, whether in politics or sport.

I found the chub a splendid quarry for the dry fly. Although we sometimes went fishing in the evenings, the early mornings were the best time.

When the weather was settled, I would set the alarm clock for half past four in the morning. It was fully light by that time, and the sky was a limpid grey.

As I dressed I could see Jack from my window, sitting on the ground smoking his pipe, his big rod in its untidy case, and the dog of the moment sitting beside him, wondering why he had been roused so early. I would steal from the darkened house where everyone slept, out into the still morning air drenched with the scent of summer.

We would walk down the hill between the two woods, Jack puffing at his pipe, his dog at his heels. An early wood pigeon would murmur as we passed. The air was heavy with the smell of that riot of summer growth, and that most wonderful of all scents, the smell of new-mown hay.

As we shut the gate into the last field behind us, our excitement would mount. The world was just coming to life, and a late cuckoo would be beginning to call. We approached the river bank with great caution, having first put up our rods out of sight. The river was deep and weedy at this point. The weeds were in jungles, though here and there they hung in long ribbons which agitated gently with the quiet movement of the stream.

Jack's form of fishing was directed to catching the fish beside the near bank, underneath the overhanging willows. My eyes were on the far bank, where I could land my dry fly beneath the shadow of a willow, or a hawthorn bush, or float it down over the cruising chub. The surface of the water was like glass, and, as we watched, our eyes became accustomed to it and saw through it. The back of a chub shows a light brown against this background. In the same light a trout shows black. Beneath the shadow of a bush, perhaps we could make out the faint outline of a back.

The Big Red Palmer would drop on that limpid stillness, pushing away a tiny ripple where it landed, and gradually the slow stream would bring it past the quarry. Quite slowly a shape would come up from the depth which would resolve itself into the outlines of a fish, fins and tail in clear relief. The big round mouth would open, the chub would float backwards, his nose seemingly against the fly. Then, without the slightest commotion on the surface, the fly would disappear.

Being used to striking, like lightning, at a rising trout, I never did more than prick the first few chub that I ever rose. It was then I discovered that you must let the fly disappear, and the fish turn down, and away from you, before you tighten. Then the languor of the river and its surroundings would be shattered by a colossal jerk at the rod, and the fish was off with the lunge of a salmon. A chub always goes straight for a hole, or straight into the weeds, and is only too likely to break you there. It is usually a short run, for he is seldom far from his lair. Then you find your rod powerfully bent, and the feeling of movement of your quarry becoming more and more indirect. You realize that he is winding your line round the tough fronds of weed on the bottom. That may be the end and, if you fish with a fine cast, it is, more often than not. But if things go right you will gradually feel him giving, and coming towards you, his weight perhaps increased by trailing swathes of weed. He will try a few more runs, but they will not have the strength of the first one, then you have in your net this great, round-mouthed, stocky fish, the colour of old silver.

As the sun starts to strike on the water and makes the dewdrops on the grass sparkle, it is possible to see farther down into the depths, to catch sight of a school of chub or roach, looking like a painting from a Chinese screen, finned and scaled in every detail. Tiny rings appear, made by the inconsequent dace, who may snap at a fly and drown it, just as it is floating towards a big chub.

The big chub will often start cruising, but slowly, like a ship with its engines only just turning over. Where the willows are close-packed on the banks beside you, it is often hard to get your fly out between them. How often does a big chub keep the limits of his cruise to such a place where you cannot get your fly over him!

Jack and I were generally carrying a brace of fish, as we breasted the slope to the manor, with the morning sun hot on our faces, after these expeditions. I would weigh the fish, and then hand them back to Jack who would sooner eat a chub than he would a Dover sole.

It was only when I went to Oxford that I started to go farther afield in pursuit of Oxfordshire trout. I bought a car for five pounds, which was almost the best bargain that I ever made. It was a Citroen. It made a fearful noise, but jogged along quite steadily at its maximum speed of thirty miles an hour. It represented a pioneer phase of the industry, and carried my Oxford friends and myself to many pleasant places on many summer afternoons.

The Colne at Fairford is one of the most difficult waters that I know, and, if we had two fish between the party to show for it, we thought we had done well enough when we gathered for supper at the Bull Inn.

Once, at Colne St. Aldwyn, I caught six good fish in an afternoon in Mayfly Week. But the Colne is a real trout stream, and most of the other Oxfordshire streams are everything in Mayfly Week, and nothing for the rest of the season.

It had always been a ritual when I was at Eton, that, on the Saturday of summer Long Leave, we went and spent the evening at Sarsden with my father's old friend, Tommy Hutchinson.

Tommy was for many years secretary of the Heythrop and died after the war, as he would have wished, in the hunting field.

That visit was a great day in each year. We had tea and then spent two hours trying a dry fly on his stretch of a small trout stream, which wanders and bubbles through the wolds. Always it was without success.

The first time that I really got on terms with these Oxfordshire and Gloucestershire trout was when I was taken to spend the afternoon with the Crippses at Ampney Crucis. After lunch, while my elders talked, I was allowed to go down to the brook that runs through the village. It was a windy afternoon and there were a few trout rising, but eventually my fly ceased to float and, after many attempts to keep it on the surface, I decided to make the best of a bad job and fish it as a wet fly. That made all the difference. When my father and my host came down to collect me for tea, I had six good trout. In 1947 I took Lew Douglas, then American Ambassador, to fish this stretch. We repeated this triumph.

The Glyme and the Windrush are two Oxfordshire rivers which

exist only for Mayfly Week. As they were much nearer at hand than the others, they were my main objectives. The Glyme is tiny, and in many places it is hard to keep a fly on the water without landing it in the ragwort or the nettles of one bank or the other. It holds not many fish, but some extremely big ones. It requires constant patrolling, waist-deep in the lush growth of the meadows, to find a rising fish. When that has been done an angle must be found, from which a cast can be thrown without landing it in an over-hanging branch or a tuft hanging over the water. In the course of one day an Oxford friend and I once lured from this tiny streamlet five trout, of which the smallest was a pound and a quarter and two were well over two pounds each.

The Windrush at Minster Lovell is a much more substantial stream, and there are a great number of chub and roach as well as some very good trout.

Just before my final schools at Oxford I took a week-end at the Old Swan Inn with a very adept fisher, and no less apt scholar, Pat Brims. As far as I remember we caught only one trout, though we lost several others. But our fishing did not lack for incident, for from one little pool I landed two chub of over three pounds each, in consecutive casts, and, as evening came on, I hooked and landed a two-pound roach; a beast which would never have escaped a glass case if he had been caught on the banks of the Thames.

When the 1939 war came, the War Agricultural Committee ordered the draining of the countryside in the interests of agriculture, and dredged the Cherwell all the way from Oxford to Islip. They brought with them a great mechanical Moloch which took huge mouthfuls of weed and gravel and mud and deposited it like a rampart along the banks of the river, to be covered with a crop of thistles and Rosemary willow herb in the spring following. To ease the way of this monster the hawthorn bushes were cut back, and many of the willows were felled. The big chub paddled their way up in front of it, mile after mile, leaving behind a canal-like river, weedless, foodless, and sterile.

Now, more than ten years later, Nature has crept back. The even, symmetrical depth has given way to deeps and shallows. The green weed has come back to give cover to the chub again.

Jack wends his way down to the bank on summer evenings and tries his bumble bee, or watches his float. From the stubs of the hawthorns new bushes have sprouted and burgeoned to shed cool patches of shade where the big chub can cruise. The wheel has come full circle again.

15

Hawking

I WAS an Eton boy when the idea of hawking first stirred me. I began to lay my hands on all the literature on the subject that I could discover, which was little enough. The strange terminology, that has come down through the ages, took a powerful hold on my imagination.

I was in my last year at Eton when I managed to get hold of a kestrel. The arrangement for the kestrel's livelihood was settled by its taking up residence in the school laboratory. It was exhibited to those who were studying natural history, in return for which its food was charged to the school funds.

This arrangement was admirable in its way but, as the science laboratory was customarily locked up at about that time on a summer evening when I had leisure to take the bird out, it did not result in it ever becoming more than a pet.

I left Eton in the spring of 1930, and that spring I got a whole nestful of kestrels. Jack climbed the tree and brought down four fully fledged young birds in his capacious pocket. They were christened Violet, Slingsby, Guy and Lionel. I cut jesses out of strips of thin leather. These are the thongs which a hawk wears on each leg. My leash and swivel were, in fact, a small dog lead, and I got a large hedging glove for my falconer's gauntlet. A lure was made roughly according to the specifications in the book, a small horse shoe bound with tow and sewn over with soft leather, to which were attached a pair of jay's wings and some bright ribbons.

It is a thrilling moment to a falconer, and particularly to a novice, when his hawks will actually fly, even two feet to his hand or his lure.

The stable where the kestrels lived was a large one, and, when they would fly the full length of it to me, it seemed worth trying them in the open air. I tried them on a fishing line for safety's sake, and it was no time at all before they were flying about the same length in the open, as they would in the stable. They seemed extremely unwilling to come any farther.

I made some blocks for them to sit on to sun themselves on the lawn. These were blocks of wood, padded with soft leather, with a ring in the top to which each hawk's leash was secured. The blocks had to be put far enough apart so that they could not get near enough to each other to fight.

Each morning, as the summer sun was rising, they were put out, with a pie-dish full of water beside each block as a bath. One by one each kestrel would scramble into its bath, throw the water over itself, and hop back again sodden wet and seemingly shrunk to half its size. Then there would be a great shaking and ruffling of feathers, varied with turning their backs to the morning sun and spreading their wings for its warmth to dry them.

My father had by that time built himself, upon the flat roof of our eighteenth-century drawing-room, another storey where he could write undisturbed, and have more room for his books. Although he would glance from the paper in front of him at the view from the window, his thoughts never left the work in hand. But the four little kestrels, having their bath were too much, even for his powerful concentration. He would lay down his pen and look at them on the lawn below, fascinated. It was not until they had bathed and dried themselves that he could bring his mind back to literature. His concentration, though profound, was never gloomy. It was the concentration of the pointer dog who senses the presence of a covey, and seeks to pinpoint their exact position.

Then one day somebody left the stable door open. The stable was empty when I went to feed them. The kestrels were loose. We saw them occasionally, afterwards, as they would come back and perch on the stable roof, but the nesting rooks used to drive them away, and after the first few weeks we never saw them again.

The small hawking coterie in Britain was then slightly on the increase. We used to exchange letters and indeed hawks as well. Gradually the circle widened to embrace one or two Italian and German sportsmen who still hawked on the grand scale. We were

of great interest to them, because ours was the country of the
peregrine-falcon and the merlin, which they coveted above all
else. In return, the Germans exchanged the goshawk which
abounds in their forests, and is probably the best hawk in the
world for enclosed country.

Hawks are of two kinds, and two natures. There are the long-
winged hawks, the tips of whose folded wings cross behind their
backs, who mount high above their quarry and stoop upon it;
not grasping it, but striking with outstretched claw with the
mighty impetus of their stoop.

Then there are the short-winged hawks, which are for all
intents and purposes the goshawk and the sparrow-hawk; they fly
straight from the falconer's fist after their prey, and grasp it in
powerful claws bearing it to the ground. Every hawk wears a
jesse of the lightest leather on each leg, the ends of which are
punctured and connected to a figure-of-eight swivel to which is
connected a leather leash, when they are sitting in the falconer's
glove.

I used to hunt my short-winged hawks sitting bare-headed on
my fist, the jesses grasped between my fingers. They always saw
the game before I did. An opening of the hand and they were
free.

The long-winged hawks are released when the falconer is
approaching his game, as when you see a covey of partridges
squatting in the stubble. They can then mount up high, and be
in a position to stoop. In order that they may not tire themselves,
by flapping after every blackbird, they are hooded. Once in the
darkness of the hood they are peaceable and conserve their
strength.

Because a hawk, in the chase, is often out of sight, particularly
in woodlands, it wears on its leg a bell of the finest make, which
must be as light as a feather and yet audible a long way off. The
hoods I used to get from an old man in Holland with a world-
wide reputation; he was one of a long line of falconers to the kings
of Holland. The bells came from India, and were not more than
the thickness of paper, but on a clear day could be heard a quarter
of a mile away.

Any really thick leather gauntlet does as a hawking glove,

except for a goshawk whose great yellow hands grip with such intensity that they will tear any ordinary glove to pieces. I had a gauntlet made of horse hide which, though it kept the claws from my skin, did not prevent my hand becoming literally paralysed when my goshawk gripped it in anticipation of the chase.

Hawks which have been taken fully fledged from the nest are less likely to desert their owner, but they are also less likely to become as good hunters as those who have hunted as wild birds. The exact reverse applies to those who are caught in a trap or a net, perhaps several years old. Except on Otmoor there was not sufficient open country to make it worth while trying to fly a peregrine at Elsfield. Even on the top of the upland there were spinneys and tall elm trees where the peregrine could sit and sulk, while I waited brandishing the lure to no purpose. Furthermore, wood pigeons were always crossing and re-crossing. The easiest way of losing a peregrine, that I know, is in pursuit of a wood pigeon in enclosed country. The goshawk and the sparrow-hawk are the best hunters for such a landscape.

I had many failures, and many tragedies, and finally bought a beautiful young goshawk, from the forests of Düsseldorf, through one of my German correspondents. Two days after its arrival I got a wire from a friend in Scotland. It said he had caught a peregrine in a rabbit trap, and dispatched her to me by passenger train. She was a screeching fury when she arrived, and her leg was badly mauled by the teeth of the trap but was showing signs of healing. She was secured at the other end of the hawk-house to the goshawk, but got loose in my absence and fell upon the goshawk and slew it forthwith. After a long period of careful training, she became quite amiable.

No hawk regards you as a master; at the best they regard you as an ally, who will provide for them and care for them and introduce them to some good hunting. You have only to look at the proud, imperious face of a peregrine falcon to realize that. In reality you become their slave. They become used to one man and he cannot easily leave them, even for a short time.

I was at Oxford by the time I graduated to the big hawks, and, although I had not burdened myself unduly with work, I had surrendered myself to the slavery of rowing. When we were in

Fishing for salmon on the Dee. Thirty years later.

Avocet, Texel Island.

Whale hunt in the Faeroes.

training for races, it was very difficult to make time to cover the five miles to Elsfield, to exercise the hawks. Jack could not be trusted to fly them, but he used to feed them, and always fed them too much.

Within range of Oxford, there was only one survivor of the once numerous race of professional falconers. He kept an inn, the Axe and Compass, at Yattendon. He would care for hawks and fly them, and even train them, for a fee. It was he who trained my peregrine, while I was heavily preoccupied with a term of rowing.

It was vastly exciting having a big hawk with which to hunt. One begins the day, at any worth-while sport, with a certain measure of apprehension mixed with one's eagerness. In hawking it is a question as to whether, when you return, you will be bringing your hawk with you. I used to take the peregrine on to the top of the upland and cast her off, and watch her describe great circles as she mounted, then watch her drop like a plummet on the lure.

The finest falconer I ever knew was Kim Muir. He was at Eton with me, though much younger, and he kept a great assortment of hawks while he was there. He had a big goshawk, also in the science laboratory. He had it loose in there, one day, when a cat appeared on the window ledge outside. The plate glass window was shut. The hawk flew straight through the glass, smashing it to smithereens: badly stunned, it recovered itself and flew up and away out of sight.

At his home at Postlip, at the edge of Cleeve Hill in Gloucestershire, Kim kept an establishment of the best-trained hawks that I have ever seen. He was a fascinating character. For he was an excellent shot, a first-class horseman, and one of the finest falconers in Europe before he was twenty. He rode eighth in the Grand National in March 1940, and fell in the field of battle a few months later. More tears were shed for hard-riding, hard-living, lovable Kim than for almost any man that I ever knew.

Once I took the peregrine over to Postlip to see what we could do with her on those bare, rolling uplands. She had a hood that was slightly too big for her, and I put her in the back of the car seated on a block. I had completed all but ten miles of the forty mile drive, when there was a fearful eruption behind me, and it

I

was only too plain that she had got her hood off. She was in a blazing rage, and by no means could I get her hood back on again. There was nothing to be done but to drive the car with one hand, which meant releasing the steering wheel to change gear.

I thrust my gloved left hand, as far as I could, out of the window opposite the steering wheel, the infuriated bird upon it. It was a hair-raising drive. At each village through which we passed the inhabitants set up an outcry as we zigzagged through it. This had the effect of throwing her into another screeching, flapping tantrum. We got to Postlip at last, the peregrine ruffled and vengeful.

After lunch we went up to some stubble fields, where we knew we could find a covey of partridges. She was plainly harbouring a grievance. Just as the winter afternoon's light was beginning to fade we saw in the next field a covey of partridges, close to a stone wall. Everything seemed ideal. We crept up to the stone wall and let her go. She mounted to no great height but began to circle above them in the approved fashion.

Wild life is far more afraid of a hawk than it is of a human being. The partridges froze into immobility. Kim and I hopped over the stone wall and flushed the partridges that got up at our feet. They took flight at unbelievable speed, as they always do when there is a hawk above them. The peregrine got her own back. She turned towards them and then turned back, and with complete indifference continued her circling. We brought her down to the lure and took her home. You do not upset a peregrine's dignity with impunity.

I lost her in the end, at Elsfield. Jack, without my knowledge, had given her something to eat which had taken the edge off her appetite. The moment she was released she flew to the top of an enormous elm, fully 120 feet high, which stood alone in a hedgerow. I stood below waving the lure as dusk slowly fell. She was not hungry and therefore not interested. She was proof against every possible blandishment. Knowing that she would sleep in that tree, I left her when darkness fell, and returned in the freezing dark of dawn next morning. I arrived just too late. She had left that tree and was quartering the country. One of the villagers coming to early milking had seen her five minutes before I arrived. I never saw her again.

Falconry takes far more spare time than I am ever likely to have again. For hours a day I used to walk my hawk on my hand. That is the only occasion that I know of in Britain when total strangers will accost you, and fall straight away into conversation. For miles around the country, people knew my hawks and me, but visitors to the neighbourhood would stop their cars, and get out to stare at this phenomenon. There were three clichés which predominated in their observations. The first one was, "How very cruel!" the second was "Is it a parrot?" and the third was, "Why don't you keep it in a cage?"

Often with a hawk in training, I would take it where there were crowds, to familiarize it with human kind. I found it excellent training to sit with it in a corner of the village smithy. Old Nappin, the smith, would work at his bellows, and hammer the red-hot horse shoes; the clang of metal on metal would make the room ring, and red-hot sparks dart hither and thither. When the hawk got used to this she would not mind anything else.

The finest hawk that I ever possessed was a goshawk called Jezebel, who was trained by Kim Muir, from whom I acquired her when he was very busy with a peregrine of which he hoped great things. She killed more than seventy head, before she was one year old. Once flown by Kim, at Braco Castle in Perthshire, she accounted for fourteen rabbits and a hare in one day. During my last winter at Oxford before going to Africa, his cousin John Hobson,* and myself, set off for the coast of Norfolk just before Christmas to shoot geese on the mud flats. Mine was not a very big car, and Jezebel and the peregrine took up a good deal of room in the back of it.

The Golden Fleece, at Wells-next-the-sea, was a place of pilgrimage to me once a year. I used to go in the midst of winter, and follow that famous wild fowler, Sam Bone, through the freezing morning darkness across the mud flats, and lurk with him in the dunes of Holkham Bay as the afternoon sun was setting.

We arrived at evening, at the Golden Fleece, and erected a hawk's perch in an outhouse. An extremely officious man followed us in and looked at these two great birds, who sat

---

* John Hobson became the Rt. Hon. Sir John Hobson, M.P. for Warwick and Leamington, and held office as Solicitor-General and later Attorney-General. He died in 1967.

unheeding on their perch. He took off one of the rabbit skin gloves that he was wearing and flipped Jezebel with it.

Jezebel plainly disliked him. She ruffled her feathers and fixed him with her cruel, yellow eye. As the rabbit skin glove touched her again, one great yellow claw snatched it from his grasp. She bent down and exerting her terrific strength ripped the glove from end to end, and finding it not eatable tossed it away. The officious man departed, much chastened.

Never have I known such an exhausting week and rarely one so enjoyable. We rose in the freezing darkness of each morning to find Sam outside the door of the inn to take us to shoot geese. We would drive for a mile or two, and then leave the car. There were one or two fields to stumble over, and then our rubber boots would be splashing in the wet mud of the marshes.

We followed Sam in Indian file until at last we came to the appointed place. A shovel was produced from his pack, and a rough grave dug for each of us. There we would lie, our heavy guns beside us, listening to the wild pipings of the birds of the marshes, and waiting to catch the drifting clangour of the geese.

A band of silver would gradually form on the horizon, and then a band of gold; then the pools that the last tide had left would turn to pink as the sun rose in the glory of a frosty dawn.

We only got one goose between the three of us, and one or two widgeon in our whole visit, but it was the adventure that we loved. We would splash back when the sun was up, in front of the incoming tide. There would be a gargantuan breakfast at the inn. When plates of eggs and bacon and beakers of coffee had been demolished, we turned to our hawks.

One or two of the local landlords had kindly invited us to come and try a flight on their land. Hawks seldom perform well in front of a large gallery of strangers. The word had been sent round by our hosts, and an enormous field of children collected to watch the sport. There were partridges and hares in abundance, but both Jezebel and the peregrine declined to give any exhibition at all except of bad temper. The peregrine, it is true, condescended to knock down one partridge. Jezebel, if she could find a tree, would go and perch in it, and glower at the expectant faces below. She

condescended on one occasion to catch a rabbit, but refused to
look at the hares.

We would drive back on these days to luncheon, terribly
tempted to go to sleep. But Sam Bone appeared after luncheon
and knocked meaningly on our door, and we were off again with
our guns in pursuit of wild fowl. As the hawks refused to keep
themselves in food we had to fit in a daily visit to the butcher to
get them some beef.

I founded a falconry club at Oxford. It was one of those ephe-
meral associations which had a dinner and a tie but, because we
had not enough money to maintain a proper establishment, we
never once took the field for falconry except for a few odd days
rabbiting with Jezebel.

Rabbiting was Jezebel's really strong suit. I would take her into
the Elsfield woods and cast her off, and she would fly straight
away into a tree. Then I would advance beating the undergrowth
with a stick, while she would fly from tree to tree beside me.
When a rabbit broke cover she was down on it with a shriek of
her bell. Sometimes she would get a grey squirrel, and twice she
pounced on a little owl. Once she went for a fox, which bounded
straight away into thick cover, where to my great relief, she could
not follow. It would have been no ordinary fight, if she had laid
her claws on it.

In June of 1934, I set off to start my career in East Africa and I
had to dispose of my pets. My tame fox had disposed of himself,
by running away. My tame badger, to whom I was greatly
devoted, and had brought up since it was a tiny cub, was now
very large and amiable. I used to take him to Oxford, and he
often accompanied me to other people's houses. I once took him
to a luncheon party in Oxford, when he was still but half grown.
He had a plate of bread and milk on the floor beside my chair and
behaved himself with great decorum. In those days at Oxford we
used to wear rather wide flannel trousers. A burst of merriment
among the guests startled the badger and, having no burrow to
which he could run, he darted straight up my trouser leg. Let no
one who has not had a badger run up their trouser leg at a luncheon party, where ladies are present, imagine that it is a happening that can be carried off with composure. It was impossible to

get the badger out of my trouser leg backwards, so that I had to stagger to a corner, badger and all, and extract him from the top.

When I came to leave for Africa, I put him down in a nearby wood, but next morning he was back on the lawn looking for me. We drove him then in the car, to a wood many miles away, where I hope he found friendly badgers and lived to a ripe old age.

Jezebel I gave to the late Lord Howard de Walden. He flew her quite a lot, until she ended her piratical career by alighting on an overhead power line. She disappeared like a phoenix, in a shower of sparks. How she made the circuit still remains a matter of primary scientific interest.

16

St. Kilda Sanctuary

MY first long vacation from Oxford was partly devoted to an expedition to St. Kilda. St. Kilda is not just an island, it is a group of islands. Of these the largest is Hirta. There are two other substantial, but much smaller islands, Boreray and Soay. The group lies some fifty miles west of the Island of Harris, and rather more than a hundred from the mainland of Scotland. It is shrouded in the mists of the Atlantic, whose rollers pound ceaselessly against its rocky cliffs.

For centuries it has been inhabited by a people whom separation from their fellow-countrymen, and the strange circumstances of their life, have turned into almost a separate race. For hundreds of years the Island had been in the possession of the MacLeods of Dunvegan. In 1930 both these chapters came to an end. The inhabitants, finding it harder and harder to support life, and the Scottish Office finding it more and more expensive to look after them, moved to the mainland where they settled at Kinlochaline, in Morven. The islands were bought by Lord Bute, to be a bird sanctuary.

St. Kilda, in 1931, was a fascinating study. Man's long tenancy had been brought to an end, and the island was left to the wheeling, screaming birds of the sea, and the small discreet birds of the land. It had become their home, and theirs alone.

If you can imagine a bay made by two long and rocky arms reaching far out into the sea with ground rising steeply from the landward end from a sandy beach, then imagine a bay very similar in size and shape but with the sea reaching up, not to a beach, but to cliffs, low only by comparison with those along the rest of the crescent; then imagine these two put together, like two horseshoes, back to back, and you have the Island of Hirta. Where the two horseshoes touch is a high saddle of ground falling sheer into the sea on either side. These are cliffs that are an alpine climber's nightmare, for the rock is rotten and the ledges are covered with turf, which comes away in your hand. At the highest point these cliffs are twice the height of Beachy Head.

The bay with the beach is called Village Bay. Here is a little quay, a little church and a manse, and a short distance away stands the village, a row of low stone cottages along one side of a rocky track. It is possible to land at Village Bay only in a north-east wind—unless one gets one of those rare moments when the Atlantic is calm. The inhabitants used to say that they caught a cold every time the boat came in. This malady was called "boat cold." In fact, they caught a cold from the wind that made it possible for the boat to lie in close.

They were a strange race of men. For their livelihood they hunted the fulmar petrel. The fulmar petrel is full of a fluid like camphorated oil, which the islanders burned in their lamps; the flesh they ate; and the feathers were used to stuff mattresses and pillows.

The islanders were amazing mountaineers, and climbed unshod, their prehensile feet clad only in thick woollen stockings. They hunted their quarry with a weapon that resembled a fishing rod, to the end of which was plaited a horsehair line with a noose. This they cast, with the precision of a dry-fly fisherman, over the necks of the birds perched on the ledges. They fished a little in the waters round the bay, and on the three main islands kept flocks of sheep who became as wild and as nimble as any mountain goat.

A small expedition was formed in the summer of 1931 of three undergraduates from Cambridge and two others, besides myself, from Oxford, to make a scientific survey of the island during that first summer after its evacuation.

Scientific survey sounds rather a grand name, but the other members of the party, notably Tom Harrisson and Bill Moy-Thomas, had not inconsiderable qualifications. We possessed enough knowledge between the six of us to make a reasonably close scientific investigation of the birds, the botany and the geology.

We had the qualified blessing of various official bodies, and we set sail from Glasgow in the boat that wanders its way slowly up through the Hebrides, on a very hot day in July 1931. We had the various tools of our trade, which included one .410 shot gun for collecting specimens. The last thing that we bought was our provisions, which we hopelessly under-estimated.

St. Kilda boasts three unique animals; the first is the St. Kilda wren, which is protected by its own special Act of Parliament. It is a small, cheerful, confiding bird, much more worthy of an Act of Parliament than many subjects that have received them in the intervening years. Then there is a unique mouse, somewhat pink as to its underside. Last of all there are the Soay sheep, dark brown in colour, cropping the green lusciousness of the grass that crowns the cliffs of the Island of Soay. I had a pair of socks made from their wool, collected from wisps that had caught on the rocks. I wore them afterwards for six years in the Canadian Infantry, and they are still the most comfortable pair of socks that I possess.

Our ship took its time wandering northwards through the islands, and then gathered itself up to cross the fifty miles of open Atlantic to St. Kilda. It pitched and plunged mightily in a heavy westerly sea. Most of us were too seasick to come on deck to see our destination looming through the veil of grey rain and spray.

We dropped anchor at the inner end of Village Bay with the swell rumbling up the pebble beach. We went over the side into a big open boat, and our stores were lowered after us. It was not many hours afterwards that we watched the stern of the ship receding down the bay, rolling into a curtain of mist as the open Atlantic caught her on the beam.

There were besides the six of us, five St. Kildans who had returned to spend the summer there. One of them was an old man, Findlay McQueen, ancient, bearded and bow-legged, but an incredibly agile cragsman in his stocking-feet. He spoke no word of English, nor did the old St. Kildan woman called Mrs. Gillies. They looked like something from another age.

We appropriated the cleanest of the houses which had been the factor's dwelling. It had a small cooking stove in one room and a fireplace in the other. There were no trees on the island, but there was driftwood and peat for fuel. The Primus stove, however, was our real mainstay for cooking. We unpacked the stores, and after careful calculation we realized we had much too little, and that we were going to have three weeks on very short commons.

When you live on a small island, if you can walk round the perimeter of your domain in a day, and can see all over it by merely climbing to a ridge, you have a feeling of living in your own universe where time does not really signify. Looking back, it is hard to believe we only spent three weeks on that island. It seemed almost a lifetime in retrospect. Rain fell almost every day, and we lived with the smell of wet moorland and the salt of the ocean blowing round us.

Tom Harrisson, David Lack* and I set off to do a bird census. Cyril Petch pegged out a square yard of ground to analyse every blade and stem that sprouted from it. Bill Moy-Thomas set his mouse-traps for his unique and inoffensive quarry, and Malcolm Stewart filled sack upon sack with geological specimens.

When we fired a gun near the bird cliffs, a bedlam of sound broke out, and such a multitude of birds took wing that, looking down from the top of the cliffs, the sea below was obscured and it looked as if we could jump from the cliff on to a great mattress of gleaming feathers.

So far as the fulmar petrels were concerned, the only census we could make was a great cosmic computation. The gannets and some other sea birds also defied any precise arithmetic, but walking the moorland slopes on the inside of the two horseshoes we made a fairly accurate survey of the little moorland birds.

As far as we could make out there was just one pair of snipe with their young. There also seemed to be one mother eider-duck who, on calm evenings, would take her family to swim in Village Bay. There were the wrens, some pipits, and occasional wading birds. When the weather was calm, the gannets would dive for fish. We could spend hours watching them plummet from over 100 feet, then strike the water with a crash which sounded as if the flat of a spade had been brought down on the surface.

Every night we returned soaking wet from our researches. The more interesting of the geological specimens were gathered together, and the rest were thrown out; some half a dozen of the

* Tom Harrisson, now Curator of the Sarawak Museum, commanded the resistance movement—largely composed of head-hunters—behind the Japanese lines in Borneo during the Second World War. David Lack is Director of the Edward Grey Institute of Field Ornithology at Oxford and a fellow of the Royal Society.

mice were trapped and skinned. My only tangible contribution was a St. Kilda wren's nest, and a young bird preserved in spirits.

There was no difficulty in watching these confiding little beasts. They had taken possession of the village. We got to know every pair of them. As the days went on, one or two wading birds, the vanguard of the early autumn migration, appeared on the beach below us and could be identified with a telescope from our cottage. One whole day was spent in search of the Leach's fork-tailed petrel. They pass the hours of daylight in holes like rabbits. We dug one out to photograph it.

Such an abundance of wild life kept us busy from dawn until dark. We were for ever ranging the cliffs in search of some rare bird, which might break the uniformity of the pattern of the thousands of floating fulmars in the air, and the puffins squatting upon the ledges. At times we would lower one of our number gingerly over the cliff, on a rope, to pick a plant off a ledge, or to photograph a young bird. There were still a few young ones, late as the season was. I have a very bad head for heights. I cannot remember which I disliked the more, being lowered over the cliff myself, or being the sole support of one of my companions.

There were a few days of bright sunshine when our horizon was enlarged and, from the high ground, we could see, in every direction, a smooth and gently undulating Atlantic lose itself in the dimness of the sunlit haze. Those days were our chance to get the heavy rowing boat out on the sea—on one day to add to our stock of food from fishing, or on another to make an expedition to the two other main islands, Boreray and Soay.

It was with a good deal of trepidation that we set out down Village Bay on these expeditions. There was room for four of us in the boat, and two St. Kildans. We took turns at manning the long sweeps. What had been a swell in the bay was a long ocean roll, once clear of its protecting arms.

Village Bay faces south, and Boreray lies to the north-east, and Soay to the north-west of the group. We hugged the shores of Hirta, to the measured accompaniment of the swell which pounded on the cliffs beside us, and sent long fingers of foam reaching far up their sides, amidst the clamour of many thousand birds.

The sound of many sea birds is not an even sound—sometimes

a dirge, sometimes almost an anthem, sometimes varying in its beat like the beginning of a score of music, ending abruptly as if the rest of the score was lost after the first line had been played.

It was awe-inspiring to look up at those rocky walls from below: they seemed to reach to the sky, seamed with green ledges and patterned by sea birds, as we sweated and lurched in the swell. Then the time came when we had to desert the foot of the cliffs and strike out across the open sea, and watch the bulk of Boreray growing slowly larger, its cliffs growing clearer in detail. It was hard to land there; it meant a jump from the rocking boat, a frantic scramble and a fastening of the rope for the others. Then came a long ascent, sometimes upright, mostly on hands and knees until we won to the grassy slopes that crowned it.

We did not add anything to our scientific discoveries by that day's trip, but the St. Kildans slew two of their sheep and hurled them over the cliff edge to the sea below, as the easiest way of getting them down. It was a very tired party that turned in to the protecting arms of Village Bay as dusk fell.

The expedition to Soay took us right round the Island of Hirta. Atlantic weather can change swiftly. It is an awe-inspiring feeling to row beneath cliffs, upon which one cannot possibly land. We circled the island slowly, anti-clockwise. It was about midday when we looked up at the cliffs of Soay. We saw some great, grey Atlantic seals. These are another peculiarity of St. Kilda—although they are to be found in two other parts of the Hebrides—Colonsay and the Monach Islands.

Getting ashore was extremely difficult. It involved a jump from the upswinging gunwale of the boat, to catch a ledge and then draw ourselves up by our hands on to a bigger ledge above; thereafter, though very steep, it was not so difficult.

The top of the island was crowned with the most luscious green grass such as can be seen only on islands where sea birds can be counted by the thousands.

We did not have to search far for the Soay sheep. Wild as deer, they dashed in all directions at our approach; no mountain goat is more sure-footed. Time and again they disappeared over the cliff edge, apparently to perdition, to reappear again having traced the network of ledges at top speed.

In a short time our eyes were on the weather, as the sky seemed to be darkening. We scrambled down and dropped the last few feet on to the last ledge, then into the boat and set off for home.

The outward journey had taken us round about three-fifths of the perimeter of Hirta. We strained at the sweeps, realizing that the sea was beginning to ruffle with the wind. We were screened by the island until the moment came, an hour later, to turn the corner of the right-hand prong of Village Bay. In one moment we saw that we were faced with a rising sea, and for five sickening minutes we steadily lost ground, and the rocky point of the prong receded. For ten more minutes we were apparently holding our ground, but row as we might we could bring the point no nearer. It was not just the exertion that made our hearts pound and our breath come short. Then gradually bit by bit we started to make headway and, with infinite slowness, brought the point of the prong nearer and nearer and rowed painfully round it into Village Bay. We were tired and wet and thankful when we set foot on the shore again.

Our isolation was occasionally broken into. A large sea-going yacht dropped anchor at Village Bay one night and pulled out early next morning. Three Breton lobster boats, which were busy evading the Fishery Authorities, ran into Village Bay in the dark and stayed all next day. We went on board one of them. She was a strange craft with a tank, full of live lobsters and crayfish, running almost the whole length of the vessel. We had some wine out of a tin mug with the crew in their cabin, and talked with them in halting French. They came ashore with us afterwards and made us a present of some lobsters, for which we were very grateful, and spared us a long cigar-shaped roll of their own hard bread. One of them fell in with Findlay McQueen and conducted, what appeared to be, a completely comprehensible conversation in Breton *patois* on the one hand, and Gaelic on the other. The three little vessels flitted in the darkness of the next night.

Two big Fleetwood trawlers put in during rough weather. The St. Kildans became as apprehensive as if they had been pirates. We boarded one, and had an uproarious evening in the

Chart Room with the big, unshaven Lancashire men, sea-booted and hospitable, and full of oaths.

There was one very heavy gale. It blew in from the west, and we watched it from the high ground. We could only see six waves back, and beyond that it faded into blowing spume. We could look down on waves advancing in unending sequence, like great towering white walls rearing up to their full height to smash against the cliffs, reaching half-way up them with fingers of white foam, to fall back again to make room for the next.

One night David Lack and I climbed to the top of Conachair, the highest point on the island, to look for petrels. It was a calm night with twinkling stars, but far too dark to see anything. A bird flew so close to me that I felt the wind of it on my face. We sat on the top of Conachair and listened to the sea booming in the caverns down below. To the north-east a bright pinpoint of light was the Flannan Islands Lighthouse; and the brighter gleam of the Monach Islands Light; to the south-east, like a tiny distant star, was Barra Head, over 100 miles distant. From the ledges came the medley of sounds that sea-birds make in the dark. Sometimes a swish of unseen wings set us staring into the night sky. It was long past midnight when we descended and stumbled towards the light of a candle, burning in our cottage window.

'We treasured the flavour of romance, and cultivated a Robinson Crusoe-like appearance. We revelled in freedom from shaving, and in every whisker that might, with courtesy, be called a beard.

The day the boat was expected was the only day of hot sunshine and real visibility. We could see all the way to the Island of Harris, from the top of Conachair, across an Atlantic as smooth as a lake, ruffled here and there, in patches, by a gentle breeze. We gave up waiting and watching, and busied ourselves packing up our belongings; and then just before dark fell there was the boat, with sightseers crowding the rails, making her way down Village Bay. We did not see the rocky islands receding behind us, for we pulled out in the black darkness, leaving the birds in undisputed possession of their little world shrouded in mist, with the endless booming of the sea in the caverns.

17

To the Faeroes

IT may have been the expedition to St. Kilda that set my father thinking of the islands of the north, but some time in the New Year of 1932 he decided that he and I should make an expedition, to the Faeroe Islands. He immediately armed himself with up-to-date literature about these islands, which amounted to three volumes in all—the first of which was published in the 1880's.

We set off at the end of July from the port of Leith bound for Thorshavn, the capital of the islands, with our rods, every possible lure for taking sea-trout in brackish waters, and with a very unclear idea as to how we were going to get back.

Our researches had yielded little detailed information, and as we pitched our way through the Pentland Firth we thought of our destination as somewhere that was very far north, was foreign territory, and was believed to be very good fishing. My father, who was immune from sea-sickness, spent a restful two days reading, and I spent most of that time alone on my bunk.

We arrived at Thorshavn early in the morning and made a heap of our belongings, which consisted principally of two large portmanteaux, an enormous suitcase filled with fishing tackle, and another suitcase in which were packed oilskins, mackintoshes and all possible devices for keeping dry, including a pair of waders that we shared.

Thorshavn is one of the most charming small capitals in the world, with its neat wooden houses of Scandinavian shape and colour, and its little church with a pointed wooden steeple. Along the stone jetty was a forest of masts of small fishing boats. The men wore, for the most part, their national dress, which is the brightly-buttoned jacket, breeches, and a cap reminiscent of gnomes in fairy-tales.

We were taken to Government House, which was a large-sized villa on the hillside above the harbour. The Danish Governor and his family were exceedingly hospitable, and made us very comfortable. They spoke practically no English. We spoke absolutely no Danish.

The Governor had made a careful plan for us. We were to do three separate fishing trips. On the second one we were to be transported by the *Dana*, the Danish Government's research vessel, which was then engaged in a marine biological survey, under the direction of that distinguished Danish explorer and scientist, Dr. Tonning. All this seemed admirable, and we spent two days in Thorshavn, re-packing our belongings and wandering round the strange wooden capital.

The first day was Saturday, and we saw a fascinating political demonstration led by the leader of the opposition, or King's Peasant as his official title is literally translated. A long procession marched through the town bearing the national flag of the Faeroes—an oyster-catcher on a white background—followed by a gathering at which speeches were made, the burden of which was a demand that the Faeroes cease to be under the Danish Parliament, and be, in fact, a self-governing dominion under the Danish flag. I have never seen a friendlier demonstration by a national movement. The Chief of Police watched it with us, and explained the fine points. He was utterly unworried, as there was no question of a breach of the peace.

Later, we went for a walk in the hills behind the town. Shooting had been forbidden by law for a good many years, but I cannot believe that that was sufficient to account for the extraordinary tameness of such otherwise wary birds. I know no other place in the world where it is possible to walk up to a curlew and a golden plover, close enough to photograph them.

The next day was Sunday and we attended church. The building, the usual wooden structure with painted wooden steeple, was filled to capacity. The priest wore black robes and, to our intense fascination, an Elizabethan ruff. From the rafters hung models of ships, many of which by their design must have been very old. They were votive offerings and had been wrought by the hands of seamen who had prayed in their extremity to be delivered from

As deckhand on a Hull trawler.

Fellow trawler-men.

shipwreck, and had survived. The congregation in their attractive national dress prayed powerfully. My father and I understood only one word of the service, the name of our Redeemer, which I imagine is the same in every language.

Next day we set off on the first of our fishing expeditions. We bundled our belongings on to a small steamer which was lying at the quay, and made our way up the coast of the main island. The Faeroes are very similar to the Shetlands in appearance. Set in the far north, they would have the climate of Labrador were it not that they are in the warm bosom of the Gulf Stream. On the beaches, strange nuts are sometimes found. These grow on tropical trees, and have been wafted by the Gulf Stream to this far northern land.

The impact of warm sea on high latitude naturally produces a vast amount of fog, but, when the weather is clear, you can see for miles through the pale sub-Arctic light. Like the Shetlands, there are many lochs from which little burns course down into long sea inlets. The sea-trout, waiting the opportunity of a spate to run up them, boil in the seawater round the mouths of the burns. There are good brown trout lochs as well. When you rise a very big fish you say to yourself, "That must have been a salmon," and then you realize that it is a giant sea-trout, for there are no salmon there.

It was just after midday that we reached our destination. We had passed several small fishing villages set close to the water's edge; between them were high cliffs that marched slowly past us. We landed at a substantial village, clambering up a jetty slippery with seaweed. Waiting for us at the end of it was a young man with a pleasant face and an almost childish cheerfulness. He had one hand buried in the white mane of an Iceland pony, which had two large panniers on its back. He unrolled a piece of paper and handed it to my father. Our two names were written on it. We nodded. We asked if he spoke English and he shook his head and smiled. He bent to our luggage and began to load it on to the panniers. A great deal was left over, after the panniers were full. Our rods we carried, our oilskins as well, and we took turns of carrying the waders, which, brogues and all, were stuffed into a large fishing bag.

K

My father, like most men who have been soldiers, was very un-happy when he could not find his destination on a map. We knew where we were, but we did not know where this charming young man was taking us, and the charming young man appeared to have no comprehension of maps. So the map was stowed away as well, and off we started.

We walked in single file along a track, which looked like a narrow garden path, and rose by easy stages to the head of the watershed. The young man was in front, the nodding pony followed him, and my father and I walked in single file behind. We did not know whether our destination was one mile away, or twenty. But after two hours walking it became quite clear that our fishing was not this side of the watershed. It is always pleasant to walk after one has been in a boat; particularly so in that clear sub-Arctic light. And so time and distance were no particular object.

At the top of the watershed was a moss, and we imagined that, as we went down the other side, a little stream would start which would gather strength and then reach some loch, from which a small burn would cascade down to the sea. We were not long left in doubt. On the downward slope a small burn did begin, and when it was not more than two feet in width we came round a bend in the valley, and there below us was a miniature loch. Beside it, all alone, was a small wooden church. What seemed several hundred feet below that was an inlet with a narrow entrance to the sea, shaped like a rocky bowl. Beyond it was a drowsy ocean, blue in the radiance of the July sun. Two little wooden houses stood together perched on the rim of the bowl.

The path became steeper. We followed the shore of the loch making for the bowl, and here and there a swirl disturbed the ripples. The nearer of the two cottages housed the family of the charming young man. The ground fell steeply in front of the wooden house, and there was the sea at the bottom of the bowl undulating gently against rock walls. There, too, was a small burn cascading past the church, and falling so steeply that we dismissed any question of sea-trout climbing to the loch above. But we were wrong.

There were four rooms in the cottage, and one had been set aside for our use. There were two beds, on each of which the bedclothes were composed of two mattresses stuffed with chaff. We slept on one mattress and laid the other on the top of us. It was quite impossible to make any variation of temperature on a hot or cold night. The only other furniture was made up of two tables, on one of which was a wash-basin and, on the other, an enormous jug of milk and two glasses.

Unpacking took a matter of minutes. It was all but impossible to discover from the family anything about the fishing, but we gathered that fish could be caught in the bowl below us—these could only be sea-trout; and fish could also be caught in the loch above us, which we assumed could only be brown trout. In the light of that knowledge, each put up a brown trout rod and sallied off to the shores of the loch.

Every fisherman has his own particular unconscious tricks of fishing. That is why two men who fish much together discover that there is a fairly constant mathematical ratio between the number and size of fish that they catch. My father and I fished together many times, and in many places, with a curious sameness in the results. In the long run I always caught more fish, and he always caught the biggest ones.

That afternoon was absolutely still. The ripple died from the loch. We basked in that wonderful, crisp, northern sunshine which does not enervate, but fills one with energy. We cast in the placid waters of the loch, let our wet flies sink deep, and worked them slowly. We got between us about fifteen brown trout, keeping only three which were about three-quarters of a pound each. We were becoming more and more conscious of hunger, as we had eaten nothing since our sandwiches in the steamer, and had been offered nothing since, except milk. At about eight o'clock, which one can tell by one's watch in those latitudes and not by the light which lasts all night long, we went back to the cottage. We had a large and intensely satisfying meal—mostly of fish, and bread and milk. We went to bed early.

Breakfast next morning included a duck's egg each, which was obviously a very special treat, as it was the product of a small flock of a drake and two ducks who were constantly walking into the front door and being shooed out again.

It was a bright, windy day. With the help of a Danish phrase book we managed to put one or two pertinent questions, which, added to much pantomime, elicited the advice that we should fish in the little loch all day and descend to the bowl of sea in the evening. It also elicited the information, which we found hard to believe, that there were sea-trout in the loch above, which somehow or other scaled that steep, tumbling burn. We took our larger trout rods in consequence, and some of the three-hooked sea-trout lures.

As the wind blew straight down the loch towards the sea, and its shape was roughly that of an egg, we decided to take one side each and fish across the wind. In no time at all we were lost in our own preoccupations. I got a rise in three of the first four casts. When we met at lunchtime I had risen over 200 trout, and the tug of their small, sharp teeth had disintegrated six flies. I landed four fish over one pound which I kept, and returned everything else.

It was one of those fishing days when there is so much incident that one is utterly oblivious of one's surroundings. We compared notes at lunchtime. My father had not counted the rises, but believed that he had risen less than half that number. He had, however, a four and a half pound sea-trout, which he had taken on a three hooked lure. The rise went off in the afternoon. I put a lure on, on a tail fly, which was promptly broken by a sea-trout, though I landed another of about two pounds.

We returned to the cottage in the evening. The cheerful young man was waiting for us. So was an aged, troll-like figure, who lived in the next cottage. They led us by a winding path down to the bottom of the bowl. It was one of those places which magnifies sound to an amazing pitch. The splashing of the burn in its last cascades before it ran through the shingle to the salt water blended with the murmur of a calm sea lapping against the foot of the cliffs. The strange, uneven cry of the sea birds added to the curious feel of the place.

We got into a boat and pushed off. The young man signalled to us to start casting immediately. The water was all in shadow as we rowed slowly round. It is at this moment of the tide that the sea-trout can be expected to take. It was like fishing for goldfish in a bowl, and being in the bowl with them. At the end of an hour I had risen one sea-trout. My father, using rather too fine a cast, had been broken by another sea-trout, which took his fly with that ferocious snap which is one of the most exhilarating things about this splendid fish. Then, apparently, the moment had passed. There was much conversation in dumb show; the boat was grounded on the shingle by the burn-foot, and drawn up; we wended our way up the zigzag path to the wooden dwelling again. Once out of the shadow of that bowl, pale sunlight still shone on the green turf. The northern air made us sleepy, and after a huge meal we went gratefully to bed.

Next day we set off to walk the ten miles back to the port. The first of our fishing trips was over.

The second missed fire. We boarded the *Dana*, the Danish Government Research vessel, and set off along the rocky coast. We passed near to the tall, sea cliffs of the Island of Fuglo, meaning the island of birds, with its screaming halo of wings that were reminiscent of the bird cliffs of St. Kilda, we spent two hours in the swell, trawling with a big plankton trawl which was part of Dr. Tonning's scientific investigation. I was very glad when the trawl came on board again, for I was beginning to feel extremely sick. We passed down a rocky coast almost like the granite jumble of the coast of Baffinland, and saw a huddle of small dwellings beside a ravine. It was a place of tragedy. Its name was Skard. Every man of that little community had been drowned a year previously in a sudden, ferocious gale, which had sprung up from nowhere and dashed their boats to matchwood against that iron coast.

We landed in a small port farther on. Much conversation broke out between Dr. Tonning and his officers, all of which was incomprehensible to us. Then it transpired that something had broken down in the engine room, and we must lie there until it was mended. Even a great quantity of schnapps didn't really make up for it. After several days' delay, we returned to Thorshavn, to spend another night with the Governor prior to our last sortie.

This time we left on a small fishing boat and set off south to the long Island of Sudero. We landed at a little harbour at its northern end, and were met by a car, a form of conveyance by no means usual at that time outside the capital. We procured a map and some kind of directions, and, as we approached our destination, saw a long loch in which we were going to fish, and beside which the road ran.

Our host was a Danish doctor from Copenhagen, a man of considerable brilliance in his own line, but who for one reason or another had decided to emigrate to the Faeroes to run a small country practice. His household consisted of himself, his sister, and a wolf-like, boisterous dog called Troll. The doctor knew nothing of fishing and could give no advice, but a small, gnome-like man was produced. He had done a spell in a Fleetwood trawler and spoke English, garnished with profanity from the same source of which, I am quite sure, he had not the least idea of the meaning.

We gathered from him that the loch was full of sea-trout and that we could borrow a boat from a nearby farm. We also gathered that over the fold of the hill, above the road, was another smaller loch running parallel, in which there were no sea-trout but enormous brown trout. An Englishman, he told us, had come there some years before and taken two brown trout, the smaller was five pounds and the larger was seven pounds, on a fly. This was an exciting prospect to go to bed on, with three days' fishing ahead of us.

Those next three days were windy, with a blowing sea mist. The first two days we fished the sea-trout loch. During the first day, we got ten sea-trout, the biggest of which was four and a half pounds. In the evening we went down to fish the little burn for the last fifty yards of its course, where it made a path through the sandy beach to the sea. The tide was not quite right and we caught nothing.

The second day my father announced that he was going to fish the loch from the shore, and I left him putting on his waders. We did not do quite so well on this occasion, but we could not be said to have done badly. We had two fish over two pounds. In the afternoon a blink of sun came out and we were casting in blue ripples.

As I brought the boat ashore, my father was splashing his way out on to the pebbles. He had a sad and pensive look. He was extremely conservative in his estimates, which always gave great force to any tale he recounted of lost fish. He was stunned by a vision of half an hour before. He had been wading deep and casting far in the blue ripples, when, quite slowly and quietly, a sea-trout which, by the extent of shiny back and size of fin and triangle of tail, could not have been under fourteen pounds, had rolled over at his fly. He had cast again repeatedly. He had changed his fly. He had done everything, but the great fish had gone on its way and never returned. When we blew out our candle that night, in our small attic bedroom in the doctor's house, his mind was still on that fish. Years afterwards he referred to it.

Next morning brought our last day's fishing. There was a blustering wind, and white caps were running on the loch. A sea mist was mixing with the rain. By lunchtime we were very wet, and had little to show for it. After luncheon we set off across the road and up the slope of ridge to the fabulous brown trout loch. There it was, like a miniature of the one we had left. It was stony at its lower end and reedy at the upper. It looked fabulous as all lochs do when you are told that they are. There seemed to be nothing to choose between the one end and the other, and I went to the stony end towards the sea. There was a strong breeze blowing down towards me, and the vision of the long-departed Englishman with his two huge trout gave wings to my feet. It was deep at the bottom end and girdled with boulders, big round stones that looked as if they had been put there by man.

The first twenty casts produced nothing at all, and the twenty-first landed me squarely into a good fish. It was not five or seven pounds, but it was a good fighting two-pounder and seemed a wonderful augury. I fished the loch for five solid hours after that. The sun had come out in the meantime, and the wind eventually faded away to an almost dead calm. There were many fish rising in the calm and I think I got about fifteen, but nothing else was bigger than half a pound. None of the natives ever fish for brown trout in that part of the world. It was only too plain what had happened. The trout had bred to a point where there were far too many for the loch. The original monsters were no doubt there, if one could find them, but the new generation were all much of a size, small fish and lean. Quite early on in the afternoon my father decided that he must go and look for his big sea-trout again. I found him up to the waist in the sea-trout loch at the exact point where he had been vouchsafed the vision of the monster. The monster remained only a vision; a recollection of a vanishing tail and subsiding swirl. By next evening we were back in Thorshavn, and the following evening we were leaving the islands.

We had always been unclear as to how we would be returning. But we had made a plan by which we would board a ship from Iceland calling at Thorshavn, bound for Copenhagen. We arranged for a fishing boat at Lerwick, in the Shetlands, to put out and meet us outside territorial waters. We were then to clamber in to it and be conveyed to Lerwick, and there we would get a boat for Aberdeen.

The ship was seen off by almost the entire population at Thorshavn, acclaiming a famous Danish comedian who was on board. As the capital receded we felt like two depressions moving south from the Faeroes, about which you read in the meteorological reports. It had been a short but magical holiday.

Our plan to reach home seemed ambitious but workable. In bright sunlight we slowed to half-speed, four miles from Sumburgh Head, in the Shetlands. There, sure enough, was a little chugging fishing boat, angling against the swell with sail and motor doing their best. We climbed down a rope ladder into the boat, which was a perilous proceeding. Our belongings were lowered after us. The Danish passengers waved to us and gave a spirited rendering of "God Save the King". Then the ship's stern disappeared in the direction of Copenhagen, and we proceeded in the direction of Lerwick.

Our arrival at Lerwick was something for which we had not bargained. We were met by a small, but impressive delegation of port officials who told us we had violated the principles of international law; that a Danish ship, by dropping us as passengers for Lerwick outside territorial waters, had in fact approached the port of Lerwick and as such was liable to various dues. My father, who was a Member of Parliament at the time, and who had once been a successful lawyer, pointed out to them that no satisfaction would be obtained by reprisals upon ourselves, and that this was a matter between the Port of Lerwick and the Danish Steamship Company, or the British Government and the Danish Government or all four together or a combination of all four. I believe it promoted a case in International Law which raged for several years, but it worried us no further.

Next evening we were rolling in Sumburgh Roost under a grey sky, bound for Aberdeen. My mind was back among the misty islands, with all their quietness and their Scandinavian charm. My father's mind was on that great back, with the big fin and the triangle of tail, and the slowly disappearing swirl.

There are few more horrible periods in a man's life than taking the Final Schools at University. At Oxford in 1933, that dreadful week of drudgery and apprehension coincided with a heat wave week. It was made more unbearable by the fact that University regulations demand the wearing of a dark suit.

I crouched at my desk in the examination school surrounded by my fellows, sitting in neat lines, their brows furrowed in concentration. Everybody looked as if they were doing better than I was, as indeed, with negligible exceptions, they were. We wrote our answers in horrid little books which were doled out to us. After I had sat for half an hour and covered three pages I was shocked to see my fellow-scholars had already filled a book, and were collecting new ones. Then the last day came, and an awful silence.

The silence lasted for weeks, punctuated by the *viva* at which you tried to assess, by the tone of the questions, how well you had done, or how badly. When mine came, I was asked one question: "Where is the Roman Wall?" I answered it satisfactorily, and regarded it as a good augury. It was not. When the results were published I, and about five other devoted souls, had been awarded a Fourth; a degree which now has a certain historic distinction, as it has since been abolished.

When that summer term ended, with weeks to go before the *viva* and the announcement of the results, I yearned for northern latitudes and the sea. A well-known firm of Hull trawler owners agreed to allow me and John Gorton,* a Brasenose friend, to ship on board one of their trawlers fishing off the Faeroe grounds. We drove to Hull in the £5 Citroen, to which I have referred before. It was a splendid vehicle and did honour to its makers. It survived for years afterwards to give good service. It went slowly and noisily, and rocked like a hansom-cab, but in its own purposeful way devoured the miles. It had long passed the point where aesthetic considerations were of any moment, so one was

* John Gorton became Prime Minister of Australia in 1968.

naturally free from any concern as to whether it acquired one more scratch or one more dent.

We arrived at Hull with very little money, and left the car at the cheapest garage we could find. At the trawler offices we signed a paper, freeing them of responsibility for anything that might happen to us. We each bought a pair of large sea boots, which by regulation had to be two sizes too large, to allow them to be kicked off if one went overboard. Not that that would avail one much in an icy northern sea.

We slept in a lodging house at the price of 1s. each that night, and spent most of the next day down at St. Andrew's Dock, looking at the very small trawler in which we had shipped. We were fascinated by the sight of two old Hull skippers, who still perpetuated the ancient British seafaring tradition of wearing ear-rings.

John and I went on board, sea-booted, with our duffle bags over our shoulders. Early next morning we were off and the Humber estuary was widening in front of us. We were singularly ill-equipped. We had no bedding and slept in the forecastle on hard wooden bunks in the clothes that we wore, and with our oilskins as our only covering. The boatswain very kindly lent me a pair of tarry trousers, which I rolled up and used as a pillow.

Later, when we got into the life, we slept like logs, and would not have exchanged these wooden couches for anything.

It was calm going down the Humber. We spent the morning getting to know some of the members of the crew. The captain was a man of note, famous as a navigator. He was also famous as being a teetotaller. It was thus the more surprising when he told us how fond he was of certain heady liqueurs, which, it transpired, he regarded as temperance beverages. The mate was shy and silent at first, but we became very good friends later on. The boatswain concealed a kind heart, behind an appearance of unspeakable ferocity. Everyone was known by a nickname. The most junior member of the crew, Ginger, was our close associate. He was a burly youth, who had an incredible appetite. It was the duty of anyone who was eating their meals in his company to see that he did not empty the pickle bottle. I was once rebuked for allowing him to do so. In fact I had watched the feat, hypnotized.

In Britain we mind our own business. In a tiny over-crowded island we naturally value our privacy. You may travel by train from King's Cross to Aberdeen without speaking to your neighbour. But the result is that the average Briton is extra-ordinarily ignorant about the lives of other Britons. It is only after a railway disaster that the public realize the weight of responsi-bility that a railway signalman carries. It is only after a mine disaster, or the loss of a deep sea trawler, that they realize how hazardous are these callings, and that in every hour of every day many thousands are winning coal and fish for their fellow citizens at the risk of their lives.

Slipping down the Humber was a fragment of enjoyment. Once round the hook of Flamborough Head, and into the North Sea, we began to bob like a cork. The next two days were purga-tory. Seasickness over a really long period eventually reduces you to a state of semi-consciousness. On one occasion I nearly went overboard. Slumped over the gunwale, black clouds and sparks chasing themselves across my clouded brain, I watched the water suddenly reach right up the ship's side, to claw me in, while I hung on the point of balance.

There are few more likeable men than the British deep-sea fishermen. Utterly immune to seasickness themselves, they had a rough but real tenderness for anyone who was suffering. Every time I was sick they forced me to eat a piece of biscuit—"Some-thing to be sick on next time", they said. After two days, the sickness had passed so completely that, bucketing in those North Atlantic rollers, in the high latitudes, I had forgotten what even the word meant. John Gorton was a better sailor and he enjoyed himself from the start.

Your body is at right angles to the horizon, as you thread your way about the decks. The horizon is the only constant. For you are always holding on, or manoeuvring to stay upright, with one gunwale slipping down deep below you, and the other blotting out half the sky above.

There are no better sea boats, for their size, than deep-sea trawlers. With the high bows, and the big air space they contain, they do not butt the seas, but rise on them like a cork. Occasion-ally one reads in the newspapers that a trawler is long overdue and must be presumed to be lost. Any sea that will sink a trawler will sink most other kinds of vessel first.

The need for space for powerful engines, and for almost all other available space for packing the fish, leaves little room for men to sleep and eat. Comfort is a comparative thing, and so great was our appetite for both food and sleep, that we were not over-nice about the rest. And you become used, after a few days, to the blend of oil, coal, smoke and fish. Hours, and even days, of spray sluicing over the vessel never seem to make it a whit the cleaner.

The silhouette of the trawler is one of the most individual of all the vessels in the world: with the high wheelhouse from which one can see over the top of the high bow, the little triangular sail to keep her steady while she is trawling, and the boat which is largely ornamental, and is lashed to the structure below the small boom. If life on a trawler is hard in summer, it is ten times harder in winter, when ice forms on the rigging, and all hands may be needed to man the steam hose to free the icy top-hamper, which, if allowed to grow heavy enough, may overturn a trawler. The incidence of pieces of sharp rusty iron and wire, coupled with the slime of fish, make the smallest cut something to be treated with as great a care as a serious wound would be treated ashore; blood poisoning is an ever-present danger. The trawlermen say that the sea goes rotten off Iceland in the winter, and adds to the danger of blood poisoning. The Vikings said exactly the same.

Our destination was the Faeroes, Bill Bailey's Bank and the George Bligh Bank. We stood well out from the north-east corner of Scotland and caught a fleeting vision of Shetland, as a point of land framed by white sea mist.

We came to the Faeroes on a beautiful clear afternoon, and passed close enough to hail a returning Hull trawler, with well-known piratical tendencies, which had got a full load of fish in an incredibly short time by trawling the breeding grounds close to the coast.

In the Faeroes in summer it is light all night, and for months on end lighthouses are not used. In that northern twilight we made our way up the coast of Sudero, plodding along at our maximum speed of just over ten knots. All the cobwebs of the Final School at Oxford had long disappeared, and apprehension about the results had evaporated with them. Next day, in cloudless northern sunshine, the trawling doors went down, and the conical net, whose mouth they keep open, was dredging along the bottom of the sea.

The trawler goes slowly when she is trawling. The net steadies her but gives her a curious circular roll. Once every two hours, in normal circumstances, the winches creak and up the net comes. The fish that have been drawn in are pressed by the forward motion to the apex of the cone of the net. When the trawl is very full, as the mouth of the net comes up to the surface so the point packed with fish will float up behind it. Usually, when the net is drawn up, there seems at first sight to be nothing in it; then the point of the cone appears, the windlass hoists it on board, and a flapping mass of fish are spilt out on the deck.

There are two pens on the deck, one for haddock, and one for cod. Hour after hour one stands and sways, going through a sequence of three movements, unconsciously adjusting oneself to the roll of the boat; one takes the fish up by the gills, and with a long cut of the knife the entrails go overboard or are caught in the air by the *entourage* of gulls. Into an open barrel goes the liver, for the making of cod liver oil, and the fish goes into the appropriate pen. Many other things besides cod and haddock fall out from the bag of the net and flap against the seaboots of the crew, knee-deep in a good haul. There are small octopuses with strange goggling eyes; small red fish called soldiers, and many others with nondescript, colloquial names. Once, we landed a fish that was almost a sphere with a tail attached, scaly as an alligator, with a good-sized haddock in a mouth which was studded with needle-like teeth. Then there were catfish which looked as if they had been cut out of lead, who fastened their teeth in anything which they encountered, whether it was a wire hawser or the toe of a sea-boot. Once we landed a basking shark.

When the fish are thick one catch will not be completed before the deck is feet deep in the next haul, and there is no rest for the crew between the catches. Our shipmates told us that there had been times when they had been gutting fish for twenty hours at a time, and sleeping at their work, still carrying on, as weary soldiers will sometimes sleep on the march.

The first day's fishing was just opposite that rock-girt bowl of sea at Saxen, where my father and I had fished for sea-trout the year before. This time, we moved our ground and moved it often. Fog and drizzle was our usual accompaniment. We came to think of the sea not as a heaving mass of grey surface, but as a screen between us and the sea-bottom, which was as a country by itself. Our comrades would talk of it as if it were a land of which they knew every inch. Sometimes we would ask why we went to one place, more than another, and be told that only some hundreds of yards away from the fishing bank the sea bottom was strewn with great boulders which would ruin the nets. On one occasion we got a great haul; far out at sea, deep down below us, they said, the bottom was like a long broad carriage drive of pure gravel. There were fish in plenty, but they tended to keep for a lesser time so that it was towards the end of a trip that the trawlermen went there.

Two new elements had just come into deep-sea fishing when we made that trip; one was the echo-sounding device, and the other the wireless-telephone. The wireless-telephone was regarded with suspicion, except in moments of danger and emergency. With only morse, a skipper could send his friend news of the fish in code, which the others could not follow. But now the time had come when he spoke over the telephone and, if he dropped one hint in his conversation that he was on to a good place, it would not be long before there was the smoke of a dozen trawlers converging on him. "Smoke chasers", they were contemptuously called. The only way that was considered safe was when a skipper met a friend at sea, and he went within hailing distance of the megaphone. We often did this with our two grimy vessels pitching and rolling in the North Atlantic swell, enclosed in their little world of grey mist, with the skipper of each with his head out of the wheelhouse window, and a huge megaphone at his mouth, conducting a conversation with his sea-booted friend pitching 100 yards away. So high was the incidence of profanity to actual information that these conversations took three times as long as they need have done, and gradually the boats would drift apart and the Yorkshire voices would be raised in a more and more stentorian shout to bridge the gap.

At the end of two weeks in that heaving, grey sea, sometimes within sight of the islands, and sometimes alone in our world of mist, we had filled our fish hold, not to capacity, but as full as we could hope to fill it on that trip. The fish were stowed and sorted in the racks, and we were headed south in a thick sea fog. The log dropped off, and we ran without noticing it for two hours. As a result we lost our bearings badly. We knew that we were close to the Shetlands, and felt our way slowly and with caution. On the sea around us there appeared sea birds in growing number, of the kind that one finds close to the shore, guillemots and little auks. Standing alongside the gunwale we were conscious of a growing feeling of something tall and solid and menacing behind the curtains of darkening mist. Then the mist began to recede and our horizon enlarged from 100 yards to four times that distance, and there was the swell breaking on the high cliffs of Denis Head. We turned hard to port, leaving a U of foam as a wake. In the chart room the skipper connected up the pencil line of course where it had been broken, and put a cross for our position. Such men are not easily ruffled.

We had a calm passage back, with no more alarms and excursions. A hot sun burned us and our companions, nearly black. Off Newcastle two tunny sported ahead of us, rolling like porpoises just in front of our bow. We came up the Humber in a warm summer sea mist.

I have seldom been so sorry to say good-bye to anyone as I was to our companions in that trawler. I never remember getting to know, and getting to like so well, a group of men, in so short a space of time, as those Yorkshire deep-sea fishermen. John and I redeemed the car, and were left with just enough money to buy ourselves a meal ashore. We drove deep into the night and slept in a hayfield till dawn. Then, wet with dew, we rumbled our way down south to reach Elsfield in time for breakfast, sea-booted and suntanned.

Sometimes, of a winter's night, I turn on the B.B.C.'s shipping forecast and listen to the voice of the announcer intoning "Iceland, Faeroes, Fair Isle, Bailey, Hebrides, Rockall—"and there comes the vision of mast-head lights rising and falling in the darkness; with the motion of those cold heaving seas; the flights of spray slapping viciously against oil-skinned backs; the smell of oil and smoke mixing with the salt; and the oaths and the good-humour and above all the fortitude of these men. "It isn't the ships that count, it's the men", so the skipper used to say.

18

Appointment in Africa

A CONSUMING desire for adventure, coupled with the stern necessity of earning my living, had presented me with something of a problem in the choosing of a job. The files of the Appointments Committee at Oxford were filled with enticing proposals dealing with *estancias* in the Argentine, ranches in Canada, tobacco farms in Rhodesia and rubber plantations in Malaya, but they all required the buying of a partnership at a substantial figure. For a time a career in the Malayan Police seemed attractive, then my father suggested the Colonial Administrative Service. In spite of my slender scholastic achievements, I was fortunate enough to be selected in 1933. I had secretly wanted to go to the Solomon Islands, but had been persuaded by my father to put down Nigeria as my first choice. I was in fact selected for Uganda.

The year at Oxford passed very pleasantly. I shared digs with Tony Richards of Brasenose, who was going to the same destination. We were twice nearly evicted from our lodgings. One occasion was when Kim Muir and Harry Legge-Bourke, who is now a Member of Parliament, arrived unexpectedly for the night. We had to house in our sitting-room a goshawk and a peregrine who spent the night perched on the backs of chairs, and which our landlady encountered unexpectedly next morning, when she threw open the door to sweep the room. This followed an incident of a month before when, for various reasons, I could not leave my tame badger at Elsfield, and he occupied a barrel in the corner. It put a strain on our relations.

In June 1934, we set sail for Africa. Although it was only eighteen years ago, anyone who then wrote a book about the journey to that continent began it the day the ship left England. It was still regarded by a great mass of the public as a land hidden and unknown. When we sailed into Mombasa Harbour, there was no job in the world that could have been offered to us that we would have taken in preference to the one on which we were embarking.

The first sight of Africa must linger in any man's memory as one of the greatest experiences in his life. There can be no more romantic railway journey than the slow climb westwards, of the Kenya–Uganda Railway, bound for Nairobi, and then on to Uganda. For the first time we saw the darkness fall on Africa, with the suddenness of a curtain being drawn across the sky. Then we awoke to the glorious African sunrise bringing a rosy hue to the Athi Plains, and herds of zebra cantering away at the noisy approach of the train. Scattered on the dry expanses were little groups of Grant's and Thomson's gazelle, and strange animals that hitherto have been merely coloured plates in natural history books. East Africa is entered by a glorious gateway.

Tony and I stayed with Mervyn Cowie* for two nights, at his house outside Nairobi. He had been at Brasenose with us, and a better guide one could not easily find. Even in those days he was regarded as an expert on African game, now he is famous for his knowledge. With him we watched great herds of wildebeest at the water holes, we saw the herds of zebra, the shape of fat Welsh ponies, but with neat bristly manes that looked as if they had been carefully clipped, and gave their heads the outline of a horse's head on a Grecian vase. It had been unpleasantly hot at Mombasa. Here it was cool and still, looking down the slope from Mervyn's house across the Masai reserve, at the peak of Kilimanjaro on the horizon.

Then we were on the train again, which takes a day and a night to cross the high range lands of the Kenya plateau, and to descend to hot, low-lying Uganda. Clifford Francis was one of our party. He was going out to take up a post as Puisne Judge. He was met by car far out from Kampala at a wayside station, and I drove the last twenty odd miles with him, along a road which wound between lines of banana trees alternating with bush. It was a smaller and much less important Kampala than the present-day town. I wandered about it in the afternoon, unoppressed by the heat, gazing at the strange, humpbacked hills covered with scrub

* Mervyn Cowie founded the Kenya Game Parks.

which surrounded it. The train arrived in the late afternoon bearing Tony Richards, and my other fellow cadet Gerald Smith.

We were installed in a small and very plain bungalow. This was to be our home for the month in which we were to be shown round the various aspects of government at Kampala, and later at Entebbe. In the course of the first afternoon we all secured native servants and spoke to them in halting Swahili which we had learned at Oxford. Our belongings were stacked up in three mountains of packing-cases. They comprised all our furniture and what was needed to set up our separate establishments for what was intended to be a career of twenty-five years' duration.

The first impact of Africa filled me, as it does almost everyone, with violent energy, coupled with a raging appetite and the facility to sleep like a log. After six months this was to dwindle, and at the end of the first year the edge is off. The appetite needs fostering, and sleep is less certain. To the newcomer, nothing is too distant, nothing is too much effort, and there is nothing which is not worth seeing. We attended the Law Courts and were given a further course in our magisterial duty. We saw each of the departments of the Government in turn, and then we were moved to the capital at Entebbe, to live in the Rest House there and see what remained.

Our arrival at Entebbe coincided with a visitation of that unpleasant phenomenon known as lake fly. Watching the blue waters at Lake Victoria lapping at the foot of that long, irregular sweep of greensward which separates the town from the lake, there seemed to be blowing down the wind great wreaths of smoke. In a few hours the whole air was full of a cloud of flies. Looking through the mosquito screens outside they were everywhere, like raindrops. They were soon in the houses, too, and in our food. They were as inescapable as a sandstorm. It was two days before the air was clear of them.

This tour of education left us a good deal of spare time, and we were always free from four o'clock onwards. In Kampala there was not a very great deal to occupy our spare time. But at Entebbe there was more scope. Charles Pitman, the game warden, suggested we might spend the day allotted to visit the Game Department, in going round some of the nearby islands, in the game launch, to try our new weapons on the crocodiles. This seemed a splendid opportunity to use my double-barrelled, hammered .450 Express rifle, which, after decades of peace in a loft in Oxfordshire, was now returning to active service. It was full of grease, and took a good deal of cleaning. When put together it resembled nothing so much as a gamekeeper's shotgun, with a rather short barrel. Its weight was terrific. Tony Richards and Gerald Smith prepared their weapons for action, and, round about ten o'clock on the appointed morning, we were at the jetty with Charles Pitman and clambering aboard his big launch, which was covered from end to end by a canopy. He had half a dozen African game scouts with him. We moved on the bosom of this great inland sea, bright sun above, and the ripples sparkling like a million diamonds of such brightness that they made us blink.

We had quite a long way to go, and little to see in the going. We did see the head of a hippopotamus, still, and seemingly unrelated to a body, which disappeared as we approached. The islands were distant outlines, disembodied by a mirage. We talked little and fell into a reverie of content, for the breeze across the lake was cool. We were drugged by the beauty of the world around us.

The islands formed a large group, but it was in two of them that we were interested. The first had thin scrubby trees and grass, but little other bush, and was ringed by a sandy beach running back ten yards from the water's edge. Crocodiles, and crocodiles only, were our quarry. They would, Charles Pitman explained, be somewhere in the grass or bush, resting. They would make a dash for the water when they were alarmed. If we got in the way of one, he would not seize us in his jaws, but give us a blow from that long, iron-clad tail.

The element we wished to achieve was surprise. The engine was throttled down. The game scouts hushed their staccato conversation, and we stole in to the beach with all the quietness that we could contrive. With Charles Pitman leading, rifle in hand, we went overboard into the shallows with all the atmosphere of a combined operation against a defended beach. Everything was perfectly quiet except for two birds who screamed from a tall tree, as jays scream at a fox.

There was a big clump of trees in front of us, which crowned the highest point of the small island. They were well set apart, and the ground was clear between them. We crept through some rank grass to the edge of the clump. Then, quite suddenly, the place was full of moving crocodiles, fanning out for the beach and the water, great beasts who levered their horny stomachs from the ground to the full extent of their bow legs, and moved at an amazing pace. Gerry's rifle went off beside me, and then Tony's. I had never fired my ancient and ponderous weapon until that moment. Pointing it in the direction of twelve feet of scaly flank passing across my vision at a bandy-legged gallop, I rocked to a terrific roar and a push which swung me half round. My crocodile disappeared through the grass; round us were splashes as they hurled themselves into the sparkling ripples. What seemed to be a baby crocodile scuffled past us, but it was a large lizard—four feet in length and coloured pale gold. The first flush was over and we had one crocodile between us. We stared at this horny creature. It looked every whit as menacing as if it were alive.

We re-loaded. As it fell into the breech, the long cartridge clinked with the same note as a shell case in an anti-tank rifle. The two were very nearly the same size. The hammer was cocked anew and we followed Charles Pitman down to the water's edge, on the far side from where we had landed. All was complete peace. The ripples lapped on the sand. The torrid stillness returned. There was not a crocodile to be seen. Not far from the shore there was a floating log—though once we were told that it was a crocodile, it was easy to see that it was one. Very little showed, but the two horny bosses round the eyes, which stared balefully from a distance of twenty yards. I fitted the sight of the double-barrel as nearly as I could between them and pulled the trigger. I was holding the rifle tightly, with my chin hard against the stock, as one normally does hold a rifle. I got a blow on the chin which made my head rock. When I looked again, there was no sign of the crocodile. From then onwards I never put my face too close to that rifle, but learned to shoot with both eyes open as with a shotgun. It fitted as a shotgun should fit, and was used only at very short range when brutal stopping power was needed.

Charles Pitman left us to our own devices for a while and went back to talk with the game scouts. They indicated that, in the grass-clad peninsula in front of us, we might well find crocodiles still asleep, undisturbed by the noise. They enjoined us to be careful.

We were not careful. We were eager and we knew nothing about the dangers. The grass was thick and about six feet high. We walked the peninsula up and down as if we were looking for rabbits. Half-way down it there was a tremendous disturbance in front of us, and the grass shook with the passage of a crocodile on his way to the water. We deemed it wise to stand still. The commotion subsided. The grass was stilled to a gentle waving under the caress of the breeze. We went on. Almost at the end of the island, Gerry stopped, held up his hand and pointed, apparently at his own toes. I came up beside him. About five feet in front of us, was a section of a scaly body seemingly about a yard in width. Which part of the body it was, and in which direction the body was facing, we had no clue. Gerry took aim at the middle of this expanse of scales. He was short in stature and the muzzle of his weapon was only a yard from the beast. At the crash of the rifle an enormous mouth opened and shut, with the force of a bear trap, not six inches from his toes. There was a convulsion as the great tail flattened an arc of tall grass, and then a stillness. We let fly one more bullet apiece and there was silence. The crocodile was dead, almost concealed in the grass around it.

Charles Pitman rejoined us, and we ate our sandwich lunch in what shade we could find. Then we boarded the launch, and made for the next island which was close by. Here a few tall trees climbed above a thick scrub. Here the ribbon of sand round the water's edge was wider. At one part the slender plumes of papyrus showed.

These islands lie within the sleeping sickness area. No one was permitted to live here. The theory was then becoming accepted that it was not necessary for tsetse to bite an infected human to convey the disease. It was thought that if it bit certain kinds of antelope, which carried trypanosomiasis in their blood, that that might be sufficient. It was a rather disturbing thought.

We bumped the game launch on the sandy beach, as soundlessly as before. The crocodiles were taking their ease in the shade of the bush. There was a very good chance of finding oneself in their way, when they woke up and made a dash for the water. We had a good deal of beach to cover. The point where we landed yielded nothing, so we stole along the beach, rifles at the ready, but there was silence except for the scolding of a single garish bird. We made our way down to the beach to the edge of a stretch of tall papyrus. It would have been quite impenetrable, but for the fact that a hippopotamus had made his way through it fairly recently, and left a tunnel through the tough stems punctuated by deep potholes where he had put his ponderous feet.

Charles Pitman went first and I followed him. Our rifles had to be ready for emergencies. It was impossible, in that narrow tunnel, in which we advanced doubled up, to avoid pointing one's rifle either directly at the man who was creeping in front, or directly at the man who was coming behind. I had my hammers down, my rifle of necessity pointing at the middle of Charles Pitman's back.

The tunnel of papyrus had fallen in, here and there, and the big stems had dropped across the path. They had sometimes to be climbed over, but more usually had to be climbed under. I was negotiating the worst of these places, when to my horror I heard my rifle click. A bent-down papyrus stem had caught my right-hand hammer, pulled it back and cocked it. Had the stem released the hammer one second before it cocked, it would have fallen back, and that would have been the end of a very distinguished Game Warden. I lowered it gingerly, and from then onwards contrived to creep with one hand covering the hammers.

We emerged into a clearing such as the one where we had fired our first shots that morning, but there was no sign nor sound of crocodiles here, so we retraced our steps down the tunnel. This time I took my cartridges out—emergency or no emergency. It had been dark in the tunnel, but the sun on the ripples was blinding when we got back to that golden beach again. We set out to explore it thoroughly. Charles Pitman decided to split our little force, and I found myself creeping along the water's edge down a long stretch of sand, alone. I had not gone twenty yards when there was a convulsion in the bush, exactly inland from me. Down the beach came a massive crocodile, heading straight for the water where I stood. I do not know where my first bullet went. With the second his belly hit the sand. His great tail gave a spasmodic flail, and there was a hole in the middle of his back where the .480 grain bullet had hit him. For me there can be no circumstance of life where the gamut of emotions can be run more intensely than in the stopping of a charging animal.

I had just re-loaded and re-cocked, when a similar commotion, thirty yards away, proclaimed that another crocodile was making for the water. There was no danger from this one and it looked easy. Two explosions of sand and he disappeared in the ripples. I heard Charles Pitman shout fifty yards away, and shouted back that I had got one. He shouted something unintelligible that seemed to suggest that I should be careful. The breeze had been dropping and for a moment a dead calm had fallen. The other islands drifted disembodied by mirage. The metal of the rifle was very hot to the touch.

I got a shot at one other, and that at about twenty yards. The first shot made another explosion of sand. The second got the top of the horny head just as it would have touched the water. The expanding bullet lifted the top clean off the scaly cranium, and the crocodile lay with his snout just touching the water. By this time the alarm was well and truly given. Every crocodile was in the water. Occasionally, a hundred yards off, a head would rise, and would submerge as I fitted the sights on it. The game scouts appeared in high glee, and set to work going over the sand, kneeling down in places and scooping it to one side. They had found what they wanted, a crocodile's nest. It is strange that these giant creatures should lay eggs, and stranger still that they should lay them in such neat lines, with as many as fifty-five eggs to the nest.

The game scouts worked along the whole length of the beach and found, in all, ten nests. They then set to work methodically smashing the eggs. Two of them competed in throwing them at the trunk of the nearest tree. Most of the eggs ran yellow yolks when they were smashed, but one nest was so near hatching that the eggs contained perfect miniature crocodiles, each with an egg-sac attached. The destruction was finished, and the afternoon was almost gone.

Charles Pitman showed us, on the edge of the beach, a little group of huts put up by some native fisher-folk who had come there in their dug-out canoes. The scouts destroyed the huts. To allow any human being to live in that sleeping sickness area was to invite the visitation of that almost incurable disease. All day long our bare arms and bare knees had been covered with what looked like small black house flies. It was a sobering feeling that we had flies on our bare flesh, each one of which was a potential killer. It is an ill wind that blows no one any good, and certainly the tsetse fly protects a vast area of Africa from overgrazing and being mishandled by man. Because of it there remains a great reserve of virgin country which, when the fly is eventually mastered, will lay new areas open.

It had been a thrilling day. The glare went out of the sun and the colour of the water changed, and we headed back, tired and happy. We had no trophies to show, except one crocodile's tooth which was loose in his jaw and which I had managed to prise away from the one that charged me. But we had memories which last.

On another occasion we went to see, as all visitors do, an ancient and repulsive crocodile known as Lutembe. His age was considered fabulous. He would leave his small rocky islet, 100 yards from the land, when he was called, and nose his way on to the beach, to take the food that was offered him.

One evening I strolled down to the jetty at Entebbe when the water was very calm to see if I could discover any tropical fish which would be prepared to take a fly. There were enormous fish there—they would have averaged about fourteen pounds—a kind of barbel. They swam slowly round, every now and then breaking the surface. I threw in a cigarette end, and one of them, cruising round, nosed his way up to the ring that it made. Then with a slow head and tail rise he took the cigarette down, only to release it a yard below the surface, for it to float up, disintegrated.

The next day we were to be shown over the Forestry Department, in the afternoon. Gerald Smith and I had a very quick lunch, took our only rod, which was a nine-foot trout rod with a reel to match, a 2X cast and a box of trout flies, and set off for the jetty. Sure enough, there was a big fish cruising. It was one of those grey days that one gets in the tropics, and the water undulated with a gentle swell, glassy smooth. The biggest fly in the box was a Blue Zulu, about size 6. One fish after another swam up and looked at it, then turned his head and finished his cruise.

Time was getting short, when, remembering the incident of the day before, we broke the end off a cigarette, and fixed it on a hook. It landed with a big satisfactory ring, and a big fish swam up to it, made as if to take it, turned away and then swung round, and opened his large mouth and sucked it in. We must have spent twenty minutes playing him. Twice he had the line almost out to the drum. He did not run, but continued his cruise in wide circles, while the little trout rod bent into the shape of a U, and the reel ran with an even note. When he did give in he gave in very quickly. I manoeuvred him to within reach, and Gerald tailed him. We took him back in triumph to the Rest House. He weighed nearly sixteen pounds. Our native boys, so far from being pleased, buried him in the flower bed in the garden, saying that as far as they were concerned, such fish were not eatable—if they were not actually poison.

Then our month of instruction was over, and we set off for our first appointments. Gerald Smith went west. Tony went to the Northern Province, and I to the Eastern. I spent a week at the Headquarters of the Eastern Province before taking the long road north to the district of Soroti, to which I had been posted. The Headquarters is in Jinja, where the Nile flows out of Lake Victoria in one dark smooth sheet of water, broken here and there by a rock on its rim, to fall in a tumult of sound and foam into a long deep gorge where it runs like a Scottish salmon river half a mile in width. It will not long hold its wild beauty. The Hydro-Electric Scheme will soon fill that gorge to the brim; but then it was possible to stand at one side of the falls and watch this tumult of sounding water, and look at that long bent sheet of thousands of liquid tons fold over the lip of the falls, looking hard and black and slippery to the touch. At my feet was a gigantic eddy where the water curved round; and there, as you watched, you saw the fins and tails of great fish slowly perambulating the whirlpool.

Uganda contains the finest eating game bird and the finest

eating fresh-water fish that have ever come my way. The latter is a fish of very modest size, averaging half a pound, the Ngege. It lives in Lake Victoria. You fish for Ngege, as you fish for roach, watching a small quill float—though the bait is not paste, but a kind of seaweed. Sitting watching the red top of that quill, I might have been sitting on the banks of an English water between the pollard willows, waiting for a roach to snatch at the bead of paste and set that red top bobbing. But if I lifted my eyes from the float I could generally see the strange, leathery visage of a hippo breaking the surface about a hundred yards off; and beyond it the tropical scrub running down to the water's edge.

That week came to an end. I packed my second-hand Morris car with all my belongings—by far the largest of which was a tin bath which could also in emergencies be used as a boat—and my native servant, Yowana, with whom I was just beginning to be able to converse with some fluency in a vocabulary of less than 100 words. Our destination was Soroti, and it was a whole day's journey to get there.

The roads in that part of Africa are of red earth, which look like the raw material of hard tennis courts. The road surface rises up steeply to a ridge in the middle. The wheel tracks on either side make ruts, into which the wheels fit, making the driving of a car like the driving of a railway train, and the passing of another car a matter which calls for thought. At one point was a swamp called the Mpologoma. Here was a large metal ferry boat, which was punted across by about a dozen natives with long poles. As they punted they sang and chanted. As I did not understand the language, I did not grasp that the burden of the chant was the expression of a hope that they would be rewarded well.

The country as we travelled became gradually freer of scrub The road was lined more often with patches of tall grass, then, as we entered the district of which Soroti is the headquarters, we were moving through lines of grass broken here and there with thorn bushes. There were, now and then, great heaps of rock piled up roughly as if by the hands of a giant, with scrubby growth sprouting from the cracks.

It was four o'clock in the afternoon when we entered Soroti.

There was the district headquarters, a modest building with a tin roof and a flagstaff outside, a small playing field and six or seven substantial bungalows widely scattered on the one side. The houses of the little township were on the other, on either side of the street of the bazaars.

I spent the night with Captain Kennedy, the District Commissioner and started to learn something of the district. As the sun went down, the darkness filled with the wail and chatter of innumerable insects. Lying in the dark under a mosquito net, I listened to the many strange noises of the night and thought of this great area of district, set in a continent so vast that it seemed to run right to the world's end.

19

District Officer

THE first time that you keep house for yourself within your own four walls, you are passing one of life's major landmarks. My bungalow was a substantial one, of the standard architecture of the Public Works Department. It had a concrete floor and a tin roof. It contained a dining-room, a bedroom and a veranda (which was a sitting-room), as well as a minute bathroom and a kitchen.

When the last packing case had been opened and removed from sight, and all my effects arranged according to their respective natures, I felt that I was a citizen in my own right. Half of what I had bought in London, nearly all of which had been bought at the urging of the cunning vendor, was relevant to the kitchen. There were water filters, pots and pans, china, glass, and a mass of other things.

The usual outfit of tropical clothing was stowed in a large austere chest of drawers. My few pictures, which were backed with sheets of tin, to keep out the white ants, were hung. In one corner was the double-barrelled .450 Rigby Express Rifle. It stood there proudly, representing a very early phase of the evolution of the rifle. But it looked the more formidable for its hammers and the heavy lever along the trigger-guard which had to be swung to one side to open the breach. It had cost £5 second-hand, and had spent three decades packed in grease in the loft of a neighbour, in Oxfordshire, whose uncle had been in Uganda in the Sudanese mutiny in the previous century. It was now, in fact, repatriated to the haunts of its youth, where it had been an up-to-date weapon. It fired cartridges which were longer than the middle finger and, even then, cost 1s. 6d. apiece. In another corner was my .318 Westley-Richards, a very accurate, hard-hitting rifle for all purposes—also second-hand. In a third corner leant my shotgun, which had belonged to my Uncle Willie who had bought it about the turn of the century. It does not eject, but I would not change it for any gun in the world, and have used it for thirty years in three continents. Two bookends on the small table supported about a dozen of my favourite books. There was a bare concrete floor; this, and the large bare spaces of wall, made it evident that the bungalow could stand a good deal more furnishing yet.

As time went on, the exposed space of concrete floor diminished as more and more antelope skins were spread about it. The horns of antelopes filled up the walls, and various African nick-nacks accumulated, such as large buckskin drums, and Nubi basket-work. When the cotton season came it was possible to have some cushions stuffed, and thus relieve the austerity of the settee and the chairs provided by the Public Works Department. To an outsider, however, this interior might have left a great deal to be desired, but I would not have exchanged it for anything in Africa, or Africa for any other part of the world.

The garden contained a rather sad-looking mango tree, and some wan grass sprouted from the hard clods of red soil. There were two small round empty flowerbeds; and the angle of the garden which bordered the T junction of two small roads was bounded by a short and skinny hedge, of some kind of privet.

Work began early in the morning. We rose before the sun was hot, and I drank my morning tea seated on my doorstep in pyjamas. The air was still and fresh as the rising sun lit the eastern sky with its flame, and the growing warmth drank up the dew. Long before midday that sun was roasting the landscape. It seemed to strike the ground and rise up and hit you in the face, leaving you blinking, until you got used to it.

The District Headquarters is always called the Boma, and thither I went after breakfast, to work a solid six hours' stretch and return for a late luncheon—finished for the day. After various experiments it was discovered that far more work got done that way, and it left that wonderful time from four o'clock onwards, when the force had gone out of the sun, free to take our exercise before darkness fell.

The long stretch of work in the morning, sitting at a table

covered with papers, was punctuated by certain routine visitors. At eleven o'clock Yowana used to appear with a tray on which was perched a large brown teapot and some cakes. Just after he had gone a native who was employed to keep the white ants in check, as far as was possible, would appear with a basin full of what seemed to be clods of earth. He would lay these out, on the edge of the concrete plinth on which the office was built; striking each with a sharp tap he would split them open to reveal a colony of white ant grubs. This daily inspection used to keep him up to his job. But it was not an appetizing sight, and it was thus the custom that Yowana should appear first.

On Saturdays there came the exacting business of checking the ledgers of accounts, and counting the cash—mostly in single African shillings. On any morning I might be required to sit in the little courthouse in the capacity of magistrate. Here hour after hour I took down the evidence in longhand on large sheets of blue foolscap paper, very conscious of my dignity when the English police officer referred to me as "Your Worship".

That district was said, in those days, to have the highest incidence of murder of any in the British Empire. The witnesses could seldom write, and thumb-printed their evidence. The women were generally the least reliable, as they went in terror of reprisals from the friends of the accused. But many a little naked African boy of nine or ten, would give evidence with absolute clarity and stand up to any cross-examination. Infinite is the variety of the duties of an officer in the Colonial Administrative Service. As a career it is a sturdy British mixture of idealism and common sense, and a magnificent life for a young man who loves wild places.

During my first year at Soroti I still had the full force of my English vigour. Those with whom I worked used to rest after lunch, and rise again at four o'clock to take their exercise, through the medium of games. A little golf-course had been made on the grassy plain. It was only necessary to clear the grass away from the rough red earth and roll it, to have a hard tennis court. The Indians in the bazaars, and the Goans, who were part of the district clerical staff, combined with my colleagues to make sides for hockey and cricket.

I had never had any great fondness for games. I enjoyed rowing at Oxford mightily. But Africa was so new, and there was so much to do, and so much to see, that I was loath to sacrifice my evening hours, or my Sundays, to anything which restricted me to the same patch of ground. Further, it seemed rather a pity to come such a very great distance to do something which one could do so much better at home—if one were so minded. My colleagues enjoyed themselves on the tennis court and the cricket field, and, every evening and many afternoons as well, and almost every Sunday, I set off with my gun or my rifle.

I acquired two companions—one was a gunbearer called Edwoko. Yowana and he were at daggers drawn, on all occasions, which was rather tedious. Yowana came from the kingdom of Buganda; Edwoko was a Lango, of the Hamitic races which run north to the Sudan. Yowana was assured and sophisticated; Edwoko was a shy creature of the wild, whose face was pitted with a pattern of tribal scars, and whose brow was always puckered in little wrinkles of concern or concentration. He did not speak much, but was none the less a wonderful companion, an adept tracker—as are all his race—and a stout comrade in a tight place, to be depended on to stand by you as long as life remained. Like all true hunters he had a very good working knowledge of natural history, covering a sphere far outside the habits of the beasts which he hunted. He had natural courtesy but could be extremely outspoken when I missed an easy shot. He had one final advantage. He could not shoot, and I never taught him to use a gun. Too many people have come to grief when they have failed to stop a charging beast with their rifle, and turning to snatch their second weapon from their gunbearer, have found the chamber empty because he had himself fired and missed.

My second companion was an enormous black and white bull-terrier called Dan. He was the biggest I have ever seen, and was as strong as an Eskimo husky dog. Natives in the remotest parts of the district who had never heard of me, had heard of Dan. He was afraid of nothing, and is the only dog, that I have known, who has gone for a leopard. But like all the truly strong, he was a gentle friend. He had a large, three-cornered smile and a tail that was always gently wagging. He and Edwoko were tremendous friends, and he would allow Edwoko's dark hand to stroke his smooth head, and smile broadly up into that scarred and wrinkled face.

The life of an administrative officer falls into two spheres. One sphere is the indoor work when he is at the District Head-quarters. His working hours are spent in dealing with corres-pondence and finance and the court work of the district. The other, and the more exhilarating, is when he is to go on safari. This district was about the size of Wales. It was sub-divided into what were known as sazas—themselves the size of small English counties. These were ruled over by the highest grade of chief-tain. These were sub-divided again, and ruled over by chiefs of diminishing importance.

On safari I was directed to visit one of these "counties" at a time, and, on one occasion, two. In the old days, and in many parts of Africa even then and in some even now, the District Officer conducted his safari on foot. But roads reached all the principal parts of this district so that we went on safari in a truck with all our belongings, and bumped and bounced along the corrugated road surface to our destination. From the head-quarters of the saza, I was attended by the saza chief from whom we received the invariable gift—of a sheep with a large tail and a basket of eggs.

I went round with him to the headquarters of all his minor chiefs. A great deal of that part of it was done on foot, tracing paths through the tall grass or between the scrub, with a retinue of attendants following in single file. If the saza was equivalent to an English county, so the next sub-division was equivalent to an English parish. Each one had its little Parliament House— a large mud hut with a grass roof. Into this building an incredible number of Africans would crowd while I sat enthroned on a dais at one end, on a wooden chair, facing the unwinking stare of rows and rows of dark faces.

I began by making a short address through the medium of an interpreter, who translated my words into the curious language of clicking sounds which is so hard for European tongues to

M

master. Swahili, which is the *lingua franca* of East Africa, was little understood by them. Then came question time, and one after the other they would ask questions which would have floored the Judicial Committee of the Privy Council. After each of such sessions, I accompanied the local chief to inspect a sad little group of humanity who were claiming total or partial exemption from poll tax on the ground of incapacity. Among them were lepers in plenty and men suffering from every ghastly variety of elephantiasis, and so on through almost every visitation of providence.

The tribal system was a very strong framework in that part of the world, and it was still possible to rule efficiently through the tribal authority, which was beginning to break down in other parts of East Africa. During a safari, any man of the parish could rise up and voice his complaint in front of the chief. Any changes in the law were made known, and all additional assistance that the Government were giving, and to which they were entitled, was shown to the people. Their many problems were heard and a ruling given. It was a simple and, I devoutly believe, an admirable form of rule.

Through these long mornings of session in the little Parliament House, Dan would sit beside me, nose between his paws. Edwoko was not idle. When Dan and I emerged in the blinding sunlight, the morning's work finished, he was there and would sidle up, leading some knowledgeable man that he had discovered. "This man," he would say, "has told me that a lion was seen ten days back a mile from here. He says further that there are many ducks in the swamp, which he has offered to show us," and so the evening excursion was planned.

When we returned, as dark fell, there was Yowana filling the tin bath, with hot water that he had heated in an empty petrol drum. The little camp table was spread in the two-roomed mud hut set apart for visiting officers. The hut was windowless and doorless, like a beehive of mud pierced with two entrances, with its thatch only too often filled with strange creatures, who made their presence felt at night, when the hurricane lamp threw a pool of light on the camp table. Bathed, and changed, I ate my evening meal, and then gingerly climbed into the creaking camp bed, with its mosquito net supported on four wobbly poles. Outside this cabin of muslin was the endless accompaniment of the whine of the mosquitoes, and the hum of the African night. Dan slept in a little bed of his own, dreaming his own dreams, but instantly alert at any strange sound. Thus we would drop away into oblivion until the first glimmer in the east betokened the rising of the fiery ball of sun and another day.

20

On Safari

IN all professions there is a routine of life, and whereas we can define what we are trying to do and the way we are trying to do it, we cannot forecast the strange things that may happen to us along the road. The greater the factor of the unexpected, the more fascinating the profession.

Thus was life at Soroti. Every day we donned our uniforms of khaki stockings, khaki shorts and khaki tunic, surmounted by a large topee to match, and went through the routine of the day's work, which I described in the previous chapter. But the unexpected would break in at the most sedate and humdrum moments, even when seated at the office table, pen in hand, flanked by a basket marked "In" and a basket marked "Out".

My office was large and bare with a concrete floor. It had an open door on either side, and two large window openings in which there was no glass, but which were protected by shutters at night. The doors faced each other, and the window openings faced each other, so whatever breeze there was, blew right through and stirred my papers when it was strong enough. The leaves of the jacaranda trees moved fitfully in the breeze outside, and the full force of the equatorial sun beat on the tin roof overhead. In a coloured photograph, this landscape would suggest a dream of beauty. But there were certain elements terribly lacking to anyone from a northern country. There were bright blossoms and a medley of birds of every brilliant hue, but no flower smelt, and no bird sang. The country smelt of dust and the birds chattered or scolded. The background of sound was the whirr of the cricket, the creak of the wheels of an ox-cart, or the interminable distant conversations in various native tongues. There were nights when I felt that I was breathing through a blanket. There were days, in the office, when my hands stuck to the paper on which I was writing, or when a puff of a scorching wind would scatter the papers and shorten my temper. But the work was full of a fascination.

One morning, when I was deep in the accounts of the district, a native appeared and asked if I would like to buy what he called, "three animals". They were small balls of spotted plush which he was carrying in a wicker basket. He put down the basket and three yellow and black plush faces peeped over the edge.

"Leopards?" I asked, for I had no wish to bring up a trio of these animals for whom I already had a wholesome respect.

"No," said the man, "not entirely leopards, they are not able to completely return their fingers."

From this I understood him to mean that their claws were not completely retractable and they were, therefore, cheetahs. I gave him five shillings for the lot of them, and he went away very pleased.

As I was busy, and the balls of plush seemed fairly contented, I put the basket down beside my table and went on wrestling with the accounts of the District. Dan lumbered to his feet and thrust his spade-like visage into the basket. He appeared to approve of them, for he gave them each a paternal lick, and went off to lie down again. At lunch-time I took them home. Yowana looked at them dubiously, but did not seem at a loss. He went off to the bazaar and returned with a baby's bottle, and we gave them their first feed. They were so small that they could all sit comfortably inside my sombrero hat. As time went on their diet was reinforced with meat, and the Medical Officer gave them lime water and Calzana tablets to strengthen their bones. Three was too many, and I gave two of them away, keeping my favourite, Sally.

Sally was the best pet I have ever had. Although a wild cheetah will slay a dog out of hand, she grew up with Dan and they were friends. As a tiny kitten she looked up into his massive black and white face, and his tolerant, three-cornered smile. Thus, when she began to grow until she was as tall as he, and then taller, there was no enmity between them, but great companionship. The cheetah is the fastest animal in the world. An

African buffalo moves fast; a lion can catch it in about three strides, but the cheetah will leave the lion standing.

Height gave Sally dignity, and she would stalk majestically about the house, purring loudly, like a tea-kettle on the boil. Her fondness for licking my hand was quite unbearable, as her tongue was as rough as a nutmeg-grater. She took a comfortable siesta after lunch just when I wanted to take mine, but it was no use trying to get on to the sofa if she had got there first. Dan would climb into my deck chair; Sally, lying on the sofa, would obscure it like a big cushion of yellow plush with black spots, and a long ringed tail like a bell-rope. She would look up at me affably, and purr, but made it clear that there was only room for one. The only place left to rest on was my bed.

The other pets were less successful—two little cerval cats which vibrated with growls when I went near them; a gigantic spur-winged goose, the largest of his race in the world; a duiker, small and shy; and last of all a monkey. The monkey eventually returned to its original owner. It had been all right when he could tease Dan and then leap to the highest branches of the mango tree in the garden, but when Sally grew up she could climb the tree after him.

On another morning, while I was sitting in my office, biting my pen for inspiration, a little deputation appeared, urging me to come with them at once to a village two miles away, where a large python had established itself in a native hut and, they said, menaced the whole community. The story had been considerably exaggerated in the course of their two-mile journey in the sun. As I approached the village there was a large crowd round a hut, keeping a respectful distance away from it. I had taken my Goan clerk with me, who begged to be allowed to see the fun.

Close to the mouth of the hut was a knot of spearmen leaning on their weapons, talking volubly, but none of them offering to go in and do battle with the python. Just outside the door was a hen squashed flat as a penny, every bone in its body splintered.

As a piece of bravado, I handed my shotgun to the Goan clerk and, taking a couple of spears from the nearest spearman, approached the low door gingerly, and peered inside. It was dark within, but light enough to see a python. There was absolutely nothing to be seen on the floor at all. There was no sign of the python round the single pole that supported the roof; but in the low rafters, just a little higher than my head, I saw him at last. He was coiled up in a knot, and seemed to be asleep. He stayed perfectly still as I went up to him. There was no sign of his head anywhere, and the whole mass of coils was as still as if they had been petrified. Then the coils started to stir, and, in the middle, there appeared a hard, wicked, V-shaped face and a mouth which opened with a hiss. Using the spear like a bayonet I ran it into his open mouth and out through the back of his neck into the thatch; the next moment coil after coil came writhing down from the rafters on to the floor. How he disengaged his head I do not know, but the next moment he was on the floor stunned and uncertain, but starting to circle the hut, his head moving from side to side just clear of the ground. The first lunge with the spear just grazed his neck, and the spearhead snapped off on the hard earth floor. Retreating in front of him I had several more abortive thrusts, with another spear. Then I got him in the back of the neck, and thrust the spearhead deep through into the earth, pinning him there. His tail went hither and thither like a flail.

On the floor were earthenware pots full of grain. At the end of what seemed a long five minutes, every one of these was smashed, but the convulsions were becoming fewer; then they ceased, except for a occasional spasmodic movement. I lifted the spear far enough to get the point clear of the floor, and hauled him out into the sunlight. A great shout of excitement went up, and the spearmen looked rather glumly on.

We brought the python back, and my clerk had it stuffed at enormous expense, coiled round the base of a property tree, inside a tabernacle of glass. It became the principal ornament of his house.

Four o'clock was a magic time of day, when the ferocity had gone out of the sun, and the strange varied game birds were on the move, feeding before dusk fell. Dan, who was often left behind when we were after larger game, always took part in these expeditions. Edwoko carried the Westley-Richards rifle should we need it—as we very often did.

Once, after guinea-fowl in a cotton plot, I saw a big bull waterbuck and hit him hard as he disappeared into the edge of the bush. Dan was after him like a flash, and Edwoko and I made all speed after Dan, terrified of what those big horns might do to him. We got there just in time to see the bull put his big horns down, as Dan charged and counter-charged. Then in one spring he was at the waterbuck's throat. Backwards and forwards these two rolled, twined together, kicking up the dust. I did not feel it safe to shoot until I could put my rifle right against the waterbuck's side. Dan did not let go until it had been dead for a full thirty seconds.

We went to a new hunting ground every night. We would drive until we came to a place bordering the road where the bush had been cut out in squares and planted with native crops. Groundnuts were the real attraction to the guinea-fowl—and we might find a covey of francolins as well, looking for all the world like small partridges. We would sometimes flush that great black and white bird, rather like the heron, who is extremely good to eat, the northern black-bellied bustard. We might be lucky enough to find the green pigeon among the flights of grey and brown doves—brilliant as a parakeet, difficult to hit as a driven partridge, and the best eating game bird that there is.

The currency in that part of the world is the East African shilling. Each shilling divides into 100 cents, and the commonest coin is the copper ten-cent piece with a hole in it, which approximates to a penny. Before setting out we would thread a number of these on a piece of string and wear it as a necklace, from which to reward the beaters. However remote the part of the country, if we shot a buck, natives would seem to spring from the ground, to help us cut it up and take their share. But in bird shooting we frequently needed help in advance, and the sight of this necklace of coins was enough to bring us all the beaters we wanted.

Sometimes we would beat three or four of these cultivated plots, separated by belts of high grass and scrub. It was rough shooting indeed, but more varied and exciting than any that I have known elsewhere. The noise as a pack of guinea-fowl get up is thrilling. There is no difficulty about hitting a guinea-fowl, but it is an entirely different thing to bring him down. So often each barrel produces a cloud of feathers, and the guinea-fowl forges steadily on its way.

The francolins were very hard to hit, as they flew so low. Now and then little button-quails, small as golf balls and studded with neat little spots, would burst from the grass, and hurtle past my head to settle again only twenty yards behind me. I never fired at one, as they were so tiny, and it would have been very difficult to find them. The bustards were easy to shoot at almost any range. There can be few birds in the world that can carry so little lead.

In these wanderings we saw many strange and beautiful birds. At that time there was no authoritative bird book from which to identify them. In that continent of perpetual summer there seemed to be no specific nesting season. At the bottom of a low thorn bush I once found a nest that resembled a chaffinch's, with two small pink eggs. Coming back the same way, later that evening, a bird that resembled a miniature brown cuckoo flew off it, but lacking a bird book I could only regard birds in this country as one more particle of the unknown.

Sometimes we had drives and would be escorted back to the car by such a chance collection of natives as we had found, carrying our varied and usually exigious bag, but more often we three wandered together, Dan and myself leading, Edwoko one pace behind with a rifle in case of emergency. Road after road we explored. If we came back empty-handed, we had usually seen something new and strange. Once I was knocking the best pace out of my rackety Morris car, to get as far as we could before shooting light went. Driving along the crown of an African road, with a wheel in either track, leaves little range for manoeuvre. Quite suddenly, and with an air of complete detachment, an ostrich, his legs hobbled by a rope, waddled out into the middle of the road. He looked scornfully at the car that was almost on top of him, now rocking and swaying as I applied the inadequate brakes. We missed the ostrich by a feather's breadth, and wound up at the side of the road, happily none the worse. The ostrich looked at us curiously and hobbled back in the direction in which it had come. It turned out to be the property of the local chief, who kept this huge creature as a shackled and unwilling pet.

All my first sorties into the bush were accompanied on my part by considerable apprehension on the matter of snakes. The question of snakes is parallel to the question of landmines to the infantryman. In time you get to know where snakes are likely to be found, just as the infantry soldier usually gets to know where the mines are to be found. An instinct is acquired for recognizing their presence. As for the one you do not see— you become fatalistic. When the grass had been burnt one could see the ground sufficiently clearly not to worry unduly, but in thick country where one's feet were invisible, however fatalistic one became, apprehension of them was always there.

The shotgun is an ideal weapon for snakes, but they will take a great deal of stopping if they are not hit in the head. On one occasion I put two barrels apiece into two spitting cobras, who were making away across the burnt ground. After the second discharge, I re-loaded slowly, but when I looked up both had disappeared down holes.

Snakes are beasts about which legend is quickly woven. Whether or not a black mamba can go at the speed with which it is credited I do not know, but the only green mamba that I have ever seen crossed a dusty road in front of me at such a speed that I wondered whether I was not dreaming. I really believed my eyes only when I saw the track in the dust.

And there was so much else that was strange. Once in a forest of thin trees, with boles charred by the fire that had burned away the grass, I saw something crouching, which seemed to be a strange bent old man. Two enormous wings opened and it floated away. It was a Martial eagle.

Writing letters, or indeed writing anything, in that climate is not very easy, but my family never complained that my letters lacked incident.

On safari there were wonderful opportunities of breaking new ground. It also gave an opportunity of talking to natives in their own villages and on their own plots; for normally one saw them only officially, when they thronged the little grass-roofed Parliament Hut at the headquarters of their chief.

It made a great difference to comfort to be able to vary the diet of rather dreary beef and mutton, by a green pigeon or cold guinea-fowl for breakfast, or perhaps a brace of teal. Dan figured in all these adventures, and twice came perilously near death. We were looking for guinea-fowl one night round the base of a clump of rocks. It was clearly the kind of place where we might encounter leopards, but it also looked a likely place for guinea-fowl as well. For some reason we left the rifle at home, and I had taken, as extra protection, a pocketful of buckshot cartridges. We were making our way slowly round the perimeter of this jumble of great stones when Edwoko, who had a special sense for danger, suggested we put Dan on his chain and that I put two buckshot cartridges in my gun instead of the No. 6's. Changing cartridges took only a few moments, but Dan was enjoying himself, and did not want to be put on his chain. We were standing close together with Dan perhaps ten feet in front of us when round the corner of the rocks came a female leopard.

She may have had cubs in the rocks, for she was in no good mood. A leopard will go anywhere to kill a dog, and she had seen Dan. I was conscious, as I fired, of hitting the edge of her jaw and knocking some fragments of teeth out; and then she came straight at us at the charge, and Dan went straight for her. I have never heard before or since of a dog attacking a leopard, but Dan was not as other dogs. As Dan surged forward, she turned in her bound and headed up the side of the rock. As she did so I fired my second barrel. She staggered in her footing and then with a great effort made the next ten feet and disappeared behind a bush on a slope. I rammed in two more cartridges and gingerly approached the bush. Behind it was a black hole—the entrance to a cave. I grabbed Dan with the idea of beating a retreat. I looked at Edwoko, who had been unarmed, to see what part he had taken. He was right behind me with his silent tread. In his hands was poised a big rock.

It was the last time he ever went out without a spear.

On another occasion in that same part of the country, I had finished in one parish, and was moving to the next. It occurred to me that, as the distance was short, I might get up very early in the

morning and walk to this next parish, and have breakfast in comfort when I got there. The chief of one parish handed me over to the
chief of the next, on the borderline. Dan led the way with his ears
pricked, while I chatted to the chief about the state of the crops, the
price of cotton, and the high incidence of evil men in the world.

The path which had taken us between lines of high grass and
scrub suddenly led us into a clearing, laid out in plots of cotton.
The world was slowly coming awake with the early morning,
and the air was limpid and cool. It is the time when animals move
about, and feed before the heat of the day. I had a shotgun under
my arm, loaded with No. 6's. As we stepped into the open we
were confronted by three ugly, tusked, wart-hogs. Dan stopped
and pricked up his ears, for he had never seen a wart-hog before.

As quickly as I could, I changed the No. 6's for two buckshot
cartridges, and then Dan was off. He went straight for the middle
wart-hog, who stood still, awaiting his charge. I had just enough
clear space to let fly at this middle one and knocked him out of the
battle. Then the two on either side went for Dan, from either
flank. Dan was a cunning and wary fighter. His eye had been on
the wart-hog that I shot. He managed to dodge the tusks of the
one on the left. I do not think he can have seen the one on the
right at all. There was a fearful scream, and he was on the ground
trying to get up, while the wart-hogs made their best retreat into
the forest. He got unsteadily to his feet, blood pouring from his
haunch, and tried to limp towards me, and fell and could not rise.
He had a hole in his haunch into which you could have put your
thumb where the tusk had gored him. In the hole were two ends
of a big muscle severed by the blow.

The Chief was a man of action. Two men were sent to pick
raw cotton which together with my handkerchief made a binding
for the wound. A plank was brought and a litter prepared, and on
this Dan was laid. I patted his head and he tried to beam. Beside
him walked Edwoko, spear in hand, his face wrinkled with concern, while tears coursed down his scarred cheeks as he looked at
his stricken friend.

We covered the distance to the chief's headquarters at top
speed. A native dresser was brought with an array of medicines,
but the wound was so deep, and the damage so severe, that mere

bandages and iodine were plainly inadequate. A large assembly of natives, who had appeared to attend the little Parliament session, clustered round. An old man came forward and said he had a weighty opinion to give, if I would be prepared to listen to it. He walked up to Dan and took the bandage off. Dan turned round as he lay and licked the wound; he could just reach it with his tongue. The old man turned to me and smiled. He told me not to worry, for if a dog can lick a wound, provided nothing vital has been touched and no bones broken, the wound will heal. And heal it did, including the severed muscle, in an incredibly short space of time. So complete was his recovery, that at the end of a few weeks there was nothing to be seen but a scar, and his speed was unimpaired.

The hottest part of the year coincided with the cotton season, and it was generally the most arduous time for the members of the Administration. It was blazing hot, and the trucks carrying the cotton turned the road surface into a pattern like corrugated iron. There were cotton-buying posts to go round, to test the scales and to see that none of the buyers was paying less than the minimum price, and to settle the hundred and one differences which arose. It was simple, good government. When the cotton ginneries had flayed away the seeds, they could be collected by any native who wanted them. He would then take them to his plot and plant them. When he came to harvest his crop a minimum price was laid down and, although he often got more for his cotton, he could not get less. It was the job of the members of the Administration to see that these various rules were enforced, and that no one was cheated.

The hot weather shrank the water in the swamps until many became bone dry, while others were reduced to little patches of open water. Then, when work was over for the day, I would find the duck-shooting at its best. There was one place which we visited periodically on safari, the headquarters of a county beside which was a lake which was covered with duck. In the hot weather it resolved itself into a long thin ribbon of water, perhaps a mile in length and seldom more than 100 yards in width. There were no crocodiles here, but there were leeches in abundance. Sometimes in the reeds round the edge we found great snipe, as big as partridges and much less erratic in their flight than others of their kind. I could buy cartridges in limited quantities only; these had to be ordered from Kampala, so I husbanded my stock, and kept them for the duck.

Half-way down this patch of water was a small grassy island, only a few yards across, on which was a small bush. Crouched beside the bush you could shoot from firm ground. When the duck were flushed they flew away, and gradually, in ones and twos, came back down the length of the water over your head. There were knob-billed geese, coloured black and white, and splendid eating. There were flights of whistling teal which were not very good eating. Then there were ordinary teal, in flights several hundreds strong. In their flocks they swooped down to the water to climb almost vertically again, and were sometimes packed so close that it was hard to pick a single bird. Sometimes there was a great flock of spur-winged geese, the largest of their kind in the world, which took a great deal of bringing down.

Wading in this murky water to reach the island my legs were assaulted by leeches. I would feel a sharp prick, and gingerly standing on one leg, raise the other one clear of the surface. I would hold a lighted cigarette against the squirming black shape and it would roll up and fall away, leaving a little stream of bright blood trickling from the hole it had made.

Twenty-five cartridges lasted a very short time, and I seldom had more than twelve or thirteen head to show for it. But meat does not keep under African sun. I could only eat a few duck myself, and the rest were given as presents to the local chief, or to those of his subjects who had helped in the shoot.

A friend of mine had an ingenious way of preserving them. He cleaned out an empty forty-gallon oil-drum. He then shot a hippopotamus, and rendered down the fat which was sufficient to fill the drum. When he had a good day's duck-shooting, he cooked all the ducks which he wished to keep and put them in the drum, taking them out later on, as and when he wanted to eat them. They were well preserved by the grease.

Dan, Edwoko and I had many happy days beside this stretch of water, and beside many others as well. We found one place which, when the sky was overcast, was reminiscent of a piece of green Hebridean moorland. Down the middle ran a turgid stream connecting two swamps. The valley was a mass of green grass, for the most part below your knees. We would walk down this stream, and many a time would flush painted snipe, as well as the commoner kind. The teal used to fly down this channel and make splendid shots, coming low and very fast. Sometimes we would get a flight of knob-billed geese to make variety. Once a bustard rose and flew across the stream, and I dropped him on the far bank. It was the kind of slow stream which one does not cross in Africa, if one can possibly find a way round. Edwoko crossed lower down and came up the other bank. As he neared the place where the bustard had fallen, he shouted the one word "Crocodile!" and pointed. A large scaly creature was making its way through the grass to help himself to the bustard. When he saw Edwoko he turned towards the water, and I rattled some No. 6 pellets on his iron hide which he cannot even have noticed.

Out here in the open I was conscious of seeing again a great quantity of sky, and there was a feeling of freedom unpenned by the tall grass and the scrub. Eagles would wheel overhead, tireless in their circling. There would be flights of locust birds like strange curlews, whose uneven wing-beats hurt the eye to follow.

Then came the trek back to where we were spending the night, and Yowana heating the bath water in a petrol tin. The darkness would close over the village outside. Against the last glow of the golden evening would be outlined the thatched tops of the famine granaries, rising to sharp points like witches' hats, and the steep grass roofs of the village huts. There would be voices carrying far, and the play of little African children. The gold would go from the western sun and the velvety darkness would descend, and the dancing fireflies and the hum of crickets was everywhere. A hurricane lamp was a pool of light on the safari table when the evening meal had been laid. Pleasantly tired with exercise, soothed by a bath and clean clothes, sitting surrounded by the noises of the night, life was pleasant. And the land under the darkness was rich with the smell of dew upon dust.

To be twenty-two, to be strong, and to be in Africa. There was nothing else that the world had to offer that I would have exchanged for that life.

21

Bigger Game

THE people of the district, the Teso tribe, numbered some 120,000 souls. A good deal of the district area was swamp. The western boundary was the marshy shores of Lake Kioga. In the south, the scrub-covered Bugondo hills were the only high ground. On the eastern side were the two fair-sized lakes, Lake Salisbury and Lake Gedge. To the south-east, and far away, rose the great bulk of Mount Elgon. To the north dry plains, covered with grass and thorn bushes, ran to the Karamoja border, which was a paradise for game. There were a good many roads.

Road-making is easy in that part of the world, for it does not involve more than the clearing away of the bush and piling up of the earth to make the crown, with ditches on either side to drain off the rains, and concrete culverts at appropriate intervals. There was very little thick scrub, and such forest as existed was composed of small trees such as the butternut, varied by the occasional stately trunk of the mvule tree. From the latter the natives made their long dug-out canoes, hollowing them out with red-hot stones, and innumerable blows from flimsy axes. It took a very long time, and was succeeded by days of celebration.

Uganda is a splendid country for game. In those days a £5 resident's licence entitled its holder to shoot more than thirty different species and over 130 different specimens in a year. This took no account of animals to which no limits were put, such as buffalo and leopards.

The first night that Tony, Gerald and I had reached Kampala we had been told the districts to which we had been posted. I was informed that in this great land of game, I was going to the only district where it was non-existent.

Sometimes, visiting a house in England, one sees a fine collection of African heads all shot, on a short safari, by one's host who has had the opportunity of going to the pick of the African game lands. Beside such places as the Tana river, there was virtually no game at Soroti. But so far as I was concerned there were quite enough varieties to satisfy me, in spite of the official label of "non-existent".

There was one herd of elephants, mostly females, that were given a wide berth by everyone. They were not worth shooting, and the shortness of their tusks was matched only by the shortness of their tempers. That their tempers were not of the best was not surprising. They had more than once been caught in grass fires, and several had festering spear wounds.

Very occasionally a lion was reported, and even more rarely a rhinoceros. But these were wanderers merely crossing the borders of the district. They had always recrossed them when Edwoko and Dan and I appeared. Of buffalo there was a handful. They inhabited an enormous swamp which went dry in the hot weather. Leopards existed in great abundance. And if anyone is inclined to think that the African big game is never dangerous, if not molested, I would suggest that he does some field work on the life and habits of the leopard. The district was almost entirely flat, but, here and there, were piles of great rocks from whose cracks sprouted scrub. Sometimes they were tenanted by a colony of baboons; but more usually they were the home of a family of leopards. In either case they often held the nests of wild bees, who are fearsome antagonists if disturbed. Buck, of several sorts, were plentiful.

I had arrived at Soroti about the end of August. The roads ran through walls of tall grass, except where a native plot of cotton or groundnuts cut out a geometrical pattern. From August onwards the hot weather intensified. In August there was nothing to be seen of animal life or to suggest its existence, except an occasional waterbuck on a cotton plot, which would be out of sight in a few strides as the curtain of high grass closed behind it. Then as the heat intensified there came the grass burning. For weeks on end the whole district smoked and, at night, on safari, we would catch the wink of distant flames in the darkness. The plains were on fire. The tall dead grass was being burned away to allow new green grass to sprout beneath it. For weeks the fires raged and the pall

N

of smoke and blowing ashes was everywhere. It did much to clean the face of the land, for the flames, racing in front of the wind, destroyed rats and snakes in myriads, and left a blackened earth from which ash rose in clouds at every footstep. Then for the first time, I saw across the plains, and became aware of the animals to whom they were home. The waterbuck were numerous, and, as they did great harm to the natives' cotton plots, efforts were made from time to time to keep them in bounds. There were a certain number of hartebeest. In the scrub-covered slopes of the Bugondo hills was the small, shy, shade-loving bushbuck; on the fringes of the great marshes were herds of Uganda kob, an occasional reedbuck, and that rarely seen beast of the swamps, the sitatunga.

Anywhere one might flush some oribi, leaping away like the wind in great surging bounds, their slim, lithe bodies looking as though they were modelled from a Grecian frieze. The tiny duiker would often bolt from our very feet, in the thicker country. These two were the smallest representatives of the antelope family, though there are others even smaller. In addition there were most of the lesser animals that form the background of the African scene, from the wild pigs to the comely and much abused jackal. Where the fires had seared the plains I could climb on an ant-hill and, with my field glasses, sweep the open ground to see if anything moved on the hot, hard, ash-covered flats.

It grew very hot at night, and sleeping was difficult. The night sky would be lit by the incessant flickering of heat lightning. The water in the swamps shrank, and the open lakes and pools dwindled in size, so that the wild fowl, having fewer and fewer places of rest, were easier of approach. The cycle of the hot season passed on its way. The sun was ferocious, though dry and crisp in its heat. We could see the country which encompassed us and hunt the game. It was the most enjoyable time of the year. Then in April and May the rain fell and the young grass came up green and strong, though coarse to the touch where it brushed our legs, and we smelt again the tang of wet dust.

When the rain fell the skies opened in unbelievable cataract. On one occasion two and a quarter inches fell in twenty-five minutes. At night a thunderstorm would often wake us—with flashes of mauve lightning which lit up the countryside like day. It was somewhat awesome driving a car in the darkness in such a storm. For the lightning seemed not to be in the heavens, but to run along the ground like a snake. It was fascinating to return after dark from an expedition with gun or rifle. The headlights of the car were none of the best, but on the margin of the road their feeble brilliance was reflected in the eyes of animals moving warily in the night. There were the eyes of antelope, yellow, or the palest green. Sometimes there were the eyes of a leopard, like two red coals. Once there was a mass of little eyes, very close to the ground, which resolved itself into a band of monkeys who had deserted the trees in search of food. On rainy nights there was a greater chance of seeing a leopard on the road; they disliked the touch of wet grass and preferred to move by the open tracks.

The coming of the rains brought coolness too, but other things which accompanied the rain were not so pleasant. Rifles had to be cleaned every day whether they were used or not; the metal collected a thin skin of damp from the atmosphere. The armies of safari ants began to march. We used to see them crossing the path in front of us like a black stain. If you put your feet in a procession they would swarm up your ankles, giving no warning until they were strategically placed all over your body, and then each one would bite. There was only one thing to do on these occasions. Quite regardless of where you were, you had to throw off all your clothes and tear the creatures off.

A friend of mine, attending a dinner at Entebbe, arrived rather late and, as he waited for the boy to open the door, was utterly unaware that he had been standing in a safari of ants. The rest of the party had already sat down to dinner; he shook hands all round, and sat down too. A second later he bounded from his chair, dashed behind a screen in the corner of the room and hurled his dinner jacket one way and his trousers the other, tearing off the ants which covered him.

The ant-hills which dot the plains and provide so fine a point of vantage from which to spy out the land, house a different beast, the white ant. They have nippers like a stag beetle. The natives, whose ideas of medicine, thought rudimentary, are often extremely effective, use them to sew up wounds. They hold the lips of the wound together and, holding a white ant between finger and thumb, they let him nip, then break off his body, leaving his pincers rigid like a stitch. They will sew up a wound this way very effectively.

But it is the big game which is one of the main fascinations of Africa, and for those who do big-game hunting, the type of weapon and the skill at handling it are all-important.

An everlasting argument rages among those who love to hunt, and concerns the relative merits of the small bore rifle versus the large bore. It is a somewhat one-sided argument among those who have had much experience of elephant and buffalo, for the small bore school is thinly represented. They are mostly in their graves. There is all the difference in the world between taking a steady shot at a heavy animal which is unaware of one's presence and lets one pick one's mark, and stopping an animal coming at full gallop, bent on annihilation. In the first place, the small bore rifle is as deadly as the heavy. In the second, you need a weapon with all the brutal shocking power that cordite and the weight of bullet can combine. A double-barrelled rifle in a moment of crisis has every possible advantage over a magazine action. I have never been charged by a lion, but I have often been told that if the first shot misses, no one will ever live to work the bolt and fire the second. With a double-barrelled rifle one can get two steady shots.

It is only in countries such as Africa that one realizes the refinement to which marksmanship can be brought.

A great elephant poacher, "Karamoja" Bell, could hit two thrown sixpences in the air, with a double-barrelled rifle. Another poacher, Pete Pearson, for long a Uganda game ranger, could probably have done the same. "Samaki" Salmon, who had killed more elephants than anyone who has ever lived, was a ranger in Uganda during the time that I was there. He was an amazingly accurate shot, as indeed anyone would needs be who could count the elephants that he had killed in terms of many hundreds. He shot with magazine rifles, but was attended by two or three faultlessly-trained native gunbearers who could switch rifles with incredible speed. None of these men, or anyone who has approached a quarter of their skill, would ever let a day pass without handling their rifle, and in no circumstances allow anyone else to carry it, once on the trail.

A friend of mine once attended "Karamoja" Bell on one of his safaris. It was one of those journeys that that intrepid character made into Belgian territory, and, as a result of the slaughter of elephants and the lightning demise of anyone who tried to prevent him, the relations between Britain and Belgium deteriorated to almost crisis point. Bell, said my friend, had a rifle in his hands all the time that he was not actually eating, or sleeping, or perhaps painting, for he was a fine artist, as well as a hunter.

On the march he would be for ever throwing his rifle to his shoulder, drawing a bead on the glisten of a wet stone, a sheen on a leaf, or anything on which he could align his deadly sight.

Big-game hunting is as dangerous as the hunter cares to make it, according to what he hunts, and under what conditions. But he is unwise to concede any unnecessary points to his adversary. If every animal stood still beside the butts on a rifle range, with a ranging rod beside him, one would very seldom miss. But one shoots at an animal probably turning to flee, with the sweat running into one's eyes, with lungs pumping with the exertion, and the sun turning the foresight into a spectrum of light. The high leaf sight, which is to be found on so many rifles, obscures most of the animal and makes a moving shot—and half the shots *are* on the move—exceedingly difficult. Thus it is the usual practice to file the backsight down, until only the smallest nick remains, so that one has as full a view of the target as possible.

It is no particular reflection on the makers of rifles, but there are very few magazines which are absolutely infallible. In my experience, by far the best magazine action is that of the Lee-Enfield service rifle, which practically never jams. The difficulty arises when any magazine is loaded with four cartridges, and one in the chamber. You may fire a series of single shots, and reload a cartridge after each shot to keep your magazine full. When you eventually come to fire the two lower rounds in the magazine, they may have had the concussion of anything up to seven or eight explosions above them. If they are hard-nosed bullets, they are likely to be drawn half out of the cartridge case. If they are soft ones, they are likely to be partly mushroomed by the shock. In either event there is the possibility that they may jam. And the possibility may mean all the difference between discovering what old age is like, or going to paradise thirty years before your time.

So much for the weapon. There remains the hunting.

There are some human beings with whom one associates nothing but happiness. Edwoko, my hunter, is one of them. After luncheon on a weekday, he would be under the shade of the mango tree, which stood close to the steps of the bungalow. On Sundays, he would be there after breakfast. He would be trenchantly eyed by Yowana, who, clad from head to foot in spotless white, walked silently on bare feet managing the affairs of the household. He would frown slightly as he eyed the slim, wild figure with the scarred, ebony face leaning on his spear, dappled by the thin shade. Dan would rouse himself from taking his ease on the sofa, and shake himself, and come to the open veranda door, beaming on his friend and comrade. Edwoko would not come until he was signalled. He had the beautiful natural manners of his kind. He would come to the doorway when he was called, and listen to the plans. He might have a better plan himself, but he would listen courteously, and then, would look up faintly smiling and say, "Perhaps the *bwana*—I do not know—might be happy to pursue a great sitatunga of which a man has told me. The man says that every evening at four o'clock this animal comes out of the forest and feeds on the edge of the swamp. He says its horns are very tall. He is a wise old man—he knows."

A feeling of exhilaration came with the clink of cartridges, as they were fingered into place in the magazine, and the bolt snapped over the top of them. Then the second weapon was loaded. That was the double-barrelled elephant gun, if we were going after anything that seemed to warrant it. But the second weapon was a shotgun loaded with buckshot if the quarry were leopards. Then the water bottle was filled, the pockets of the bush shirt crammed full of spare cartridges, and we were ready to climb into the car to take the road to the hunting ground.

We were a curious trio. Fashions change in the tropics, but then the usual headgear was the double terai hat, two sombreros fitted one upon another, khaki bush shirt with no sleeves, which was worn outside khaki shorts; khaki stockings, and a pair of desert boots which the Eighth Army were later to make so widely known. You cannot better these boots in a hot country on hard ground, with their thick crêpe and soft uppers of untanned buckskin. Edwoko was clad only in a pair of old khaki shorts. He would be beginning to smile to himself at the adventure which was coming. Then there was Dan, sitting up on the back seat, his forehead pitted with almost as many scars as Edwoko's face, his cheerful black and white visage quivering with a wide grin of anticipation.

The car would be left behind, Edwoko would shoulder the second weapon, a cartridge was brought into the breach of the magazine rifle, and the safety catch snapped on. From then onwards my thumb rested on the safety catch, to snap it down as my rifle went to my shoulder.

How many paths we three friends followed together. Sometimes Edwoko would pick his way unerringly, across ground like pale, red concrete, and I could not resist the temptation to ask him how he knew the beast had gone that way. He liked being asked that question. He would give a broad smile, bend down to pick a blade of rank grass, and hold it up. It was easy then to see that it was bent, as it would not be bent in nature.

Although we did a hundred hunts together, the mystery of the African tracker's skill always remained something very near to magic. Our first hunt took place before the grass was burnt. It was the first time that the Westley-Richards rifle had been purged of grease and put in order for the chase. It was exciting to follow Edwoko down a narrow track between the high grasses, with the rifle slung and its magazine loaded. We were after waterbuck which were doing much damage to the natives' plots of cotton. It was blazing hot. To his great mortification, Dan had been left behind. The path led us to a big clearing in the grass and scrub. It was planted with cotton which looked, at first sight, rather like neat lines of rose bushes bearing woolly white roses.

We had hoped to surprise a waterbuck here, but the clearing was empty. Edwoko quartered the ground and, in a moment, was beckoning me. He pointed with his spear to fresh tracks in the soft earth. We followed these tracks for two hours of the late afternoon. Where the beasts had gonè through the tall grass they had made a little ravine through it, along which we could walk quite easily.

Always the tracks crossed and recrossed plots of cotton, and once they were so fresh that loose earth was still crumbling into the slots when we got there. At every moment of these two hours we were expecting to come upon our quarry. The excitement was perhaps the greater, as I had then no idea what a waterbuck looked like. They were moving at about the same speed as ourselves, but just how far ahead we could not say, Several times we climbed up on tall ant-hills, but there were merely the tops of the grasses to be seen, a few scrubby trees, and nothing else.

Quietly, and apparently from nowhere, an elderly native joined us. He occasionally exchanged observations, in an undertone, with Edwoko. We plodded on and then came the unmistakable sign of the gathering of dusk. It seemed tragic if two hours of such exhilarating tension were to be crowned by darkness and anticlimax.

The tracks led us into a country where the grass was shorter, and more sparse, and we could see for twenty-five yards or sometimes further. We had covered many miles. Edwoko suddenly stopped dead in his tracks and pointed. I could see nothing. Beside us was an ant-hill perhaps five feet high. From the top I looked over the spear points of the grasses and there, forty yards away, were the horns of a waterbuck; its head with its pricked ears, its neck, and the arch of its back were visible. It was that last look that an antelope gives before he decides on flight. I fired. I thought I had missed, but after ten steps the horns disappeared in the grass and Edwoko was bounding forward with his spear in his hand, to halt motionless. The buck was dead. A big beast with a good pair of horns.

Four years before, very nearly to the day, I had killed my first stag in the mountains above Little Loch Broom in Wester Ross. The circumstances could not have been more different; the feeling was the same. But now Africans seemed to spring from the cracks in the ground. They parted the grasses round us and, as they got to work skinning the buck, darkness fell, like a curtain suddenly drawn. Edwoko suggested we make our way home as we had a long way to go. He said that he had given instructions that the head, hide and the four haunches of the beast should be delivered to me at Soroti the next day. He stood for a moment like a pointer deciding his direction and then off we moved. Against the sky, still lit by the last glint of the dying sun, was silhouetted his dark head and the point of his spear.

Soon we were walking under the stars. We found a path which joined another path, and then another path, and yet another path. We were weary when we reached the road where we had left the car.

I bestowed a haunch of the waterbuck on my colleagues next day. It was not accepted with any marked enthusiasm. I understood why when I came to try the meat, after my cook had done his best with it. Great efforts were made to render the skin into a suitable rug. But after a very few days I gave it away. The waterbuck is a rank creature and its smell is ineradicable.

It was several months afterwards that the depredations of these beasts in that part of the district caused so much harm to the cotton crops that permission was sought by the local chiefs to hold a buck drive. The grass had been burnt by then, and I often walked round of an evening among the cotton plots and perhaps accounted for a dozen buck.

The buck drive was much talked about. A great gathering of natives took place. I asked one or two of the senior chiefs whether they were going to attend. They smiled sardonically and shook their heads. Their smiles conveyed a great deal. They explained that high office makes enemies, and a scene of milling animals and flying spears was no place for a man with enemies. The local chief, who was one grade below them, announced his intention of coming, and took full control of all the arrangements. I took two police *askaris* with me. They appeared dressed as for parade, in their uniform jerseys, belts and shorts, blue puttees and marching boots, their heads crowned with a fez. They brought their .303 Lee Enfield rifles. Edwoko took my shotgun loaded with buckshot in case we met a leopard, and I took my Westley-Richards. Dan was left at home. He, too, might have a few enemies. I hoped that I had none.

The drive took the form of what seemed an army of natives,

each man with a spear and a throwing stick, advancing in a crescent formation with the horns thrust forward. They had beaten ten miles of the bush when we joined the flank. The object was to push the waterbuck steadily forward and corner them against a piece of swamp, some five miles farther on.

The sun shone blisteringly hot. Here and there spidery trees threw a dappled shade. At the start, the waterbuck did not extend themselves but loped along, halted and looked back from two or three hundred yards ahead, at the advancing hunters. Occasionally, one more curious than the others would let his fellows canter on and stand, ears pricked, to get a better look at the advancing men. The askaris and I picked off three of these inquisitive stragglers. There was a great deal of incidental excitement. From patches of unburnt grass would burst, every now and then, an oribi or a duiker. There would be a tumult and shouting, a few spears and throwing sticks would fly, but seldom with any effect. The sun scorched our faces and arms: the metal of the rifle was almost too hot to touch.

A family of bush pigs stampeded into a patch of scrub and, losing direction, became mixed up with the advancing line which immediately lost its formation in knots of leaping men and singing spears. There were many interruptions and halts to the steady advance of 100 pairs of bare feet. Thus it was early afternoon before we reached the spot where the climax was to take place.

At the swamp the waterbuck began to come back towards us, only to shy away from the line of spears; and then the semi-circle was a prison, with its horns on the edge of the swamp enclosing a herd of perhaps sixty buck.

This was the moment; I got down on one knee to get a steadier aim. The range was about 100 yards. There was only one direction in which I could shoot, without danger of hitting a spearman. That was in the direction of the swamp. I dropped three buck in five shots, took my eye off them for a moment to push five more cartridges into the magazine, when a terrific cry went up and there charging for the centre of the circle, head down and horns pointed wickedly forward, was one of the biggest of the buck travelling at a tearing gallop. As he reached the circle I saw two men leap apart to give him way, and a spear struck him just behind the shoulder. The next moment all was pandemonium, dust and shouting. Two more buck followed their leader, horns outstretched. Then the whole herd galloped after them for the gap in the broken line. The air was full of dust and spears and shouting. And the spears seemed to be going in every direction. It was certainly no place for anyone who had an enemy.

The *askaris* fired several times with a fine disregard of where their bullets were going. Then the sound of hooves was getting fainter, the dust subsided and the shouting took on a different tone. Men were gathering in knots round the fallen beasts. There were very few. Only three had fallen to the spears, and there were the three that I had killed myself. Men were stabbing and hacking at the carcasses. They shouted continuously and were deaf to anything but their own voices. The chief suggested we go back with him. He led the way, Edwoko followed behind. It was a day to reflect on: a glimpse of an ageless Africa in all the hardness of its outline.

I had one safari in the Bugondo hills. A rest camp was set up on the hillside where we could look down across the waters of Lake Kioga, sparkling with a million diamonds in the breeze. There was thick thorny scrub over most of the little group of hills, with, here and there, grassy slopes where the bushbuck came out to feed of an evening. "Watch your dog," said the local chief as I started to climb to the rest camp. "There are . . ." he used a word with which I was not familiar, adding in parenthesis, "animals which look like men."

I glanced up the slope to where the grass-roofed hut just showed over a fold in the ridge above us. Climbing slowly and methodically in front of us was a baboon, looking rather like an elderly and short-tempered clubman. To the right of him on the edge of the scrub were several others. Edwoko attached the chain to Dan's collar, and we kept him close during our stay.

It was pleasant to tread sloping ground after the dead flat of the rest of the countryside, and strange to look for our quarry above or below us, instead of peering across what seemed to be an everlasting flatness. I did not get a bushbuck, but fanned the ears of two which we had surprised in the open, as they darted for the safety of the scrub. Like all true forms of sport, there is a great deal of pleasure to be got from a blank day in African hunting. Like all forms of sport that I have ever followed, blank days out-numbered days of success, in a ratio which made success the sweeter.

I had many days, and one or two nights, after leopards. Provi-dence watches over the novice, or he would never live to gain experience. There was a leopard whose depredations won him great notoriety; and he was soon the subject of legend. He lived in a great mass of rocks, which were piled 150 feet high and were perhaps a quarter of a mile in perimeter. The lower slopes of this rock jumble were thick with scrub. In a cave on one side lived the leopard.

It was the hottest part of the afternoon when Edwoko and I reached the rock. By this time we had acquired a large following of natives who had come to see justice done to the murderer of their flocks. We turned them back, but they crept forward again to points of vantage. The ground was bare round the base of the rock. To a stunted thorn tree was tied a hapless goat, and Edwoko and I took a stand in the lee of a boulder twenty yards away. I had my Westley-Richards, and Edwoko the shotgun.

When the preparations were complete, we leaned against the boulder, screened by it from the scrub climbing up the mass of rocks above us. The sun beat down blisteringly hot. An unnatural silence seemed to descend. Suddenly the goat, which had been looking at the ground round him with a view to grazing, was struggling at the extreme end of his tether. Then a great beast, seeming almost black, was upon it, and it was down, and dead. The leopard's teeth were in its throat, one big velvet paw was across its body, and there was silence except for a low, liquid growling.

My rifle went off, without my even being conscious of having aligned the sight on that spotted, slowly gyrating neck. In a trice four threshing paws seemed to be in the air. Unconsciously I snapped another cartridge into the breech. Suddenly, swift as a nightmare, the animal was on all four feet with a swishing tail, a dark line across the back of his neck, where the bullet had merely grazed him. In a split second I was recognized as the author of the blow and, as the leopard seemed to take wings towards me, my rifle went off half-way to my shoulder, and there was a line across the top of his head, as the second bullet grazed it. For a trice he halted, shaking his head, like a boxer with concussion, and then the bush at the bottom of the rocks hid him from sight. Disappointment and relief are rarely mingled, but they were at that moment, and in full measure. That was the last I ever saw of that leopard.

Edwoko and I went back to that rock many times. Once we sat up for him in the moonlight, with all the noises of the night around us. That was the first time I had seen that strange African nightjar which trails from each wing a long plume, an eerie bird to see by the light of the moon. The night was full of noises, but the beast we sought went on velvet paws while we strained our ears until they buzzed, and blurred our eyes peering in vain for the movement of that sinister, graceful shape.

The day comes when one catches the wariest animal off its guard. A fellow cadet in the service, Armine Wright, and I were hailed from our office one day by an excited man, who told us that there was a leopard asleep in a tree beside the road, not two miles distant. We got into my car, taking our rifles.

We disembarked and, not twenty paces into the scrub, there was the tree, and sleepily regarding us on a lower branch was the leopard. He was so close that he could have sprung on to us with ease. We had tossed up on the way, to decide who was to have first shot. Armine had won the toss. His heavy, soft-nosed bullet crashed through the leopard's skull, and it lay in the fork of the tree, its tail swinging, its position unchanged. We gave it another bullet to make sure, before somebody climbed the tree and hauled it down by the tail.

When the grass was short, Edwoko and I had several sorties after the few buffalo that lived in the wide area of dried swamp on the eastern side of the district. It was fifty miles of driving to reach there, and miles of walking under a torrid sun in dry grass with hard clods beneath. Edwoko could walk all day, if he could get water. But water was hard to come by in that vast, dry plain, and, on one occasion, when my bottle was empty, he was almost at a standstill.

One of the most unnerving things about big African game is

the deadly quietness with which they can move if they wish, and the thunder of their going when they charge or flee. The first time we flushed a buffalo, and a big bull at that, it looked like the engine of the Flying Scotsman freed from its rails, as it galloped away sending the dust flying. We followed that buffalo for a good fifteen miles, before we decided to halt. I shelled a hard-boiled egg, and greedily put it in my mouth all in one.

Edwoko climbed on to an ant-hill to spy out the country. He was twenty yards in front of me. To the right was the big area of high grass. We imagined the buffalo was still keeping ahead of us, but he was awaiting us. He burst from the thick grass, wicked horns back and nose outstretched, straight for Edwoko. It is very hard to shoot with a complete hard-boiled egg in your mouth. Furthermore you cannot shoot a .450 express rifle kneeling, unless you want to be thrown on your back. How much delay there was before I was on my feet with one hammer of the rifle up, I do not know, probably not more than a second, but the beast seemed almost at the ant-hill as the rifle went off. The crash of five fingers of cordite, and the thud, as the .480 grain bullet struck him somewhere on the flank, seemed to fill the world with noise. He faltered, turned half right and was lost in the long grass. If you wound a buffalo you must follow him immediately. You must follow close enough so that he cannot turn on his tracks, lie down beside his trail, and ambush you. If you stay where you are he will stalk you.

We set after him at the best speed that we could make, but he seemed to be travelling fast, for all the thud that bullet had made. Here and there Edwoko bent to pick a blade of grass, and pointed to the spot of blood on it. Once we came to a place where he had circled his tracks to ambush us, but he must have had a good lead, for his patience had evidently run out, and he had forged ahead again. When darkness fell we were not up with him, and his tracks did not suggest that he was unsteady in his gait.

We were very tired when we got back to the car. We explained the circumstances to the local chief, and he assured us he would take out fifty spearmen next day to search for the buffalo. They did not find him. Some weeks later he was sighted in his old haunts again. He seemed to have taken no harm from the bullet, except that his naturally short temper was even shorter than before. A party of natives crossing the swamp encountered him, and had to take to the thorn trees for their lives. He drew off and left them, after they had had a long prickly sojourn in the sun. I went after him several times again, but never saw him. On one of these occasions I got a beautiful Uganda kob. It was the only head I brought back from Africa.

Many a hot day saw Edwoko and I and Dan in single file on the hunt. Many and varied were our adventures, although our successes were not spectacular. Sometimes it was the edge of the swamps; sometimes it was the tall grass country; sometimes burnt stretches of the plain with the thin shade of the occasional thorn bush. Sometimes it was the patch of thin scrubby forest, but always it was new, and always it was exciting, and always there was the mystery of the blazing sun which hung like an inverted blow-lamp over the land, to be suddenly quenched in the dusk. Then the stars would twinkle in the pall of night, while we three friends trudged, wearily, and happily homewards.

22

Convalescence in Kenya

IN June, 1935, I had a very bad attack of amoebic dysentery. The nearest hospital was eighty miles away, at Mbale. It was a small building which catered for sick Europeans. There were three others beside myself, and we filled it to capacity. We were made as comfortable as possible, and any friends and colleagues who were in the vicinity would drop in and see me in the cool of the evening. There are few more depressing diseases than amoebic dysentery, and the various forms of cure are both dreary and drastic.

My nurse was an Irish girl who had been in Labrador with the Grenfell Mission, and possessed a very agreeable tame monkey. After three weeks of treatment I began to come to life again, and to take an interest in the subject of sick leave. I suddenly found myself about to go on leave, and with nowhere to go. I sent two telegrams to addresses in Kenya where acquaintances of my mother lived, and before there was any time for any answer to come back, packed my belongings and was driven down to Tororo to take the train. My nurse presented me with the monkey as a present. I placed it in a cardboard box—much to its rage—for the purpose of travelling. On the platform at Tororo Station I met Lady Bourdillon, the wife of the Governor, who was going off to England on leave. While I was talking to her there was a sudden eruption. The top flew off the cardboard box, and the monkey made a flying leap on to my shoulder and sat there chattering. I hastily excused myself and clambered into the train.

I had not much hope of my telegrams reaching their destinations, so I took my ticket to Naivasha where there was a pleasant little hotel, and where it was possible to get some bass fishing in the lake. One of the families to whom I had wired lived close by.

The high altitude of Naivasha was not easy to get accustomed to immediately, and I spent the first day limply lying on my bed, marvelling at the contrast and the coolness. Next day at lunch-

Altercation in Africa, over a goat.

First crocodile, 1934.

Dan and I in Africa, 1935.

Typical Teso country with Mount Kamalinga in the background.
Uganda, 1935.

time I was told somebody wanted to see me. There were Hugh and Rebecca Ward, with my telegram which they had collected at the post office five minutes before. They were kindness itself. My belongings were packed in their box-body car, and my servant, Yowana, was wedged in. The monkey perched on my shoulder, as we set off up the side of the plateau.

The hard-packed earth road took us up the side of the long grassy escarpment. As we moved upwards, ridge after ridge unfolded, until it seemed that we must soon reach some kind of grassy peak. The next ridge was steeper, and as we crawled to the skyline in low gear there was above us no peak, but in front of us a rolling prairie resembling Salisbury Plain, and beyond, and miles away, the ground rose to the tree-covered peaks of the Aberdare Mountains. Just below the forest line stood Hugh and Rebecca's house which they had built themselves, looking across that great stretch of rolling grassland.

There was not much wild life to be seen. Here and there we passed those pretty little antelope, the steinbok. Now and then we saw that strangest of all birds, the wida—the size of a sparrow, with a long billowing tail, like a piece of tape, undulating behind it.

The house was roughly the shape of an E, lacking the middle stroke. It was of one storey. The grass pasture in front of it fell suddenly and steeply into a wooded ravine, at the bottom of which ran a little stream. Most of the trees there were dead, and covered with thick lichen. The stream wound its way through deep clefts of rock. The water might be three feet across in places, and five feet in depth. From the house one looked over the tops of these trees, and over miles of rolling pasture to the horizon which was the edge of the plateau, and which looked like the edge of the world.

The upland air brought a wonderful return of appetite. To see fireplaces which were not merely architectural ornaments, but which sputtered with burning logs in the evening, was a wonderful change. Strange to remember how thrilling it seemed to wake up and see frost patterns on the window pane, and to sleep without a mosquito net. But dysentery is a weakening disease, and the first few days energy was quickly expended. It was not for a week that I came to life again.

My monkey made himself very much at home. He ran up and

down the tin roof making a noise like stage thunder. The love of mischief, which belongs to all his kind, led him to steal into the drawing-room where we were sitting after lunch, and snatch a Dresden china shepherdess from the mantelpiece; with three bounds and a scramble he was running up and down the roof carrying it under his arm. Eventually he released it, and, to our unspeakable relief, it fell on the soft earth of the flowerbed. Next day he stole an egg from the kitchen when the cook's back was turned. The cook looked round and saw him, and tried to grab him as he rushed out of the door, with the egg carried under his arm as a three-quarter carries a rugger ball. He dodged the cook, and carried the egg up on to the roof. Rebecca was faced by a deputation of her staff who said that the visiting *Bwana's* monkey made their lives almost intolerably burdensome. Then he started to range further afield and frolic in the high cedar trees on the edge of the forest, where he could do no harm.

It was a wonderful thrill to hold a trout rod again and soak a cast of wet flies. The path to the water is something you always remember. At Lareko, you went over the edge of the grassy mantelpiece, on which the house stood, and descended a steep winding track through the trees. You did not see or hear the little stream until you were right beside it, and there it flowed brisk and clear in its rocky cleft. Foliage hung over it from the banks, and there were only one or two possible casts either almost straight upstream or almost straight down. Even with a rod in one hand and a landing net in the other, it was hard to believe that there were really trout in this continent, but at the second cast there was a kick and a plunge and a running of the reel, and there was a fish nearly three-quarters of a pound in all the glory of red and black spots—Africa fell away, and Peeblesshire was there in its stead. I never caught more than three or four fish on any of these expeditions.

During the first week I was so limp that I found the climb back up the hill a heavy pull. When the fish were not taking, I would sit beside a little waterfall for the pure pleasure of hearing running water. My monkey attended me closely. Sometimes he would see something which would frighten him and he would come bounding back and leap on my shoulder, or perch on my broad-brimmed hat.

There was little life in that forest except for the colobus monkeys, with their long coats of black and white. Now and then they would come through at full tilt in the tree tops, with a cracking of dead branches and falling of twigs, looking like flying hearthrugs. My little monkey, who was less than a quarter of their size, would rush to me for protection whenever they came by, and sit chattering on my shoulder. At night a strange beast called a hyrax rabbit would set up a whirring noise, like a fishing reel running at full speed. But otherwise, there were few beasts.

Most of the days at Lareko were like an English May, but sometimes there were those distinctively African days when the sky is that strange pearl grey and everything is still. Occasionally we would ride up to the Aberdare forest at the back of the house, and follow paths among the dark cedars, of that peculiar twisted grain that looks as if a giant had taken them between his finger and thumb, and given the whole trunk a sharp twist. There were lions in plenty in the forest and much else besides, including that shy antelope—the bongo. There were also Scottish red deer, although no one ever saw them. They were introduced with the idea that they would become an animal of the plateau. The red deer will always become an animal of the forest if he can, and they disappeared into the darkness of the cedars and were believed to have multiplied mightily. Sometimes on these forest trails our horses would sense something they feared. Then it was right about turn, and hard work to keep our beasts at a controlled pace.

One day we went over to lunch with some neighbours. They were noted horsemen, and had been knocking a polo ball about when we arrived. I noticed our tall, lean host cantering, with a back like a ramrod from years of service in a cavalry regiment which had never seen an armoured car. After lunch we stopped beside the road to fish their little stream. It was bigger than the one at Lareko, and it wound its way through the folds of the open plateau. It was said that trout fry had been put in here a number of years ago, and that within the space of two years they were catching fish of two pounds each. The year following, a trout of six and a quarter pounds was taken, but from then onwards the stream had become so full of fish that they had tended to stay small. My third cast, beneath a little waterfall, produced a fish just over half a pound, and the afternoon some half dozen others.

I discovered that in these deep and narrow streams, it was a great advantage to get your flies as deep as possible. Then, instead of a tail fly, I often used a little fly-spoon, smaller than my little finger nail. I have done this since, with great effect, in both Canada and Scotland. Very few of the fish take the spoon, and nearly all the dropper fly.

Our host of that day had moved himself from Yorkshire, and was in process of making Kenya as much like his native country as possible. I shook hands with his Yorkshire gamekeeper, who found Africa a very impressive place. He had made himself very much at home. He was watching over a consignment of pheasant eggs brought out from England, which he hoped to rear. But they never hatched.

Those days at Lareko passed swiftly and happily. It was with the deepest regret that I said good-bye to Hugh and Rebecca Ward, and drove across the plateau, and over its rim down to the little railway station beside Lake Naivasha. I felt greatly improved in health, but not completely recovered. I took the train to Nairobi and stayed with an old friend of Brasenose days, who was teaching there. I reported to the hospital and was given another week's sick leave, most of which I spent with Mervyn Cowie, and looked again from his house, over the flat thorny plain of the Masai reserve, at the pointed cone of Kilimanjaro, breaking the level horizon. With Mervyn I watched the great herds of animals on that sea of land. It was only for a week, and then I was headed westward to Uganda once more.

I had not been long in Uganda when my dysentery came on afresh. During the months that followed, I was more often in hospital than out of it, until, on one hot morning at Kampala, I said good-bye to Edwoko and Yowana and Dan and set off for Mombasa, with England as my final destination.

That was an Africa where you seldom heard the expression "Race Relations". The races got on with each other quite unselfconsciously. But with the weariness of the war, a poison entered the blood-stream of the world and it is coursing now in the arteries of Africa. Peaceful Lareko is a miniature fortress. But the poison will work its way out in time.

23

In Search of Health

IT was February of 1936 when I reached England from Africa. Amoebic dysentery brings you very low, and even the sharp tang of English winter brought no return of energy or appetite.

The previous summer my father had gone to Canada as Governor-General. My brother, Alastair, who had left Eton early and was waiting to go to Oxford, was with my parents in Ottawa. My sister Alice, and her husband, and my brother Billy, were in England, and with them I spent a few weeks before going north to Peebles to see my Scottish kin.

There was a fine spell of warm March weather in the Borders. I borrowed a rod and fished the Tweed above Peebles Bridge. The hot sun had brought a faint touch of colour to pallid cheeks. But I walked carefully like an old man. So much do the Scots regard the world as being their parish, that going to the ends of the earth, or returning from them, is hardly a matter even for comment, so that during that week of March sunshine I was back in their pleasant round of life, as if I had never left it.

There followed, on return to London, dreary weeks in the Hospital of Tropical Diseases. The various courses, which were as drastic as the disease itself, had become not only wearisome, but also hateful. Lying in bed gazing at the ceiling, or through the window, at the dreary roofs and sooty chimney pots, became less and less tolerable.

It was the end of March before I set out to join my parents in Canada. My mother met me in crisp April sunshine, when the boat docked at Halifax. She could well be excused for not recognizing me; I hardly recognized myself.

The dusk gathered as the train rumbled westward, until all silhouette was lost except the tops of the pines marching past like an endless regiment of soldiers. Early next morning we looked at

Quebec mounting up its steep hill, shrouded in snowy gloom and separated from us by the width of the St. Lawrence, where the ice floes ground and swirled with the break-up of the winter frost. We reached Ottawa that evening, and reunion with the family was complete.

From Government House, at Ottawa, one looks out on a little park with scattered trees, the homes of no fewer than three kinds of squirrel. With the grey and red squirrel everyone is familiar, but the black squirrel is a curious novelty to the newcomer. When the snow goes the chipmunks appear. Little beasts who have much furry charm.

Just beyond the gates of the park, and beyond the roadway, the ground falls almost sheer to the Ottawa River. It is hard to believe that this great body of water, several times the size of the Thames at London, is itself only a tributary. But it is a tributary to a stream so huge that it drains a quarter of the continent.

Spring was on the way. The April sun was throwing long shadows on the snow, sometimes thawing it at midday, for it to turn to ice as dusk fell.

Spring comes at a bound in Eastern Canada. Almost in a day the snow is gone and the birds return, and the buds on the trees grow sticky and then burst. In the forest the bears are afoot again after their winter sleep. The moose, reduced by winter to a bag of bones, has become little more than a famished wreck. His coat becomes covered with ticks, and you can see where he has shaken himself as the snow is marked with little flecks of blood. But when the ice goes out of the lakes and there is fresh food about, the moose can wade into the waters and cleanse himself, and bring flesh back to his enormous frame by cropping the verdure of spring that has come to the world again.

Spring comes some time at the beginning of May. The frost goes from the land. The fish, which have spent all winter long under the icy shield, where just enough oxygen remains for them to support life, come to the surface and glory in their revitalized element.

As the sun warms the forest, the birches shimmer with green once more, and there are two glorious weeks when one thrills with the wonderful aromatic freshness of the pines, unvexed by the mosquitoes and the black flies which will drone in their myriads when a few more weeks have passed.

My father's duties as Governor-General were many and responsible, but he managed as far as possible to maintain his Elsfield régime of life and get through his work in the mornings and evenings, and leave his afternoons free for the open air. We used to walk together in the afternoons, though not very far, because my strength, which was once greater than his, was now far less.

We had had many fishing expeditions in the past, and now we fished again. It is possible to say much about Canadian hospitality, but it is virtually impossible to exaggerate it. Kind hosts in plenty offered us fishing, and we had many happy days together amidst the silence of the pines. We had to go some distance for our fishing, and it meant a few nights spent at a fishing camp in the forest.

The whine of an outboard motor will always remind me of those days. Many mornings did we set off together, sitting amidships in a big dinghy clasping our rods, the bow tilted up in the air, and the stern weighed down by the motor and the sunburnt, taciturn guide who was steering.

As we set off down the long lake which stretched away from the fishing camp, the water was usually as calm as a mirror, and we could see the ring of the rising fish half a mile away. The pines mounted up the steep slopes from either shore, until they lost themselves in the wreaths of mist which writhed like smoke as the growing power of the sun melted them, and turned the colour of the pines from sable darkness to every tint of green. Behind us the long wedge of our wake spread across the still water, and a thin haze of blue smoke hung round our stern. There were few birds to be seen. On one little lake, that we went to frequently, was a pair of wood ducks, the drake looking as garish as if he had been daubed with paint.

When the sun disappeared, and the mist pressed down the slopes on to the tops of the pines, and the whole land smoked with rain, the only sound of life was the clear untroubled monotone of the *rossignol*, the Canadian nightingale. Often, beside the shore, we would see in the top of a birch tree a strange object, which, at a distance, resembled a large fur muff. It was a porcupine which had laboriously climbed the tree to help himself to the fresh buds.

We stayed in a comfortable log dwelling with a stone fireplace, where the roaring fire kept out the chill of the evening air. The smell of the pines was everywhere. We woke each morning to the sound of the lake water lapping on the sandy beach beside our window. We caught great quantities of trout, but came home none the less happy when we had caught none at all.

We had so much to talk about after a separation of nearly two years. I far outran my puny store of strength on these fishing expeditions. Somebody once said that they thought I would go fishing even if I were dying. It is perfectly true. I was supposed to be dying, and I went fishing with unabated keenness and no diminution of enjoyment. But it was like being a very old man. However much I husbanded my strength, weariness would drag at me after a few hours.

Back at Ottawa, long periods of fatigue would come upon me, and for days I could do little but lie down and rest. I sometimes went with my father on his various duties. June in eastern Canada is a very hot month, and the hot weather seemed to sap my strength. Together we visited many Ontario townships, and went down to the eastern part of the province where there is no forest, but a network of farms that have been long settled. When the blossom is on the fruit trees, in spring, it has a beauty that few places in the world possess. This is the country of the United Empire Loyalists who came north after George Washington had triumphed, as they preferred to remain British. The little stone farmhouses, with the fanlight over the door, are the homes of many a family of this proud descent. I had the great honour seven years later of commanding a battalion of them. A people cheerful and kindly, as they are sturdy and resolute.

About the middle of June, according to custom, my father moved to the Citadel at Quebec. The road climbs to a good height before passing under the old stone gateway of the perimeter of the Citadel walls, which served as the barracks and parade ground of the Royal 22e Regiment. The Governor-General's residence has a small and inconspicuous entry; there is only a short flight of stairs before the upper floor is reached. After a passage, and through a small anteroom, a visitor enters what must be one of the most intriguing chambers in the world.. As he comes in he faces the windows, and he is looking at the country on the far side of the St. Lawrence. As he approaches the windows the St. Lawrence widens before him, and then he looks down to find that the ground falls sheer away below the wall to the edge of the great stream which washes the foot of the cliff beneath.

It was somewhat farther upstream that Wolfe's Highlanders forced the Heights of Abraham in 1759.

On the landward side, the city slopes away downhill. Due north the forest begins, undulating with the slopes of the Laurentian hills. Downstream the river is divided by the long Isle d'Orleans and thereafter widens towards its great gulf. Some of the finest salmon rivers in the world, the Restigouche, the Grand Cascapedia, the Moisie, and many others, enter this gulf from either shore.

The Citadel itself is surrounded by the city of Quebec, but we made expeditions along dusty roads on the north shore of the St. Lawrence. This land has long been settled and much of the forest has been uprooted to make way for farms, but inland are the pines, with the occasional farmhouse standing on its little square of cleared land. This is old France, a France that has never known a French Revolution, In every village the dominating building is the church whose wooden steeple rises high above the middle of the village. On a Saint's Day, many a horse and buggy can be seen on the dusty roads, bearing a family in their best clothes to visit their neighbours, and farther into the forest there are the real "habitants", the sturdy sunburnt man and wife, weather-beaten with the toil of wringing a living from the land, and with their large family grouped around them.

There are clear unmistakable legacies from those men of Wolfe's Highlanders who conquered and stayed to settle. They are the families who have not spoken a word of English for generations, and whose names are McNichol and McDonald, and many another of Highland origin. Once, of an evening, my father and mother and I watched what is known as a *veillé*. The people of the village gather together to sing and dance. A man, in a red-checked mackinaw and lumberman's boots, crossed two fiddle bows on the ground and did a Highland Sword dance. A girl sang a ballad in French whose lilt was unmistakably Highland. For hours we watched, too enwrapt to notice the fury of the mosquitoes.

All over Canada curling is a sport far more general than it is now in Scotland. They curl mostly with irons and not with granites. Perhaps that is because they learned to curl with metal here. For Wolfe's Highlanders, in the tedium of the first winter of occupation, filled kettles with water, froze them, and used them as curling stones. Many of the French Canadians, both of the city and the land, with whom I made friends that summer, I was to meet again in the Canadian Army. On more than one occasion, on the battlefields of Italy, I saw them go into the attack. Their enemies regarded them with unspeakable dread. It was not difficult to see why.

As June gave way to July, the heat became more and more intense. It was a dry, crisp, northern heat in which, if I had been full of vigour, I could have revelled, but it drained my small accumulation of strength until at times I was an invalid for days on end. But in spite of this I can look back happily on that first Canadian summer. I was taking seisin of a country that was to become my second nationality.

24

The Canadian West

WE set out from Quebec about the beginning of July for a visit to the West. It was an official tour such as the Governor-Generals undertake every year. The party was my father and mother, my brother Alastair and myself. Our two railway coaches formed a remarkably comfortable home. We were going over old ground as far as Ottawa, but from then onwards all was new. Canadian trains are large and enormously powerful. They cross the continent at a steady, but not frantic, pace. For a night and a whole day, after we had left Ottawa we travelled through forest; every now and then the march of the pines was interrupted, and we had a view of a lake, and the ring of a rising trout. Sometimes for miles, the line was foggy with the smoke of a forest fire. Here and there we rumbled over a bridge as the forest divided to let a river rush beneath us. Then, on the second morning, we woke up in a different world. The pines had thinned, and finally ceased; in their stead was the flat Manitoba prairie, which at that time of the year is a golden ocean of grain. When the wind blows, it ripples the wheatfields like the waves of the sea, running from the horizon to break at your feet.

Somewhere on the horizon was always the tall angular shape of a grain elevator. Here and there were little patches of scrub, which no one had bothered to clear, and which helped to hold the moisture and break the wind. It is from this same flat prairie that the finest grade of hard wheat in all the world is grown.

We stopped awhile at Winnipeg. I was destined for a time to be a citizen of Winnipeg, and trudge to an office every morning, clad like a fur-bearing animal, against the wind whose cold steel edge was sharpened in the passing of hundreds of miles of snowy prairie. But on this first visit the temperature was over 100° F. in the shade.

At Saskatoon we halted and drove out to Carlton, over miles of dusty prairie road, to where the Cree Indians were having a great rally. My father talked to the chiefs, who were clad in their gala finery of feathers. He spoke to one, who was evidently of great age, and asked him how old he was. "I do not know how old I am," said the chief, "but when I was fully grown the prairies were still thick with buffalo." His recollections went back to a simpler, sturdier era, for the last buffalo faced the guns of the buffalo hunters at about the time that the last spike was driven into the Canadian Pacific Railway, and that was at the turn of the 1880's.

We continued our course across this great land ocean. At Regina, we visited the depot of the Royal Canadian Mounted Police, where they still used horses in the course of duty. To the south, Saskatchewan was in the grip of the worst drought in the history of the wheat lands. No rain had fallen for about six years, and the soil had turned to drifting dust. There were places where we saw the chimneys of farmhouses appearing out of a dust dune which suggested the Sahara. The people were clinging grimly to their homes, and the land had gone almost sterile. No desert dust storm was worse than when the winds picked up the powdered ruins of the farmlands, and carried them to erode what still remained of fertile country.

At Edmonton we were well into Alberta, off the flat land and into the foothills of the Rockies. We stopped at Banff among the high mountains on our way through. We had no time for fishing, but we looked at an amazing fish hatchery composed of ponds full of big fish of various varieties, which were fattened on a diet of chopped liver. Not long before, a Chinaman had come upon this chain of ponds and, believing it to be a part of the natural forest, had hurried back to get his bamboo rod and line. Later, the enraged custodian had found him with an enormous pile of fish on the bank at his side, and a smile of celestial happiness on his face.

At Kamloops we had an afternoon's fishing for that hard fighting fish, the Kamloops trout, whose beauty is in the sheen of pink down his sides. We were driven to a lake on the edge of the Douglas ranch, and fished there happily in the rain for several hours. It was a relief to be in the high air again after the sweltering heat of the prairies. It was pleasant to see a cowboy cantering along the road, as we set off home, with his lasso at the horn of his saddle. Cattle countries are attractive the world over.

Of all Western Canada, I think that there are few places where I would rather live than in this high ranch land of Kamloops, unless it be in the Kootenay or the country of the Caribou trail.

Two days later we were running down the Pacific slope of the Rockies to, what was, for me, the first sight of the Pacific. We went from there to Vancouver Island and had a day's fishing for steel head trout among some of the tallest trees on earth, the great Douglas firs that have stood for nigh upon 2,000 years, and which are nearly 400 feet in height. It is a hackneyed phrase that in these groves you feel that you are in a cathedral; but that was exactly the feeling that we had in that green gloom among those pillars of timber. We spent two happy days salmon fishing at the north end of the island at what is known as Campbell River.

Then we were getting into late summer, and it was time to return across the continent to Ottawa. We stopped at Calgary, within sight of the high Rockies by day, and of the distant flames of the natural gas gushers by night.

That was my first view of the West. I had seen it from the vantage point of the top rung of the ladder. I was to return later to look at it from the bottom rung. Much has happened since then. Oil in quantities, then unbelievable, has made many men rich. Soil has recovered in the wheat lands and the price of wheat and the price of cattle has rewarded those who held on doggedly in those dark days of drought and low prices. The essential character of the West does not change. It is a land with big cities, that have grown over an incredibly short span of years; for Calgary was only founded in 1875, the year my father was born. It is a country where those who make their living from the land are far more often under the skies than under a roof, a country that harbours every kind of pleasant individualism which goes unquestioned among a race of hardy individualists, people of unbounded hospitality, who in the depths of disaster can never be made to lose their sense of humour or their friendliness.

But in that year of my visit, 1936, there were men alive who, in their distant youth, had seen the veil lifted from that half of the continent, and the rush of adventurers stampeding to the golden West.

I had the good fortune to fall in with not a few of them, and have listened absorbed for many hours while they told of the old days. When they had first come to the West, the country had looked very different. On the rangeland the prairie wool was everywhere. It had been the natural grass of the prairie, and got its name from the fluffy appearance. There had been no barbed wire, and the land had not been touched by the plough.

By 1936, except on the remoter stretches of cattle range, there was little prairie wool left, and hundreds of thousands of acres of rangelands had given way to the plough.

The conversation of the old men took you back into a vanished world. In those days you would never have been quite sure where you stood with the Indians. The Blackfoot Confederacy was a powerful force, which included three strong and warlike peoples of the prairie Indians. They had beleaguered Calgary, within ten years of its foundation, and had only been prevented from destroying every white man west of Winnipeg, by the far-sighted statesmanship of their chief, Crowfoot. In the Ranchman's Club in Calgary there is a portrait of Crowfoot. His dark, hawk-like face has a most striking beauty.

The last war in Canada against the Indians was the second rebellion of Louis Riel, the half-breed, in 1885. South of the border, the Sioux had fought their last fight, at the battle of Wounded Knee, seven years later. The old days lived in the recollection of those old men.

There was an aged chief who lived on the prairie near Prince Albert with his little band of Sioux. He had escaped thither when his people had been massacred by the Blackfeet. He had been little more than a boy at the time. He was now old and wrinkled, and deep in his nineties.

On another occasion, in those early days, a tribe of Canadian Indians had ridden south to take fire and sword to the tribes of the American West. Some kind of order was eventually restored, and an arrangement was made between the Governments of the two countries. The Americans were to escort these wild horse-men, now satiated with blood and plunder, to the Canadian border.

Several regiments of United States cavalry accompanied them. The agreement called for their being met at the border by an adequate Canadian military force. The bargain was carried out faithfully, for they were met at the border by two Royal Canadian Mounted Policemen and escorted back to their own lands with-out a hint of trouble. One of those mounted policemen, "Peaches" Davis, was still alive in Calgary when I was there. That was the last year, too, of Pat Burns's life, the cattle king of so great a stretch of rangeland. A big man, he greeted his guests sitting down, for he was bowed with age and not far from his end. He sat in the sun in the garden of his house in Calgary, which he had seen grow from a few shacks to a great city. That winter, an old man was burned to death in his shack not far away. Far back in his youth, he had ridden with Buffalo Bill Cody against Chief Yellowhand.

One of the most remarkable survivors of that old roaring world was Nigger John Wade. He had been born a slave in the Southern States and, as a boy of four, had been taught to ride by his master. He had ridden a bare-backed horse round a corral, in the centre of which his master had stood with a stock-whip. Then the Civil War had come, and he had gone North and West when he had grown up. He was believed to be one of the only two men on those prairies who had never been thrown by a bronco. In his case, it was said, that the strength of his legs was such that no horse could pry him loose. He was very deeply respected, and much loved. It was said that if darkness caught you on the prairies six miles from a white man's abode and ten miles from Nigger John's it was to Nigger John that you would go.

There were many strange stories that I heard told by the old men, and some who were only middle-aged. Most of the stories were slow in their telling, as we sat on a wooden doorstep in the summer evening, or round a camp fire in starlit darkness. They were seldom told as stories, but came out as explanations. There was a short, stocky man with whom I shared a meal one evening. He rolled one cigarette after another, using only one hand. He completed the cigarette with a snap of the fingers which was fascinating to watch. He anticipated the question. "Guess it's got to be a habit," he said. "Used to be a stage coach driver once upon a while. You only got one hand free then—that was in Montana—I quit the same year as the comet, 1910, or thereabouts."

In those days there could be no ambiguity as to what was meant by the Comet.

The old days of the Canadian West were every bit as romantic as their counterpart in the United States, but never a fraction as lawless. If you want the difference between the two, talk to an old-timer who remembers the roaring days of the American West. Listen to a man who knew Dodge City, Kansas, when it was a wide open cow town, and it was said, "West of Chicago, no law; West of Dodge City, no God."

"*Maintiens le droit*" is the motto of the Royal Canadian Mounted Police, and maintain the law they do. Recently I came upon a report of a corporal of the Royal North West Mounted Police, which was their old name. Any man who can write a report like this is going to see that the law is respected.

"On the 17th instant, I, Corporal Hogg, was called to the hotel to quiet a disturbance. I found the room full of cowboys and one, Monaghan, or 'Cowboy Jack', was carrying a gun and pointed it at me, against Section 105 and 109 of the Criminal Code. We struggled. Finally I got him handcuffed behind and put him inside. His head being in bad shape, I had to engage the services of a doctor, who dressed his wound and pronounced it as nothing serious. To the doctor Monaghan said that if I hadn't grabbed his gun there would have been another death in Canadian history. All of which I have the honour to report.

(S.) C. Hogg, Corporal."

How much real change have these men seen? Gone is the old open range where the cattle of several ranches would graze together distinguished by their brands. It was then that the rustler really flourished. For if your neighbour's brand was an O

Sally, my cheetah.

Rapids on the Grand Peribonca.

Alastair and I in British Columbia. Summer, 1936.

and you chose a Q, it was not difficult to fake the difference. If you killed and skinned a steer it could be done in a way that would defy detection. It can be done from the inside of the skin with a needle and milk weed.

Now much of that prairie has been put to the plough. Much of the rest is fenced. Gone are the buffalo since the early 1880's, although there are still wild horses in plenty in the Ghost River country. But the cowboy is still there. As long as beef is eaten, there will be cowboys. Under the prairie sun, they still seek the shelter of the broad-brimmed hat, and wear a big handkerchief round their necks that they can pull over their faces when the dust starts blowing. And men who ride scores of miles in a day are not likely to desert the big wooden stirrup and the high-heeled boot that they settle into, to take their weight on their instep. They need leather chaps to shield their legs when they ride through bush country. And so, little changed, the cowboy lives on, though his race is far less numerous than it once was. If he disappears it will be a tragic loss, for there is no other vocation, and no other part of the world, that produces quite the same kind of human being.

Once I looked into a junk shop in Saskatoon. Its wares were deep in dust. The small, shabby, old proprietor stood eyeing me hopefully. He plainly had few customers. There was the usual *bric-à-brac*. But there was a pair of cowboy boots, the carefully tooled patterns on the leather almost defaced by usage. There were old banjos, lacking most of their strings; a repeater watch or two, and a mother-of-pearl handled sheath knife, of strange design. It was a curious glimpse of the old West. These things had once meant much to their owners. Now they slumbered like those who had possessed them, under the dust, and the same prairie sunlight blazed down on the street outside.

The West is not a geographical expansion. It is a world of its own.

A friend of mine, riding the Alberta prairie, came upon the ruins of what had once been a homesteader's shack. It must have been occupied for quite a long time, for at the back were one or two graves, evidently of its inmates. A wooden cross still stood upright. It marked the grave of the homesteader's wife. Her

P

name, and little epitaph, had been wrought on with a red hot poker with loving exactness. The epitaph ran: "She was so pleasant." All that the world knows of love were in those few words. It conjures up a vision of a sturdy, good-natured, pioneer woman, who could do everything her man could do, and make him a home as well. To this day, a woman needs a man's strength to be a homesteader's wife.

High above the mighty Peace river, which is cradled by one of the most delectable valleys in the world, is the grave of a man famous in those parts, called "Twelve-Foot Davis". He, too, has an epitaph of one line. "Here lies a man who never locked his cabin door." Now the earth encloses them and a line commemorates the quality that men prize in the West.

The English "remittance men" were the great feature of the West at the turn of the century. They had their place in that free and easy community, for it was not lack of courage or lack of intelligence that made England too hot to hold them. The 1914-18 war accounted for most of them. "They may have been green, but, by God, they weren't yellow," was the verdict of the West.

Like all really right-thinking human beings, the people of the West have a great tolerance for pleasing eccentricity. Once in the Peace River country I saw a wooden board outside a homestead. On it was boldly painted in large white letters, "Machine salesmen will be shot." My companion chuckled. "That's an old time cowboy," he said, "he can't abide machines." Which was a pleasing glimpse of the obvious.

What of the Indian? The white man and the Indian each has his own civilization. Two civilizations cannot live side by side. One is bound to borrow from the other, and sad has been the fate of many an Indian tribe, beside whom towns and cities have arisen.

But when Indians have room to range and hunt as they do in the forest, or ride and herd cattle as they do on parts of the prairie, they are a people in their own right. The feather headdresses and the beaded buckskin clothing, are worn only on high days and holy days; for the workaday life of the trap or the herding, they are attired like their white neighbours, but with what a difference! No white man can walk as a cat walks, or imitate that peculiar seat on a horse that Indians have.

The Indian languages are as numerous as the tribes themselves, but if you follow the forest belt, the Cree language will take you almost from Labrador to the Rockies. I have sat for hours listening to it, to the laconic, musical sentences as well as to the sharper, more staccato tongue of Chippewyan.

Indians live in time, and the white man lives in space. There is no greater conserver of wild life than the Indian trapper. He kills only what the territory can afford to lose. He does not scour a place of life, with the idea of moving elsewhere next season. He probably traps an area that his forebears have trapped for centuries and means to leave his descendants a population of wild life as abundant as he himself found it.

An old Indian, nearing his century, which is not uncommon among this long-lived people, once described to me the whole vista of his life. He saw his first white man when he was a child. The white man rode a horse, and had a cocked rifle across his saddle. Then came more white men, and they built roads, and then came the stage coaches. Then Donald Smith, later Lord Strathcona, laid the two lines of steel across the prairies to the Pacific, and the railway ran. Then came motor-cars, and last of all came aeroplanes. "You white men are always trying to go faster and faster; we live, you are still trying to learn how to live."

In the year of 1936, an Indian came to a wayside station on the Canadian Pacific Railway, and set about boarding the train without a ticket. When he was asked to buy one, he said quite simply that he had no need of such a thing. "I once did Donald Smith a service," he said, "and Donald Smith said to me, 'When my railway is finished I will let you ride on it for nothing'." That had been a long time ago. The railway was finished in 1881. But to the eternal credit of the Canadian Pacific Railway, they honoured the promise, and the Indian had reason to be thankful that he had once done the great Donald Smith a service.

The treaty that secures the right of the Indian is probably the most durable of any that has ever been made. It ends like this . . . " . . . these things shall be, as long as the sun shall shine and the rivers shall run."

There are many varieties of the Canadian West, from the flat prairies of Manitoba and Saskatchewan, through the foothills of Alberta, to the eternal snows of the Rocky Mountains, and their westward slope to the Pacific. But there is an outlook on life that embraces them all.

The smell of the first warm breezes of a prairie spring is something that I shall not forget, for this is the coming of life to the land, and the great wedges of geese drive north, headed for the nesting grounds of the Arctic. Then there is the burning sun of the summer months, and with the grain turning to gold and running like the waves of the sea before the breeze. And in the cattle country, dust flies from the hooves of the ponies in the round-up. Then it cools to the crisp tang of autumn, and the grain is cut and the cattle are settled, and the geese come south again, heading to the sultry swamps of the Mississippi. The winter lays its mantle of snow, men seek their firesides for six whole months, the fly screens are laid aside and the storm sashes fitted, in their stead, to take the shock of the icy wind. For all its big cities with their tall buildings, and their bustling traffic, the West is a country of the open air.

It is a world with its own way of life. Once, after a long hard day in the open, I sat down to smoke and rest with a companion, while our dinner cooked. It was a summer evening. My companion's face was like leather from decades of exposure, but it was a very kindly face adorned with a long drooping moustache. His legs were bent from a lifetime in the saddle. He fell to talking about his remote youth in Wyoming. "In them days," he said, "if you got up against a feller, and had a quarrel, you shot him. And the folks said, well—it's the West. What happens now" he continued. "You get up against a feller, and you have a quarrel with him, and what do you do? Why, as like as not, you shoot him. And folks say, well—it's maladjustment, or lack of privilege, or some darned thing." Then the wrinkles relaxed into a broad smile, and his eyes twinkled. "But, bless you, son," he said, "it all amounts to the same thing in the end."

25

The Turn of the Maple Leaf

I HAD come to Canada in April, 1936. The chill of that early spring had done much to bring me back to life, particularly the expeditions into the forest, which is the most glorious outdoor existence in the world. I now knew that I was going to live. The heat of the summer in Quebec, and the sultry days on the Western tour with my father, had brought me pretty low at times. The first faint tang of autumn, and the slow turn of the maple leaves in the forest to their hour of matchless glory, brought with it an increased vitality.

Once or twice I drove out from Ottawa, with my mother, to MacGregor Lake, which was the haunt of that hard-fighting Canadian fish, the bass. The bass is not a thing of beauty but he is a doughty fighter. The impression he gives is of a coarse fish which leaps and leaps as if actuated by a spring. As well as a hard-fighting fish, he is very good to eat. My mother used to sit in the stern of the boat while I rowed and fished. The lure was a curious one called a bucktail. It resembled nothing so much as a moustache on a large hook.

We were driven by a chauffeur who had been with us ever since we went to Elsfield. Like so many Oxfordshire country folk of his generation, he had a Biblical Christian name. Few can have had the fortune to have had a servant so faithful as Amos Webb. He did not long survive my father's death. He had a stroke from which he partially recovered, and returned to Elsfield to die some months later among his own people. He was a keen fisherman. On our visits to MacGregor Lake he used to go out in a boat, by himself, and row round trolling a spoon. One day a big pike seized the spoon, and the rod, which was not properly secured, disappeared overboard into the depths.

Each morning and evening the tang in the air bit a little deeper.

The maples turned to their glorious hue and, in pursuit of the goddess of health, I accepted an invitation to spend a few weeks at a hunting lodge. It lay in the forest, south of Quebec City, and within a mile or two of the American border. To reach it we left the main highway and drove along a dirt road which wound through the forest. Down the centre of it ran a ridge of grass, and we could see a ruffed grouse picking at the seeds of the Timothy grass, to scuttle away into the bush at our approach. The road ended at a lake. The car was left in a shed, and there was half a mile of water to traverse, and then round a bend to the right was a promontory on which stood the wooden lodge, with a group of cabins round it. The trees running down to the water's edge were mirrored in the lake when the water was calm. There were deer in the forest, and an occasional bear, and red squirrels scurrying along the branches of the pines. There were ruffed grouse—that curious partridge of the forest—which roost in trees, and shelter in the winter in a bank of snow. There were a few duck on the waters of the lake, sometimes reinforced by others from neighbouring stretches of water. There were the commoner Canadian varieties, the black duck and the blue bill.

So fertile is this soil for timber that you may cut the forest to the ground, and return in twenty years to find a new generation of trees, as tall as their progenitors. My host kept a large staff of woodsmen at this time of the year. I know no one whose company is pleasanter than those quiet, sunburned men with their perfect, natural, good manners.

Their leader was an old Scotsman in his seventies, Albert Cathcart. He was deeply beloved in that part of the world. "Père Albert"—the French Canadians called him. There were two men from the Maine border whose Christian names bore the stamp of the Quaker community into which they had been born —Philander Wintle was one, and Alphaeus Cunning was the other.

My chief companion was a tall Westerner who had moved East after the 1929 crash, which had ruined him. He had that wonderful poise that so many have who have lived in those new lands. He was a good man on the trail, and a good handler of a canoe, but he had learned these arts later in life. To look at him you could see the life to which he had been bred, for his legs were bent with years on the back of a pony.

At mid-day, we would stop beside the forest trail and light a fire, and cook our luncheon in a clearing, where we could feel the autumn sunlight on our faces, and see it enflame maples to a vision which is one of the greatest glories of nature. He would talk about his youth in Saskatchewan. There were a lot of new settlers then from a number of European countries, flooding into that part of the country. He used to carry a pistol, he told me, "just in case somebody started something, I felt I would kinda like to start square. Ninety-nine times out of a hundred you wouldn't want the darned thing, but, when you did want it, you'd sure want it like hell!"

Sometimes we went out in the canoe, with a shotgun and rifle, to take the forest from a new starting point. Sometimes we followed the trails that radiated from the camp. I had shot so many African antelope that I had no desire to kill one of those beautiful deer, whose tails flashed like white banners as they cantered away into the darkness of the pines.

After one abortive day of trying, I never pursued the ruffed grouse with a shotgun. They never rose from the ground until they were deep in the forest. You could not get a flying shot at them. The .22 rifle was the weapon. They would run along the ground, between the naked boles of the pines, then hop on to a log and turn for three seconds to treat you to a fixed scrutiny, and then run deep into the forest out of sight. With a .22 rifle they were great fun, as there was time for one quick shot when they turned to look back. We generally came home with two or three every day. When it was blowing hard, and the lake had turned from a mirror to grey ripples which gradually swelled to waves, we would get a duck or sometimes a brace, if we were lucky. One night there was a storm, and when we woke next day the maples were bare, the ground beneath them carpeted with the glory of their leaves. The Fall advanced and, with the deepening tang of the frost, I began to feel better and could make longer expeditions as each day passed.

We had two tragedies when we were there, which cast a blight over that golden autumn. We returned one night to find a curious silence brooding over the encampment. My host's son, Ian, came down to meet us as we beached the canoe. "Père Albert" was dead. He had been paddling the canoe against a stiff breeze while a friend of mine had been sitting in the bows, rifle in hand. My friend had turned to Albert, and asked him if the exertion were not too much. Albert smiled, and said he never felt better in his life. Two more strokes of the paddle and he fell face forward, stone dead. The back of his head struck the thwart in front, smashing it with the force. The canoe had almost capsized, but not quite, and my friend had paddled it back. Reverent hands had lifted the body of the well-loved old man, and now he was laid on his bed and round him stood his companions of the forest. There were stains of tears on the weather-beaten faces that looked down at him.

"Père Albert" had gone to his long home. To those who stood round him, the forest would not ever seem quite the same again.

Ian was a keen and expert woodsman. We had many pleasant times together. He had an old dog who had the curious facility, that many dogs have, of almost invariably being in the wrong place at the wrong time; but for all his ineptitude he had great charm, and was much loved. One night Ian came back without him. He had been after a deer, and the dog had encountered a porcupine on the trail. Not knowing when to leave well alone, he had snapped at it. The next moment his muzzle and throat were studded with those wicked sharp quills with their unseen barbs, which make them work inwards when they have pierced. In a second he was a raging Bedlamite, foaming at the mouth and shrieking in agony, until a merciful bullet ended his troubles for ever.

Ian was taken prisoner a few years later, in Hong Kong. In the horrors of that confinement, in the hands of the Japanese, his mind must have fled back frequently to the peaceful beauty of the Canadian woods that we had shared that year.

When we had packed up our traps and traversed the lake by boat for the last time, and were headed for the City of Quebec, I felt better than at any time since leaving Africa, but there was a barrier that could be instinctively felt to the recapture of real health and strength. Two weeks later, after a lengthy examination in a hospital in Montreal, it was discovered that the amoeba which I had carried with me many thousands of miles from Soroti was still there. Strange animal instinct whispered that the amoeba could only be laid by the full rigours of an open-air life in the sub-zero world, and so it turned out.

26

Winter Expedition

PREPARATIONS for a winter expedition did not take long. A friend had planned an expedition for himself, and suggested that I accompany him and stay on after his time was up. I spent an afternoon in the Lumberman's Stores in Ottawa collecting a great deal of warm clothing, much of which turned out to be unsuitable. What you need in the forest, you discover only by experience, for what one man may need, another man can do without. My father lent me his stalking rifle (a .240 Holland and Holland), and the last requirement was to arm ourselves with sufficient literature for the railway journey across the continent. Our destination was Price Albert in North Saskatchewan, and the month was November. Three days of railway travel is full measure. The whole of the first day we read and watched the pines passing in procession through the forest.

During the second day we were crossing the open prairie which resembled a great calm sea of snow. Here and there were farms, intersected with a thin tracery of fences. At the stations there was always a gathering of folk to watch the train come in, clad in wind-breakers and close-fitting leather bonnets with flaps over the ears. The temperature inside the train was warm and suffocating. By the time we had reached Saskatoon I had finished Gone With the Wind, which I had begun when we left Ottawa, and thereafter dozed and watched the snow-covered expanses gliding by. At Prince Albert we spent a night in an hotel, and the next day drove to Waskesiu Lake. It was the centre of the National Park, and in summer is thronged with visitors, but in winter it is as solitary as any part of the surrounding forest. There was a post there of the Royal Canadian Mounted Police. There were also the forest rangers. There had not been much show, up till then, and the going on the roads was passable. Next day was mild.

We talked things over with Phil Hughes, the R.C.M.P. constable and his assistant, who was a special constable. The latter, Wallace Laird, was a Scotsman from Fife, and a well-known hand with dogs. Our guides were to meet us at a lake just north of the park which was some distance away, and the journey was complicated by the fact that not all the ice on the lakes was safe. We spent the next night in a ranger's hut beside a big lake. The lake was frozen, but the wind whipped away the snow, and it was a smooth sheet of ice. It was very still when we got into our sleeping-bags, but at intervals all night long came booming sounds, as of cannon shots. It was the ice cracking under the pressure of its expansion as it deepened with the frost.

It was clear next morning, and a high wind had got up, but what was more serious, a large rift had opened in the ice in the big lake. We were forced to find another way. Coming down a small lake with the dogs, we were travelling at high speed over a patch of clear ice when we hit a rough patch and the sledge overturned.

Wallace Laird and I hit the ice pretty hard, and, although we slid like curling stones, we were a good deal shaken. It was lucky that we had made an early start for we had a long way to go. The two mounted policemen knew every inch of the country, and we traversed the lakes on ice that would bear the weight of a sledge, and put our shoulders to it to help the dogs over steep portages which separated them. Twice we had to circumvent unexpected stretches of open water.

It was evening, and we were tired when we met with the first of our Indian helpers. Together we carried our belongings on our backs over a short portage to a small lake, Adjawan. On the opposite side was a comfortable-looking cabin. That lake and cabin had become celebrated, for they were the home of Grey Owl and his beavers. Grey Owl was away from home, but in the North you do not lock your cabin door. Such is the code that you leave your shack so that any wayfarer may stretch his sleeping-bag on your bunk, and make a fire in your stove, and it is part of the understanding that he leaves it in precisely the condition in which he found it. By the same token you leave your belongings and goods on which you depend, cartridges, matches and furs, and they will be respected. It is when this code is broken that drastic retribution follows.

As we approached the log cabin we noticed barbed wire twined round the boles of the nearest trees. This was to prevent the beavers from felling any tree which might fall on the shack. Fifty yards this side of it, a canoe had been put up for the winter, keel upwards, supported by two trestles. A beaver had felled a tall tree which had fallen exactly across it and cut it in half. We advanced to the cabin and pushed open the door. At first sight it appeared to be stacked with firewood, for a great heap of logs and branches started just beyond the sweep of the door and reached to the ceiling on the lakeward end. The lake shore was only a few feet beyond that wall.

A brief investigation showed that this was not firewood, but a beaver lodge. Half of it was in Grey Owl's occupation, and the other half ran down to the lake, ending in the water itself. His house, and the house of the beavers, formed two complete semi-detached residences. There was not much room in his end of the shack, but there was a bunk and a table, a couple of chairs and a stove. There was a Winchester rifle supported on two nails beside the door, and below it an old-fashioned six-shooter, hanging from a nail, by its trigger guard. There were sundry boxes and *bric-à-brac* lying about, and, on the window sill, was an English dictionary, the pages thumbed almost black.

It was not yet dark, and while the Indian lighted a fire in the stove, we strolled round outside. The birds, little black and white shrikes—whisky-jacks as they are called—seemed extraordinarily tame, so did the few squirrels that we saw. One ran on to the roof of the shack and looked down at us curiously. The Indian put his head out of the door and gave us a handful of crumbs. "They are tame," he said. "Grey Owl feeds them." And sure enough, after a moment or two of shyness, and some manoeuvring, we each had a little bird perched on our open palms. A squirrel ran down the eaves of the shack and accepted some food.

There was no doubt that Grey Owl was a very remarkable man where animals were concerned. The Indian told us of a tame moose who would come to the door of the shack, but we did not see it. We had just finished dinner, and were contentedly puffing tobacco, when quite suddenly and quietly the door opened and gave a glimpse of stars twinkling outside. We had expected a man to enter, and looked up from where we sat at the height at which his face would have been. But it was not a man; it was a beaver, dripping wet from the waters of the lake. He was followed by another. The door moved easily, with enough bias to close itself when it was released. It closed as quietly as it had opened and there were two large beavers, in our midst, trailing their flat scaly tails and inspecting us closely. They treated us to a long look, decided we were harmless, and moved over to two boxes which stood in a corner. From one they took an apple and from another a crust of bread. They were used to rummaging for their food in the shack and did not seem to be worried by us. Then one of them put down his food and waddled over to the bunk. I had thrown my buckskin on it and the corner hung down to within his reach. He reached up and took it in his teeth, dragged it down and trailed it towards the door. I put my foot on it as it passed. He dropped it and stood up and treated me to another long stare. He was not pleased, for he gave me a hiss. He had enormously powerful teeth, as an animal must needs have that cuts down tall trees. Then he picked up his food and, with his companion, opened the door and disappeared into the freezing darkness.

I had met Grey Owl before, and was to meet him afterwards. I have always been sorry that he was not there that night, to interpret all these strange things to us. He had at that time made a great and deserved reputation as a writer. He was probably the only man who has ever written a first book and then, after allowing a few months to elapse, travelled a great distance to the nearest post office, expecting a cheque for it, and found one waiting! He was half Indian only—indeed there are very few full-blooded Indians to-day—but his appearance was wholly Indian. He was one of the handsomest men I have ever seen, and had the most musical speaking voice of any human being to whom I have ever listened.

The Indian who had kept house with him at one time, told me that he would often look up in the dictionary every word of paragraph after paragraph. It was that same thumbed and blackened volume that lay on the window sill; but on one occasion he saw him sit down and write for nineteen hours without stopping. On that occasion he wrote the best book of all. He was not strong, having been wounded in the 1914-18 war when he was a sniper. He died just after the 1939-45 war began. Having been a trapper, with a professional indifference to the lives of animals, he had become madly fond of those that formed his immediate circle, his beavers and the small birds round Adjawan lake. They became an obsession with him. He kept the same hours as the beavers, rising at five o'clock in the evening and going to bed at five o'clock in the morning. My father visited him in the summer that followed, and went out on the lake in a canoe. A beaver broke the surface beside them. Grey Owl put a duck-board over the side, and the beaver ponderously climbed aboard. He was a strange man in many ways, but one who made a contribution to literature, and in his own way, a great contribution to his native Canada.

It was half-past six next morning when we left. One of the beavers was just outside the door and was turning lakeward, down to the patch of water that they kept open all winter long. We gave him an apple which he accepted.

It was early afternoon when we reached our destination, having shed the Indian. Then we met the rest of his family, the brothers Jimmy and Tommy, and another Indian called Settee. We looked at the camp which they had prepared for us, and we looked at one another, then we admired each other's weapons. Jimmy was middle-sized and very powerful, with long hair. He had a big nose of the classic Indian shape; but where Settee was dark, Olympian and silent, Jimmy had a continual fund of cheerful conversation. His brother Tommy was darker, with eyes that danced with humour. Jimmy loved to be chaffed and loved to chaff other people, and his beady eyes would twinkle incessantly at his own jokes. They had put up two tents, and had cut balsam branches for beds. Furthermore, they had acquired two stoves from a ranger's hut, one for each tent. We sat down on the balsam branches, warming our hands at the stove, to an enormous meal of venison, and talked far into the night—Jimmy boasting of his law-breaking, and the two mounted policemen, taking it in good part, chaffed him about the day when they would catch him.

I went to bed that night to the wonderful resin smell of the balsam branches that were our beds, in the comfort of the eider-down sleeping bag. The wilderness was beginning to take a powerful hold on me.

This camp was our base for nearly a fortnight's wandering in the winter woods.

Wally and Phil left next day with the dog team, and this intensified the quietness. Sledge dogs are companionable creatures, and their furious scrimmage at feeding time is always worth watching. We fed our dogs on one of two kinds of food, either on white fish, in appearance rather like chub, which were thrown to the dogs solid as rock with the frost, or with moose meat which was chopped up with an axe. We had to be very careful to keep the axe blade well out of their way, for if a shred of moose meat stuck to it they would pounce upon it, and if a dog's tongue touched the steel of the blade it would freeze it solid. The wretched creature would try to wrench itself free, shrieking in agony and sometimes tearing part of its tongue away in its writhings.

Our camp was in the midst of splendid game country. The forest was full of small timber, thinning at times where the muskegs occurred. A muskeg is an unlovely phenomenon. It is a swamp of glutinous mud, which represents a stage in evolution some-where between timber and coal. Interspersed throughout the region were many lakes, which now were white expanses of snow-covered ice, the forest that bordered them seeming black by comparison.

The principal game were moose and caribou and the small black-tailed antelope which they call the "jumper". In addition there were wapiti, like huge overgrown red deer. These caribou are forest dwellers, unlike their cousins who migrate in tens of thousands every year to the barren lands north of the timber line. Wally had once encountered them when he had been fur trading farther north, a few years earlier. He had been driving his dog team across a frozen lake and found himself confronted with a forest of horns. The dogs had bolted straight ahead, almost drunk with the scent of so much game. The army of caribou had opened a lane in front of him, down which he had hurtled. He had an eerie recollection of being surrounded by thousands of antlered heads, no longer shy creatures fleeing from the sight of man, but a multitude who allowed a man to live and pass on their sufferance.

Night after night, we would hear the wolves howling, day after day we would see their tracks. But we never saw one in the flesh. That is rare. Often we would see the tracks of moose and caribou overlaid by the sinister pad marks of a pack of wolves, usually five or six in number. For a wolf pack, like a covey of partridges, is a family. Sometimes, as with partridges, several families will pack together. The wolves can keep up their deadly remorseless lope for mile after mile. The moose will run until he finds he cannot shake off his pursuers. Then he will seek for something against which he can put his back, and prepare to stand and fight. The wolves will range warily round him. A big bull-moose weighs about a ton. His armament is his great bladed horns and his splay hooves. He can kick forward like a mule, and if he lands one of these pile-driver blows he can sheer a wolf's muzzle clean away. But he has no chance with a pack. Three will snap at his nose and engage his attention, while the others will steal round his flanks and snap at his hind legs to hamstring him. Then he has no hope, for his power of manoeuvre is lost, and his noble bulk is overborne by the snarling mob, and in a little while the forest is silent again.

The weather was still and frosty during our stay. We woke each morning in the half darkness of a winter's dawn and fell to breakfast, sitting on the floor of the tent round the stove. It was a chill scramble to get into your clothes when you deserted the warm snug folds of the sleeping bag.

I knew, now, instinctively, that the African germ was defeated, for appetite and strength were returning. Jimmy and I made our plans at breakfast and it would be getting light when we emerged from the tent. On the branches beside the camp would nearly always be a spruce hen, sitting solemnly regarding us. They are like dark partridges, and can perch on trees. They are preserved by Canadian law as they may be the salvation of those who are lost in the forest, for they can be knocked down with a stick if you approach them warily.

The forest was very still as we set off down one of the many trails into the snowy silence. Jimmy would lead, and our eyes would search the carpet of snow for fresh tracks. At midday, we would halt and light a small fire. We would sit with our rifles within easy reach, while we toasted bread and bacon for our midday meal. We would boil up some snow in a can and make black tea. Jimmy always retrieved the tea leaves afterwards, and put them in a twist of cloth, frugally using the same leaves several times over. And we would talk, in the warmth of the crackling sticks, and from Jimmy could be absorbed much of the lore of the wilds.

Our bag was negligible. Once when the snow was falling heavily, we walked right up to a moose. It was cropping twigs from a bush. The bush obscured its head and neck and we had no means of telling whether it was a bull or a cow. There it was, with the snowflakes settling upon its flanks, a huge head-less bulk, not twenty feet away. We stood like statues. The single metallic discord of the cocking of our rifles did not disturb it. Then the head lifted, and we were regarded by two eyes down a long curving nose. It was a cow moose. We did not fire, and in a moment the timber and the falling snow hid her from our gaze.

Once we followed a big bull-moose for many hours. It joined a number of others, and still the chase went on. The sun went down in a cold orange sunset behind the pines. It was getting dark and the outline of the trunks was dimming when we caught up with him. The range was about a hundred yards. The big bull, towering over the others of his kind, was a strange, ele-mental outline against the darkening forest. The flash of my rifle lit up the firmament for a split instant, but there was no answering thud of the bullet striking home. Like shadows the great beasts flitted, and there drifted back to us the clash of their horns against the pine trunks as they forged their way through the forest.

With Jimmy I fished one long cold day through the ice for

pike. We hoped to vary our diet, but we caught nothing. It was cold, and overcast with snowclouds, and although we stamped our feet they ceased to feel as if they belonged to us.

A single human figure came to the edge of the lake and watched us, a half-breed named Baptiste. He was one of a family of homesteaders, who lived little more than a mile away in a shack, with his father who was a veteran of the distant days. The old man had the scar of a Pawnee arrow wound in his leg. He had got it as a small child when he had crouched below a wagon, one of many that were laagered in a circle, watching his mother beside him kneeling and firing between the spokes of the wagon wheels at the charging, wheeling horsemen.

From Jimmy I learned why Indians have such white teeth. They chew resin as if it was chewing gum. I learned how to make a not unpalatable syrup from the birch as well as the maple, and last of all, how to build a really warm fire. It is the habit of white men—so Jimmy explained—to build a large fire and sit far away from it and never get warm. He would sit on a log and light a fire between his feet. Beside him would be a large pile of twigs that had been gathered and heaped before he even lit the fire. Quite mechanically he would add a handful of twigs whenever the little fire burned low. The warmth would rise up and suffuse his whole body, and he would sleep quite restfully, replenishing the little fire without fully awakening.

Gradually the cold intensified. When we started out on the trail each morning our brows and our eyelashes would whiten with frost. A lock of Jimmy's raven hair, which had escaped from below his fur cap, would be whitened until it looked as if he had suddenly, by enchantment, grown old.

The forest was no longer silent, for the trees crackled like gunshots in the cold. We were far from home one afternoon when we came to a frozen muskeg. We had started to return to camp and were trying to take a short cut. The frost was like iron, but ice on a muskeg is notoriously tricky. We were almost across when I went through it. Jimmy hauled me out. The touch of water at 80 degrees of frost is like the feel of vitriol. We staggered on to firm ground, but I was like a knight in armour from the waist downwards, with a skin of muddy ice an inch thick from my moccasins to my waist. Jimmy knew the answer. He pushed over three dead tamarack pines and, with his knife, stripped armfuls of dead and lichened twigs from them. In less than a minute, a fire was roaring and crackling higher than our heads.

Darkness fell. My fringed buckskin coat acted as a rug and on it I sat completely naked in the warmth of the flames. We were in the circle of light and warmth and the leaping flames illumined the ring of pines surrounding us. The smoke spiralled up in the sub-zero darkness, and the sparks wandered up to the tree tops. My clothes steamed and dried. There were my buckskin breeches, two pairs of stockings and a pair of socks, moccasins, chamois leather under-garments and all the paraphernalia with which a man must shield the naked skin from the air of the winter north.

Then we hit the trail for camp. The ball of my right foot had been frozen. Every time I put it to the ground, it felt as if I were stepping on a tin tack. It was a long nine miles to camp. There was no sound except the cracking of the trees in the frost. Then an owl began to hoot, and gradually, from fatigue and discomfort, I started to shout abuse at the owl, to relieve my feelings. We were thankful to reach the camp, and we relaxed in heavenly warmth and drew off our thick outer garments, and lay and smoked and listened to the sizzling of bacon and venison frying in the same pan, and the bubbling of the battered coffee percolator. It was luxury so complete and so satisfying as to be rare this side of paradise. Outside, the owl hooted again. Jimmy turned to his brother, his eyes twinkling, "Johnnie got real mad with that owl," he said, "He bawled the hell out of him for the last two miles home."

There was never a dull moment with Jimmy in that frozen fairyland.

Crows were a great plague in the province at that time. The Saskatchewan Government, with great ingenuity, devised a plan for reducing their numbers. They captured a number of crows alive, and fixed metal rings to their legs, each marked with a sum of money. At the least it was about a dollar, but there were a few crows which were marked 500 dollars each. One still cold day, when a bright sun was making the snow glisten on the branches, a crow flapped over our heads, and it was so low that we saw it had a ring on its leg. We pumped two magazines of rifle bullets at it, but they droned away into the frosty blue infinity, and the crow winged his way out of our sight.

Jimmy is a man that I will never forget. That autumn he had acted as a fishing guide for my father and they had formed a great mutual attachment. Jimmy and his brother are the half-breeds described in my father's last novel *Sickheart River*, while he himself in that instance is the central figure—the man who goes north to die.

We parted just before Christmas in 1936. I was now well on the road to life and strength.

In August 1939, I came south from a year's isolation in the sub-Arctic. A complete year of letters arrived for me in a sack. and these were two of them. The first was from a mounted police friend, writing in turn to another friend, a copy of which had been sent to my father who enclosed it to me.

17th June, 1939.
Royal Canadian Mounted Police,
Saskatchewan.

"I thought you might be interested to know that the law finally caught up to. . . . Jimmy, and he won't be poaching for some time to come. Last month, I got a call to go up to the National Park with the tracking dog to help investigate a case which involved the breaking into the Warden's cabin. . . . A quantity of Government stores had been stolen and Jimmy was suspected as he could not be found at his home camp. I worked the portages north, trying to pick up tracks while H and G — (Wardens) headed S.E. through the bush looking for signs. Two days later G — located Jimmy, D — his brother, and an Indian, about eighteen miles inland from the narrows. . . . They had the stolen property as well as illegally caught beaver and muskrats, so he put them under arrest and started walking out to the highway. They travelled all night and at dawn made a fire and boiled the kettle. There they attacked G — beat him badly over the head with clubs, tied him up, stole his revolver and escaped into the bush with their packs. I got down with a dog, eight hours later, picked up the scent and tracked for two hours—by that time we knew they were heading home and a party went ahead to the E. boundary of the Park and picked up the three as they came in late that night after having travelled on foot through the bush that day for thirty miles. They were all very meek when brought in. The trials were held . . . last week, Jimmy and his brother were sentenced to five years each with hard labour in a penitentiary, and the Indian got twenty-eight months.

"So ends the saga—until 1944, anyway.

"I used to tell Jimmy that we, or at least the law of averages, would catch up with him eventually, but I did not think it would be as drastic as it turned out."

In my father's letter which conveyed this sad enclosure, he commented as follows:

28 June, 1939.
The Citadel,
Quebec.

"I enclose a letter which contains sad news. Our dear Jimmy has been pinched at last and tucked away for five years, along with his virtuous brother. He was too great a spirit for our effete times!"

27

Logging Camp

THE sojourn in the forest of North Saskatchewan had been the turning point. The tenacious amoeba that had preyed on me since Soroti days had proved itself no match for open air life in 80 degrees of frost. The steady return of strength brought with it a longing to tread the snow again in the winter woods.

Jack Fraser, an Ottawa friend and I, arranged a trip to the logging country of the upper Ottawa River. His father had owned vast stretches of timber limits, and was still alive at a great age. Jack was one of the finest horsemen in Canada and a great lover of the forests.

We boarded the night train at Ottawa in our city clothes with a ragged assortment of luggage—our sleeping bags rolled up, a duffle bag apiece to carry our clothes, snow-shoes, and our rifles in blanket covers. We went to sleep to the rocking of the train, rumbling its way through the farmlands and into the deep forest.

We had arranged with the guard to stop the train, and let us out, at a little halt called Moor Lake. Sitting on our sleeping berths next morning, our city clothes rolled up in bundles and thrust into the duffle bags, we attired ourselves in buckskin breeches, two pairs of thick trappers' stockings and Indian moccasins. As well as that we had an assortment of sweaters, surmounted by wind-breakers. I topped all that with a buckskin coat which I had got in the West, and which I always wore in cold weather. It seemed strange in the light and heat of the sleeping car, surrounded by passengers travelling correctly attired from one city to the next, to be donning the livery of the forests.

Then the train began to slow down and ground to a halt. The guard flung the door open, and we scrambled down into six inches of snow beside the track. Our sleeping bags and duffle bags were thrown down to us—rifles and snow-shoes were passed down more gently. The coloured sleeping car attendant waved good-bye, and banged the door above us. There was a creak and a jolt. The great train gathered itself up and the wheels ground past us. Coach after coach with darkened windows passed, and then we were looking at the end of the last one disappearing round the bend of the forest, and with it the world of the cities. Slowly the noise died away. We were standing in a glade through which ran those two ribs of steel, while big flakes of snow drifted down in the silence. We collected our luggage.

The halt was an empty wooden shack. The snow was falling steadily, and the last vestiges of darkness were fading. We put on our snow-shoes and shouldered our belongings. Jack knew the way and we headed along a narrow trail. It was pleasant to be in that silence again, and to break it gently with the cushioned thud of snow-shoes on soft snow. We arrived at a shack and had breakfast with two taciturn lumberjacks in red-checked shirts.

Everybody knew Jack Frazer in these parts. We were close to the Ottawa River, which is of great width in these parts. It was a sheet of ice, smooth here and rough there. On some of it the snow lay to the depth of a few inches, but for the rest it was a mirror of ice. River ice is not uniformly trustworthy, as you may find what is called "a honeycomb" where the ice will not bear you. Jack had nearly lost his life on this crossing once, through driving a horse-drawn sledge into a honeycomb. It is a poor outlook if you fall through the ice in sub-zero weather, and the river drags at you to pull your numbed hands from their hold.

We crossed after breakfast without incident. The heavy snow had stopped, and a light breeze was driving it in white powder in little spirals along the glassy surface. Our first destination was the Lumber Depot. It was the base for the logging operations in those limits, on the north shore of the river. There were several lumber camps in the forest, cutting the timber which climbed the slopes north from the river bank. The custodian of the depot was an old man called Alfred Allen. He had eyes of such unusual blue that they were startling.

We spent the day with him getting used to the forest and unpacking and repacking our various belongings. Next day we set off and slowly climbed the uphill trail to a shack which we intended to make our headquarters, at Teapot Lake. We had acquired a third member of the party, a woodsman, Théophile Rabishaw. It was very still when we took to the trail, and frosty without being cold. We had not far to go, and after perhaps an hour's steady plodding, we had reached our destination. The sun had come out and made the billowed snow dazzling, with splashes of palest gold where it glanced. The frost on the twigs glistened from an infinity of tiny rainbow specks. We saw little sign of game. The tracks of two deer and no more. Now and then a squirrel would shake down a small shower of snow from the branch of a pine.

The shack stood on the edge of a small lake. We had been climbing steadily since we left the depot, and the lake lay on a flat ledge surrounded by forest. All round it the dark pines thronged the edge, and their shelter had left the snow unblown, smooth and soft as a carpet.

There can be nothing that exceeds the comfort of a log cabin in winter, and few things come near it. When you have brushed the powdered snow from your moccasins so that the warmth will not melt it indoors; when you have shut the door behind you, and the stove is crackling and roaring, and you have spread your sleeping bag on your bunk and sorted the rest of your few belongings, you have a feeling of comfort which few forms of living can match.

We decided to devote that afternoon to adding to our supply of fresh food. To this end we took the handle off a syrup tin, cut it into lengths, and fashioned them into fish hooks. A piece of twine did for a line, and a piece of fresh meat for a bait. Fishing through ice is a cold job, and we wrapped ourselves up with everything we possessed. The preliminaries are lengthy. You need an axe and you need a pole. You clear the snow from the ice, and then you hack away at it. Then after what seems hours of effort, suddenly your axe goes through and the water boils up, fizzing like champagne. You lay aside your axe, but you must always be prodding with your pole to prevent the hole freezing up again. If you leave your hole, it is the etiquette of the woods to plant a pine branch beside it, to show that the ice is not as thick there as elsewhere.

The fish, whose world has been smothered by this layer of ice, are galvanized into life by this sudden inrush of oxygen, and come close around it. We fished for an hour and a half, stamping our moccasined feet to warm them. We lowered the bait through the hole and waited for a bite. Many of the fish fell off as we were lifting them out. One, who seemed bigger than the others, would not come through the hole which had grown too small in spite of prodding with the pole. The line came up rigid as a walking-stick—the wet threads frozen stiff. When we had finished we had between us about a dozen fish. They were red trout, thin with the privation of the winter, but splendid eating for all that.

That night we had a huge meal and sat toasting our feet round the stove when we had done. Théophile, according to the custom of his kind, wore his fur hat indoors, removed it to eat, and immediately replaced it afterwards. It was strange, until I got used to the habits of the woodsmen, to find that they wore all their outdoor clothes indoors, and went fully clad from the atmosphere of the log cabin where the air is roasted by the heat of the stove, straight to the sub-zero frost which grips the world outside.

Thus Jack and I spent many happy days. We covered a great deal of ground on our snow-shoes. His were the more conventional kind, resembling a tennis-racquet. Mine were built for me, by an Indian in Saskatchewan, out of straight-grained birch, pointed and turned up in front like a ski, and made for my weight. It was possible to jog along for hours, once I got the hang of them.

We visited several lumber camps, and had our midday meal there. The whole life of the lumber camp is fascinating. They were hauling the timber down from the higher levels. The trail down the slopes was beaten hard as a highway. Very slowly the two cart-horses would take the strain of the timber sloop, which is the big sledge with solid runners, upon which is lashed several tons of timber. Perched on the summit of this load of timber, ribbons in one hand, long whip in the other, was the teamster. A wire hawser was attached to the rear of the sloop, which was paid out round a pulley wheel to stop it gaining momentum with the steep slope, and becoming a juggernaut. Jack had often seen it done the other way, when there was no wire hawser to take the weight. Then the sloop would steadily gain momentum, while the teamster standing atop of the load of logs, on which his spiked boots gave him a purchase, would lash the two horses to a downhill gallop, they with their eyes rolling and realizing, as did the man who lashed them, that if they stumbled the three living things would be ground to extinction under this juggernaut of timber.

Once at the foot of the mountains, the logs lie until the spring and the break-up of the ice. Then comes another hazardous chapter, when they are floated down the waterways, and the lumberjacks are wet from morning to night in the chilly water that has not long shaken loose the grip of the ice. I have stood for hours watching timber going down a rapid river, bumping and jarring in the swirls.

A long jam across a rapid is a fearsome thing. A bridge made from a forest of poles, at every angle, with the drifting logs piling up behind. That is the moment for the man of experience, who must be as surefooted as he is daring. By looking at the jam he is able to see what is known as the "key log"— that log which, if moved, will set all the others moving. He must steal out across this jagged mass of timber, with his iron-shod peavie, jerk the log free and then run madly for the shore, as the forest shakes itself loose and starts to grind its way down the rapid with the force of the pent-up water behind. Sometimes it is done that way; sometimes he goes as near as he dares, and casts a stick of dynamite. There is one thing for which he prays as he scrambles back, that the rapids will not make the logs go end over end, for then he has no hope.

We saw much of the men who follow this dangerous and exacting calling, men warmly and variously clothed, with many days' beard on them; men who did not speak much, but when they did, there was a tone of Quebec and England in the accents, the intonation of several countries of Europe, and always a broad Scots voice somewhere. The foremen were men with whom to be reckoned. It would be a foolhardy man who picked a fight with one of them. In the log cabin where we had our midday meal, a notice was pinned to the wall—"No Talking During Meal-time". It was obeyed without question, and we ate our food in silence. At the end of it, the cook's helpers would put all the knives and forks into a series of sacks, soak them in water and then shake them, and take them out miraculously clean. A lumber camp cook commands very high wages, for unless the food is good the men will not stay. Nowhere else will you see pork fried as it should be fried, followed by that wonderful delicacy, raisin pie.

Our wanderings took us over a good deal of country. Once, when we were unarmed, we found a lame deer. It was making slow progress in the soft snow. I went after it, but the bridle of my right-hand snow-shoe broke, and, losing my balance, I put my moccasin down in the soft snow. In a moment I was up to my waist, for the snow falling in the protection of the trees does not pack hard, but stays soft as down. I managed to reach the bole of a tree and pulled myself up by it, and then spent much time fishing for my loose snow-shoe. The deer was a long way off by the time I had my foot back in a new bridle.

Sometimes the sky seemed grey with snow, and seemed to press down to the points of the pines. Sometimes there was sunlight, and dusk would come, and with it a frost, and a sky of a still pale orange.

We visited the depot several times and supped with old Alfred Allen. Occasionally he could be persuaded to reminisce about the old days of logging in the Upper Ottawa Valley. He remembered the men who had borne great names in those days, and who are now historical characters. He was taciturn, but like all of his kind, had a tremendous gift for picturesque language. On asking him about a notorious bad man who had achieved notoriety in that part of the world, some years back, he said; "Old Nick's got him now," adding in parenthesis; "He was a pretty hard ticket."

Once we went down to a little logging village on the shore of the big river, which had seen several generations of lumbermen—men with spiked boots and red jerkins, who can jump on a log to cross the river, spin it with the spikes on their boots, holding their peavies in their hands horizontally like a tightrope walker. They come in every human shape and size to follow this dangerous profession. In the saloon of that little village there are marks in the beams of those spiked boots, where men, either for a wager, or to show their *joie de vivre* had jumped in the air and kicked the beam above their heads, and left the nail marks.

Alfred Allen would sometimes talk of the old days of square timber. Those were the days of the broad axemen, who handled a big axe with a double head, and would walk slowly backwards down a pine trunk as it lay on the ground, each blow of the axe bringing the blade within two inches of their toes. When they had reached the end of the trunk, one side would be levelled off as if it had been planed.

In this logging village beside the river, I was taken to see an old man who was dying. Lumberjacks are so much in the water from the moment the ice breaks up, that in later years they are racked with rheumatism. It is a strange and embarrassing proceeding to be introduced to a dying man. He lay in a two-roomed shack, a great human wreck, his knees drawn up underneath the bedclothes, his big hairy hand resting on the coverlet, his eyes fixed on the ceiling above him. He was one of the last of the broad-axemen, and now his time had come. A faint flicker of interest passed over his gnarled, kindly face as I was introduced to him. He was very weak. I laid my hand on his big hairy paw, which had held the haft of so many an axe. It was very still in that room. A cheap clock ticked over the fireplace. There was little furnishing and less ornament, but a section of spruce log not more than a few inches across had been carved in the shape of a moose. He must have spent many happy hours working on it. It was a fine carving and had a great deal of life about it. My eyes must have rested on it for rather a long time, because he followed the direction I was looking. "Would you like it?" he asked. I murmured something about not wishing to deprive him. He smiled with all the wisdom of the ages and shook his head. "No more use to me," he said. The last of the square timber had long gone down the river, and he was going down the river himself. I have that carving to this day and treasure it greatly.

Then it was time to return to the cities, and again we shaved and prepared ourselves to return. We mounted the train in our woodland clothes. Next morning at Ottawa we donned our city garb—much crushed from its sojourn in the duffle bags. That last spell in the woods had put the stamp on my recovery. The pursuit of health was now complete, and it was time again to set about making a living.

28

Fur Trading Post

A N idea was beginning to form in my mind. The winter forests had begun to take a powerful hold on me. Adventure, combined with a career, had led my father to suggest the Colonial Service. Now that a microscopic germ had denied me life in Africa, strong became the desire to start life again in this northern fairyland.

About twenty-five miles away from the police post at Waskesiu was the Hudson's Bay Company's post at Montreal Lake. Phil Hughes and Wallace Laird were going that way on police business, and I needed no second bidding to accompany them. It was December 8th, and the temperature had risen to the point where we were glad to leave aside our heaviest garments when we were snow-shoeing. The mail appeared. There were a few letters for me, but in such places mail always appears astonishingly irrevelant.

We set out in two parties. Phil and I donned our snow-shoes and took the trail to Bittern Creek, where there was a ranger's shack half-way along the route. The trail was of soft new-fallen snow, and a narrow one at that. The green arms of the pines, on which the snow was billowed, reached across the trail from either side. Wally had to make a later start with the dogs. We covered twelve miles in a very short time and were in the ranger's cabin, with our midday meal sizzling in the frying pan, when he arrived. The warmth and comfort of a log cabin is always difficult to leave on a winter's day, but we fought off that delicious feeling of well-being and sleepiness, tidied the cabin, to leave it as we had found it, and followed the dog team as it threaded its way along the winding of the trail. In that atmosphere you could keep up a gentle plodding trot on snow-shoes, slowly eating up the miles.

Snow began to fall gently at first, and then in a drifting curtain, through which the tops of the tall pines showed only

indistinctly. We came on our destination at last, round a sharp
corner of the trail. It was the conventional wooden store of the
Hudson's Bay Company, with the name written in old letter-
ing, and under it the short eloquent inscription "Incorporated
May 2nd, 1670". Close to it, snuggling against the skirts of
the pines, was the post manager's house, with a thin column of
blue smoke rising from the chimney and losing itself among the
falling flakes. There was just enough breeze in the open clearing
to stir the company's flag at the top of the pole—the red ensign
on which is inscribed the letters H.B.C., which in jest they say
stands for "Here before Christ". Beyond these buildings there
was a vista in the pines, and dimly seen through the snow was the
white blank of the frozen lake. At the door of the post was the
Hudson's Bay Company's post manager, Cecil Lockhart Smith.
He was a Scotsman, like so many of the company's servants.
He helped us to unharness the dogs and unload the sledge, and
we followed him to the veranda of his house, and took the stiff
broom that stands outside the door of all houses in the north, to
brush the powdery snow from our moccasins. It was very
comfortable inside, and we took off garment after garment
before we sat down round the crackling stove in the well-
furnished living-room. He had a good library of books, and the
room was comfortably furnished.

We had given no notice of our intention to visit him. It was
left to me, as the novice, to ask him how he was ready and
waiting when we arrived, when no message had been sent.
"Moccasin Telegram", he answered and shrugged his shoulders.
At about nine o'clock that morning the Indians had told him
we were coming. That was about the time when we had made up
our minds to come! Such is the curious telepathy of that people.

It was fully dark now, and the falling snow hid the stars.
Outside the dogs were tied up. Occasionally a whine or the
noise of movement would come from them, as one shook the
flakes of snow from his coat. The crackling fire and the large
meal left us sleepy after our day's travel. We had covered about
twenty-five miles since breakfast. We played cards till we yawned,
and then sought our sleeping bags.

The snow had stopped when we awoke next morning. Our

tracks of the day before were buried deep under a smooth white quilt. Wally and Phil left with the dog team at midday, in search of a trapper who was wanted for some minor infringement of the law. He had three places of abode, separated by many miles of snowy trail. As chance would have it, they went to the wrong ones first, and scoured a great many miles of forest trail before they found him. The snow was soft and the dogs were tired to the point of a slow plod, which is less than a man can do on snow-shoes. They banged on the door of the trapper's shack, and for one moment it looked as if the inmate was going to turn ugly, but, instead, he resigned himself to sullen acquiescence.

That day I spent in the trading store. When you opened the door you were met by the same smell that greets you in every village shop in Britain. It was a compound of the smell of cheese and biscuits and soap, with overtones of coffee and plug tobacco, and undertones of gun oil and sacking. It was the apotheosis of the village shop. Shelves ran the length of the walls. On the floor below the bottom shelves were sacks of tea and coffee and flour, and boxes of biscuits. Above them the shelves were lined with cans and cartons and packages, containing all manner of food, cartridges, matches, and plug tobacco. Elsewhere were bales of blankets and clothing, packets of needles, skeins of wool, and reels of thread. From a projecting rail hung rifles and clusters of fox traps. In short, there seemed to be everything that a human being could desire within the compass of life in that white wilderness of winter, or in the pine-shaded silence of forest, and lake, under the summer sun.

Upstairs was the fur loft. It was a moment or two before one's eyes became accustomed to the gloom, and the furs hanging from the rafters excluded much of the light that came through the small window. The furs were hung up in bales, like by like, strung by the nose, the tails hanging downwards. There was a bale of wolf skins of every shade of dark and light brindle, beautiful to look at, but coarse to the touch. There were the dark foxes with their frosting of silver. There were red foxes of every shade from rust to orange. There were cross foxes with the dark intersection on their shoulders, just visible in the gloom. There were lynx and a few fisher, and a vast agglomeration of the tiny pelts of red

At Teapot Lake, Ontario. Winter 1936–37.

Montreal Lake post, Saskatchewan.
Left to right—Constable Phil Hughes, R.C.M.P., Cecil Lockhart-Smith, H.B.C., and myself.

A trapper trading his furs in a Hudson's Bay Company post.

Montreal Lake post. *Left to right*—Myself, Phil Hughes, Cecil Lockhart-Smith.

squirrel. This was the wealth of the wilderness, which supported the solitary lives of the tiny human population scattered throughout the great, tree-clad spaces.

Down below, once more, we built up the fire in the stove and went through the books of the post. The whole of this harvest which came over the counter and was sorted to hang in the loft above, was reduced to columns of neat figures. Looking round the store at the array of trade goods and smelling the intriguing smell of all that was there, was to look at the whole economy of this forest world.

That evening, two Indians came in from the trail with a magnificent bunch of skins. They brushed the snow from their moccasins before they entered, then each shouldered a sack from the birch-bark toboggans which they hauled by hand. They wore the strange, decorative clothes of the winter world. Their hair was long and dark, but where the light from the lamp caught it, it had the sheen of a raven's wing. From one sack came two red foxes, several coyotes, red squirrels innumerable, and a beautiful lynx. From the other sack, rolled up like a parcel, there was a bear skin. I sat by the stove and watched the trading go forward. The factor folded each fur over his arm and held it up to the light, to see how straight and strong the guard hairs were. He probed with his fingers, to inspect the under fur, and gave a careful examination of the pelt to detect a blemish. The Indians seemed to speak in monosyllables, more a language of nods than anything else. They seemed satisfied with the price the factor put on their furs, for they put their elbows on the counter and ranged the shelves with their dark eyes. They savoured every moment of their buying, asking to look at things, and after a scrutiny which seemed to take a full five minutes, handing them back shaking their heads. Finally the sacks which had brought the foxes bulged with shapes of the many different purchases that they had made, and the door shut behind them as they disappeared into the dusk.

Several days went past in this pleasant mode of life. Wally and Phil left for the police post at Waskesiu. They made an early start and the sky was clear enough to see the stars twinkling above the tree tops. Our minds were only partly on the harnessing of

R

the dogs. When it was complete we went into the house again, and stood round the wireless and heard King Edward VIII make his abdication speech. Wally and Phil set off down the trail right away. Cecil and I did not speak much that day. We didn't feel like it.

The remaining days passed pleasantly. An aeroplane landed on the lake with skis, part of a two-man air line, owned and piloted by two expert bush pilots who made an excellent living out of flying between that string of posts. We brought the pilot up for a cup of coffee. He was a striking-looking man. In spite of his flying clothes, and all the apparatus of the machine age, he seemed as much part of the wilderness as all the rest.

One day a tractor-driver appeared, towing down the lake two huge sledges which looked like lorries on runners. His was a cold and hazardous calling. Sitting up on the seat of his tractor there was no shelter from the bite of the sub-zero air, and the cutting winds, on the expanses of frozen lake; uncertain, too, for his vehicle weighed several tons, and ice is not all of an even thickness. Twice that day, he told us, he had jumped off his tractor seat when he heard ominous cracks of the ice below the caterpillar bands. He spent the night with us and summed up his profession as "A son of a gun of a cold job, but no kick about the pay".

A sudden unusual mild spell descended. Chopping a hole in the ice to fill a pail of water—which we did several times a day—could make us inconceivably warm under layers of winter clothing. Sometimes the temperature rose even above freezing, and there would be a musical tinkle of a cascade of falling crystals, from the snow on the branches of the pines. Then Wally and Phil returned bringing the dog-team. It was December 14th. Phil went back by himself on his snow-shoes, and Wally and I put all the baggage on the sledge. You would not need a dog-team to reach the post now. For they have built a road to it, and the frontier has moved further north.

We had an uproarious evening before we left, and next morning we harnessed the dogs, with the temperature falling and the whole white mystery of the winter forest asparkle with fresh frost. The trail to Waskesiu had been crossed and re-crossed several times since the last snow fell. Thus running beside the sledge, we could discard our snow-shoes and run in moccasined feet. Wally, who had a great eye for sledge dogs, had acquired a tiny husky puppy which was put aboard the sledge, where it peered about it with little beady eyes. It looked as if it were made of plush.

It was not too cold to run, and we jogged along behind the sledge, the sound of our moccasined feet lost in the swish of the snow along the runners and the thud of the dog's paws. We covered about ten miles without hardly a stop. Running with moccasins on a good surface of snow, it is possible to cover distances which would be quite out of the question in any other garb, and in any other part of the world.

The leading dog was old and had shown signs of failing on that run. As we boiled a kettle up beside the trail, I became conscious of having pulled a muscle in one leg, which was going to be a nuisance. The sky began to darken with unshed snow, and soon the flakes were drifting down through the branches, and there was a curtain across the open trail in front of us. We had come less than half-way when we halted for lunch, and we had not gone five miles on when the sledge was going at a snail's pace. The old leader had slowed to a walk, which every now and then became a stagger. Wally tried coercion and then kindness, but it was no good. The leader was failing. He was making his last trip. He floundered on, falling frequently. My own leg was beginning to be very painful. We took the leader out of harness, and moved the dogs up one. We lifted him on to the sledge, and his eye fell on the little puppy. He gazed at it. His eyes that were getting dull but, for a moment, a spark seemed to come to them which conveyed the impression of infinite sadness. It seemed to say: "I am an old dog now; look at me; I am finished. Once a leader is taken from harness he never recovers. You are only a little puppy; you don't know what that means; one day you will."

The sledge moved very slowly now. The leader kept on scrambling off the sledge and staggering and falling beside it. I made a very slow pace with my strained leg and the gloom intensified. The snow got softer and deeper as we went on. There was only one thing to do, and that was to keep moving until we got to our destination.

Hour after hour we plodded, and the pine trees marched past us like a slow procession. It got dark but there were no stars, just the flecks of snow faintly stinging our faces, in a world where we could tell dark pine from white snow but no more. We did not speak much.

We were utterly exhausted when we reached the police post, and saw the lights twinkling from the windows of the big log-cabin, and the door thrown open showing the flames flickering on a comfortable interior. We unharnessed the dogs, who were dead tired. The leader was very far gone. I believe his sufferings were far more mental than physical. He did not look where he was going, but walked into tree trunks. Life held nothing more for him. He died the next day.

It was a difficult trip down to Prince Albert for there was a lot of fresh soft snow, and the motor-car that Phil drove frequently skidded into a drift. When we got on to the road which goes through the little village of Tweedsmuir—so different from the hamlet in the Borders—the forest gradually thinned, and then we left it behind us for the prairie of North Saskatchewan and the twinkling lights of the bustling town of Prince Albert. Next day, sitting in the train crossing the snow-covered prairie, studded with occasional brown dots which were Hungarian partridges, or sometimes prairie chicken, my mind went back to those weeks in the winter forest. I knew now, for a certainty, the profession I wanted to follow.

29

The Hudson's Bay Company

IT was almost inevitable that I should seek employment with the Hudson's Bay Company. The northern forests of Canada and their few, but fascinating, inhabitants had taken such a firm hold on me. I wanted the opportunity to press even further north to where the forests stopped and the barren lands began, and on to the Arctic Ocean, and the Arctic Islands beyond.

The Hudson's Bay Company, with its long and romantic history and its enduring Scottish connection, offered all this and a profession too. At their suggestion I returned to Britain and spent the summer of 1937 doing a course at the School of Economics and Commerce at Dundee, to learn something of the framework of business. In the autumn of that year I joined the company's head office in London, and for two months worked as an apprentice clerk. It was one simple routine job after another. The name of that building is Beaver House, and beneath it is a large, cold chamber where the furs are stored. Whenever the opportunity offered I would slip down there, and there were furs of such beauty, and in such quantity, as you could see assembled nowhere else in the whole globe. It was fascinating to think of the great catchment area of Northern Canada from which they flowed into this pool. The hand of many an Indian, many an Eskimo, and many a mackinawed trapper had gathered those furs in that vast patchwork of forest and barren lands, hundreds of thousands of square miles in extent.

The company of "Adventurers of England trading into Hudson Bay" was formed originally by the great Prince Rupert, with its main headquarters in London. The headquarters are still in London, but much of the executive direction is decentralized to Winnipeg. Thither I was dispatched on New Year's Day of 1938.

For six months I was a citizen of that city which has a most inequable climate but an extremely hospitable population. I was set to keeping the books at one of the fur trade districts. I do not know whether they ever got these accounts in order afterwards, for I was not cut out to be an accountant.

After some months of this employment, at which I was about as much good as would be a blacksmith trying to repair Swiss watches I was sent for and told that I was to be posted to Cape Dorset in Baffin Land. I was immediately the envy of all the others who were waiting for posting, as, of all Canada's Eastern Arctic, Baffin Land is the Naboth's vineyard of the fur trader. Some leave was owing to me and I spent three days of it fishing with my father, at a camp on the Montmorency River, above Quebec. It was wonderful fishing.

My mother was in England, on a short visit, and I took ship and spent four days at Elsfield with her, before setting off on my adventures. Alastair came back with me on his summer vacation from Oxford. We crossed the liner coming the other way on which my father was travelling home for a few months' leave and exchanged greetings by wireless.

Montreal was blazing hot when I reported for duty there. Our little ship was lying loaded and ready at the dock. Ralph Parsons, the fur trade commissioner of the company, gave me dinner that night. He was of the mould of the men that had built up the company, over two and a half centuries ago. Our ship was the R.M.S. *Nascopie*, which was the company's supply vessel in the Eastern Arctic. She was an ice-breaker who had done that hazardous journey for many years. She is now no more. She struck a reef in Hudson Strait a few years back. She is deeply missed by those who knew her. It was pleasant to leave the torrid heat of Montreal and launch out on the broad bosom of the St. Lawrence in that little crowded ship.

It was to be slightly more than a year before I was to see civilization again.

In sunlight we dropped down the river, which is more like a moving sea than a stream. In darkness we passed beneath the heights of Quebec, where the lights made waving paths of radiance across the water. My brother Alastair, and Pat Campbell Preston, one of my father's A.D.C.s, came out in the pilot boat and shouted good-bye. Then we were voyaging on, down the greatest body of fresh water in the world, to the salt of the Atlantic. Just clear of the Straits of Belle Isle, we saw our first big iceberg. As we ploughed steadily up the coast of Labrador the villages got fewer, and the trees got sparser, until we were following a jagged coastline of bare rock.

We turned into the inlet at Hebron, a company post built a century before by the Moravian missionaries; it was a solid building of heavy ship's timbers. Before we reached the trading post of Port Burwell on the northern tip of Labrador, pans of ice were beginning to appear, and imparted a chill to the air. If they were small we took them on our ice-breaker bows, and sent them lurching and foaming to one side, otherwise we avoided them.

Once clear of Port Burwell we were at the mouth of Hudson Strait, and headed west and north for Lake Harbour Post on the Baffin Land shore of the strait. Here and there were big fields of ice. When you were down below you felt the ship check, and very gradually lift, and as gradually subside. If you were in the bows, when we were running through ice, you watched the stem mount on the rim of the ice and then a great jagged crack would open ahead, and icy foam would hiss up through it, and the crack would widen into a channel and the ship would be on her way again. The presence of the ice called for warm clothes.

At Lake Harbour we went through the same age-old routine of unloading stores for the winter, and taking on the fur catch of the year that was passed, as we had done at the Labrador posts. But this time it was varied; for my father delivered his Chancellor's address at Edinburgh that day. I listened to it on the ship's wireless, by the light of the midnight sun. Then we slanted along Hudson Strait and headed for Sugluk, on the southern shore, and all night unloaded cargo without lights to help us, for there was no need of them. Navigation was by knowledge rather than instruments.

I was in the chart room, one evening, with the captain, and asked him to show me where we were on the chart. He looked rather scornful and pointed to a chart pinned up on a board. "That's the latest," he said, "and by that we're 150 miles inland."

A great character was Captain Smellie. He was said to be the finest ice skipper alive.

Our other calls completed, we turned to run for Cape Dorset. It was a beautiful day, still and warm, when we arrived. Chesley Russell clad in a red duffle coat, and a fur hat, strode up the gangway, red-faced, stalwart and friendly. The Eskimos paddled their kayaks up to the ship's side, and stared at us smiling.

It is an interesting moment when you meet a man with whom you are to spend a year alone, with your nearest neighbour some 350 miles away. We became fast friends very soon, and often laughed together over our first impressions of the other. Chesley's impression when we shook hands, was that I should certainly not live through the winter. My impression of Chesley, a Newfoundlander, was that he was about the toughest-looking customer I had ever seen; I was soon to learn that he was also one of the most kind-hearted of men.

Two days later, about midnight, the *Nascopie* awoke the echoes as her winches hauled up the anchor. Her engines started to churn the still surface as she slowly went about. She wished us well with a long, strident shriek of the siren, and, in a matter of minutes, we were looking at a silent empty bay, with a mountain of trade goods on the rocky shore beside us and another mountain of timber with which to build a new dwelling house. The old house had been pulled down as it was falling to pieces. The Eskimos gathered, intrigued by the sight of a new white face, cheerful and inquisitive. There was a stillness that seemed to brood over the whole land, not matched by anything that I had ever known before.

Cape Dorset Post stands on a small, rocky island, separated from the mainland by a bay less than half a mile in width. The bay opens into the strait on the east, and on the west the tides race over a narrow rocky bar. Behind are granite slopes, whose hollows fill with grass and herbage in the summer. Across the bay the mountain rises high and steeply. It is part of the rocky rampart that runs the length of the south coast of Baffin Land. Once this barrier is penetrated there is an undulating plain of tundra beyond. In the summer we needed a dinghy to cross to the mainland; in the winter the ice made island and mainland into one. There were three other white faces beside Chesley and myself, as we took stock of each other and our tasks next day.

There was Tom Manning, the explorer, and his bride of a day old. This wedding on board the *Nascopie* had been my first experience of being a best man. The ring was a copper washer out of the engine-room. They were packing up Tom's schooner to set off to explore the coast of Foxe Basin, the western boundary of Baffin Land. Then there was Herbert Figgures, whom I was replacing. He had been Chesley's companion of the previous year, and was posted to Lake Harbour. They soon went their way, leaving Chesley and me together.

When there is no darkness, there is no set period to the day's work. The mountain of trade goods on the shore gradually diminished and the store began to fill. The heavy boxes of ammunition went to the small, sentry-box-like building. The petrol and kerosene went to the fuel store. All else went into the long, low building along whose front ran the sign: "Hudson's Bay Company Incorporated 2nd May 1670". The bottom floor housed the trade goods, the loft above housed the furs. These buildings are always separate so that no single fire could destroy the ammunition, the petrol and paraffin, the trade goods and the furs, and the post manager's dwelling at one fell swoop.

The Eskimos were awaiting their annual outfit. Each Eskimo is advanced, in kind, what he needs for his hunting and trapping for the season. The measure of that advance is his proven ability to hunt and trap. They thronged the store. There seemed to be no end to the business. Rifles, ammunition, traps, tea, coffee, sugar, thread, duffle, and skeins of wool went over the counter. As fast as they emptied the shelves we had to rip open new packing cases, to meet the demand. But one by one they went their way and there were fewer tents on the beach and the pile of empty boxes grew greater. Then, when the great demand was over, the trade goods were tastefully displayed on the shelves, giving the likeness of a well-stocked general merchant's establishment, in a Scottish village.

Hither came the Eskimos from 100 miles or more of coast to trade. Those farther east traded with the post at Lake Harbour. The great company was to them one of the elements of Nature, something that seemed as old as humanity. I would defy anyone to resist the charm of the Eskimo. Ignorant of the existence of

anything but their own little world, they are the most good-
humoured of all the Queen's subjects. Childlike in many ways,
they are yet not without their wisdom. Their language is so rich
that English is a mere primitive dialect by comparison. Their
ivory carvings show a remarkable gift for creative art. But perhaps their greatest quality is to have mastered the art of always
being happy.

In addition to the trading, there was the work of sawing up
planks, and the eternal knocking of nails into boards, as our new
dwelling house slowly took shape. Then it was a non-stop life
with very little time for sleeping. The air was as keen and in-
vigorating as that of my own border hills. We felt like
work.

There was one interlude. I accompanied Herbert Figgures to
Lake Harbour. We went in the bigger of the post's two vessels—
a Peterhead schooner, which carries mainsail and jib and is
powered by an engine. We had a number of Eskimo families on
board, and their dogs as well. We hugged the granite coast of the
straits in blazing northern sunshine; loaded to the gunwales.
We came back, three Eskimos and myself, in mist and rain. The
Fur Trade Commissioner had lent me his own rifle, a sporting
model .303 Lee-Enfield, and this was my first chance to use it.
Two whole cartons of ammunition were used up on the seals who
rose to watch our passing, but with no result. I bought from the
store a .22 rifle. These were the total extent of my armament.
For shotguns are little use in the Far North; they are too easily
damaged, and you are seldom within shotgun range. You shoot
the seal and the goose with a high velocity rifle, and the hare and
the ptarmigan with a .22.

They say in the Far North that you have nine months' winter and
three months' bad going. You have in reality three seasons, and
not four—spring, autumn and winter. We had roaring gales with
rain, which brought the rollers crashing in from the straits and
pounding against the rocks of the little bay. Torrential rains
swelled streamlets which ran down the little stony glens in the
granite hills. Winter was not far off. It is the season of significance
in the North. It is then that the trapping takes place, and to trap
you must travel, and your dogs must have food.

An Eskimo husky dog may weigh anything up to ten stone, and can exert a maximum direct pull of about a quarter of a ton, He needs strong meat, and so he must have the walrus, or else the fish that the Eskimos catch when they run up the rivers in the open season. But walrus meat is far the best.

It was July 24th when the *Nascopie* arrived at Cape Dorset, and it was September 1st that we set out for the annual walrus hunt. Two days before, Jock, the policeman from Lake Harbour, had pulled into Cape Dorset, on the same errand, with his top-heavy police boat which seemed to dwarf our little schooner. It had a little brazier on which to cook, and a proper cabin, which seemed an almost Byzantine luxury. We had only a tiny fo'c'sle which was merely a covered-in space in the bows. It had a little cupboard for food, and a raised platform above the bilge running into the V of the bows, the half of which was covered by the serpentine coils of the anchor chain, and on the other half of which I slept. It smelt always of oil and bilge and of anything that might be stowed in the little hold the other side of the partition.

Our destination was Salisbury Island in Hudson Strait, which is noted for walrus. We had with us one or two Eskimo-owned boats from Cape Dorset. It was dusk when our little fleet, tumbling in an oily swell, passed under the tall crags of Salisbury Island, and we ran up a long inlet which curved at the end, and gave us a covered anchorage. Apart from the police boat, and our little Cape Dorset fleet, there were several Eskimo boats from the south side of the strait, and thus the walrus hunters assembled. We lay in that inlet for seventeen days, issuing forth early every morning, except for the few days that gales raged, and the heavy swell drove in from the strait and pounded on the rocks round us.

Jock and I would go ashore on those days, finding the rocks hard to the thin soles of our seal-skin boots. The wild geese were flying south, as they smelled the advent of winter, and there were days when the air was full of their clangour. Sometimes they would pitch close to our anchorage, in a marshy hollow, and then rise and form their V, driving south for the warmth of the south latitudes. But when the gales were not too fierce we hunted the walrus.

It was hard to keep our footing on the slippery lurching deck, when the hunt was on, as we chased the hard-pressed herds of walrus from the rock on which they lay. I have a vivid memory of ivory-headed harpoons with their seal-skin lines attached, drawn back for the throw; the crack of carbines; and the all-pervasive smell of petrol, oil and blood.

Gradually, after many adventures, we got a full load, and the night that we ran for Cape Dorset, we were perilously near going to the bottom. A raging gale blew up from nowhere, and the cold darkness was a nightmare of tumbling black waters. Autumn was on its way out.

Chesley and I had settled down to a routine of life, and there was still much to be done to the new house. But there was at least one day a week when we could take our dinghy with the outboard motor and go among the inlets, hunting seals. Chesley, like all Newfoundlanders, was a genius at handling boats. They were his true setting. At a tiller he was sublimated—a character from the Norse sagas.

We looked forward to our day's hunting. We dressed warmly, for it was getting chill. Otoochie, the Eskimo who lived beside the post, and was our one permanent employee, always came with us. He was a crack shot, though a very slow one, and would dwell on his aim for a whole minute. We would set off in the dinghy with Chesley at the outboard motor. Once clear of the little bay we had the choice of several rocky inlets to explore. Seals would put up their heads to look at us. Chesley would cut the motor and three rifles would be aimed at the strange, whiskered, wistful face looking at us so inquisitively. Sometimes, in a likely place, we would drift, waiting for them to show themselves.

The hares go white long before the snow comes. When we saw a white patch against the dun-coloured rocks we would land and pursue. We usually came home with three or four seals, and perhaps as many hares.

Between the mouths of the inlets and the bay was open sea, and an icy spray would soak into our duffle garments, so that getting back to our warm kitchen, a change of clothes, and our evening meal, was all the more delicious.

A powdering of snow came and went, and came again, and gradually the air got colder. September and October arrived and, before November was in, there was a leathery scum of ice collecting on the edge of the tides. We drew up the boats on to the shore. Gradually this scum hardened into a yielding sheet, and then into a shield, and by the second week in November we would cross the harbour on foot, on ice that was slowly deepening to its winter thickness of nearly eight feet. Autumn had gone, the days were getting shorter and the snow more frequent. A deep stillness lay over the whole land, from which life had gone. The rivers were empty of fish. The birds had sped south. There remained only the animals and the raven, the great snowy owl, and the ptarmigan, who alone of their kind face the Arctic winter.

The caribou herds had retreated deep inland. The Eskimo hunters had to go far to find them now. In that country they often encountered wolves. The Arctic wolf is far more formidable than his cousin of the forests, and the Eskimos were afraid of them. Polar bears are not very common in that part of Baffin Land. They are beautiful beasts. Against the snow they are not white but the palest of pale gold. They are almost a maritime animal, as they can swim for miles, and even for long distances under water.

For the rest, there is the white fox and the occasional blue one, the ermine weasel, and the big white Arctic hare. Then there is the humble lemming, who occupies that invidious position in the animal pyramid of being the prop and stay of the next most numerous animal, and whose function is to turn herbage into flesh to become food for the fox, the weasel and the great snowy owl. Last of all come the beasts of the sea, the walrus and the seal, and the small white whales.

30

Baffin Land in Winter

CHESLEY and I settled down pleasantly for the long dark winter. We were proud of the house that we had built. It was warm and windproof and of good proportion. We had a bedroom each and a small living-room where we had our meals, a little office where we kept the books, of which we had a fair number, a kitchen with a small kitchen range in which we burnt Nova Scotia blue coal, which the ship had brought up for us, as there is no driftwood in that part of the world, and no local fuel except seal oil. There was also a large room where the Eskimos, who had come in to trade, could sit and drink a mug of tea, and a larder. We had a very wide range of tinned food. Every Saturday night Chesley used to bake bread. We once took the temperature in the kitchen when the baking was at its height. It was 114 degrees. We supplemented the bread by caribou meat, which is better than the best beef. We also had seal meat, which, though not the finest food one can imagine, is perfectly eatable. We shot ptarmigan occasionally, and managed to get Arctic char, cousin to the sea-trout, at holes in the ice. Being winter-time, they were not at their best. In their due season we got geese and eider duck eggs.

As winter deepened so we saw less and less of the sun. By mid-winter it was not fully light until ten in the morning, and the low sun cast long mauve shadows athwart the dunes of snow. It would start to decline at two in the afternoon, and it was dark by a quarter to three. Thus we had many hours indoors in each other's company, and we found that company did not pall.

With the coming of winter our clothing had grown heavier and heavier. When we went outside now we pulled our hoods, fringed with husky dog fur, well over our faces. It was the only part of our bare skin that was exposed to the elements.

As the cold increased, so the sky seemed to change. On the

coldest days on the island trail the sun shone with a hard, yellow light with no vestige of warmth. On either side of it stood what the Eskimos call the sun dogs—two perpendicular shafts of yellow light. When they disappeared over the horizon and before night fell, the world was covered with a still, immovable orange sky, which darkened until the snow gleamed pale under the bowl of night.

The Eskimos were hard at work at their trap lines, and few came in to trade. I savoured to the full the wonderful intellectual luxury of knowing that you were completely free from any outside interruption. On the island, where the post stands, and on the mainland opposite, we had what was called our short trap line. It was about a ten-mile journey on foot to cover it, and we could just do it comfortably in daylight. Chesley's long trap line was shaped like a hairpin, and was about a 240 mile journey to get round. By the time we had done this journey often enough, the trail was dotted with the snow houses that we had built along it. We were very careful to put back the block of snow when we left a snow house, and often used the snow houses twice, and even three times to save ourselves the trouble of making new ones.

Sometimes we would be together at the post for a week, but more often we alternated—one at the post, and one on the trail for a week at a time. When we were both at the post we would wander round the short trap line together.

One of the hardest people to describe is your greatest friend. Chesley was an almost elemental figure. Strong as a bull, ungainly except in a boat, Rabelaisian, generous in the fullest sense of the word. A sturdy and most lovable companion. Opuktuk the Eskimos called him. It means "the Red". It was a reasonable name for his face was brick red, particularly about the nose which had been broken in a fracas and many times frozen, and he always wore a garment of red duffle. He was the son of a Newfoundland fisherman and at thirty-eight years of age had had twenty years in the company's service. He had very little education, but in the course of twenty northern winters had done more deep reading than many professors. He had even battled his way through to the end of *The Decline and Fall of the Roman Empire*, and other such works in which I had shamefully fallen at the first fence and never remounted. In a boat he was a Viking, taking risks for the fun of them with gusts of laughter, and roaring songs at the top of his voice. Among the Eskimos he was a leader, and not far short of a god.

Together, we sledged or we trudged on foot over many miles of snow. Together, we built the house, we traded, we did endless odd jobs, we took turns at the cooking and, with hands roughened by hard usage, grasped pens to wrestle with the accounts.

He had had many adventures. He had spent a year on Devon Island which lies north of Baffin Land. It is a dangerous country, for it has an ice cap and all the hazards of crevasses and avalanches. Once he woke up in the night there, in a snow house, and felt that his ribs were being crushed in. He lit a match. It went out. A blizzard had drifted the snow house over, and the air was almost exhausted. He managed to wake the Eskimos who were with him, who were almost drugged by asphyxia. He cut through the roof as far as his arm would reach, and then supported on his shoulders an Eskimo to reach higher. At the full extent of the Eskimo's arm the blade of the snow knife reached the outside air and they clambered up to the world of the living again, and found themselves alone under the night sky, their sledge dogs dead and buried seven feet deep.

Once he had camped with companions, beneath a precipice, and as they settled for the night, divested of their heavy clothes, had heard above them the gathering roar of an avalanche. Chesley had hurled himself against the far side of the snow house and through the breech they escaped, the first wave at their heels. They had nearly frozen to death for their warm clothes were buried under tons of snow when the fury of the avalanche subsided.

He was intensely resourceful. Once the baulk of timber, which formed one of his sledge runners, broke along the line of the lashing holes. He had taken his rifle and shot a new line of holes in the runner. That broke as well. He and a companion harnessed the dogs to a bearskin and rode home on that, clinging to their belongings and each other. They were black and blue for weeks afterwards.

Top—Chesley Russell and myself, 1938.   *Bottom*—Our schooner.

Hudson's Bay Company post, Cape Dorset, Baffinland.

Our dog-team resting, while a snow-house is built.

Eskimo encampment.

Sir John Franklin had gone down that strait by Devon Island on his last expedition. Chesley was running down the sea ice one day with his dogs. He came on a stretch of shore where Franklin had evidently stopped for a while. Four stumps showed where a wooden shack had been built. A small flag pole still stood. There were two graves. The crosses were made of ship's timbers and the blizzards of nearly a century had worn away the wood, except where the names were painted on. Thus the letters stood out embossed and readable for many yards distant. They were John Hartnell, H.M.S. *Erebus* and John Torrington, H.M.S. *Terror*.

In 1945 I was walking to Westminster to make my maiden speech in the House of Lords. I stopped to look at Franklin's statue beside the Athenaeum Club. On the plinth is inscribed the names of the crews of the two ships. I read those two names and thought of Chesley. I felt that anyhow John Hartnell and John Torrington would wish me well.

At the post I cooked the breakfast on weekdays, and Chesley on Sundays. When that was cleared we put on our heavy clothing, grabbed our rifles from the outside porch, our trapping bags and our long snow knives, and trudged off down the slope and through the rough ice, and over the ice in the bay, to our traps on the mainland, returning to do those on the island later. The rifles lived in the porch the whole winter long. They were never brought inside, as the frost in them would condense to drops of moisture which would rust. Every drop of oil was removed, which could freeze and hold the striker or jam the bolt, and instead we would graphite the inside of the breech with black pencil, which has a lubricating effect.

We carried rifles whenever we moved abroad, but except for an occasional ptarmigan or a hare, there was little to shoot at that season. We would plod together, puffing and blowing as we stumbled through the shore ice, and up the steep slope to the trapping grounds beyond. When it is really cold you must never exert yourself to the point where you puff and blow; for if the air is sufficiently cold and you draw it too fast into your lungs, it does not have time to get warm by the time it reaches them, and will cover them with white frost.

S

On we would trudge round the traps, stopping here and there to study the fresh track of a fox, or perhaps an old trail of a polar bear. Sometimes ptarmigan would rise at our feet, and we would watch their flight, until they alighted and we tried to get within shot. The sun was sinking when we got back to the post, in time for a late luncheon. We always had venison for luncheon when we could get it. We cut it into slices and put it in a large basin which was placed on top of the porch, so that the husky dogs could not get at it. Also on top of the porch reposed an enormous Christmas cake, a present to me from my father's cook at Government House. Few Christmas cakes can have survived longer than that one. It was taken down from time to time, frozen as hard as concrete, thawed out in the house and two large slices cut, which were as fresh as the day the cake had been baked. Then the cake was returned to the grip of the frost, until it was wanted again. After luncheon we would perhaps do the accounts of the post, if there were any new entries to make, and darkness would settle outside. Most of us in this busy world wish that we had more time for reading, but when your evening starts at a quarter to three in the afternoon, you find that you reach a point where you do not want to read any more. I kept a weekly diary. I have since published it, under the title of *Hudson's Bay Trader*. It was my father's suggestion. He pointed out that a beginning and an ending are the hardest tasks in literature, and no man could hope to accomplish each of them every day of the year. But it was within the bounds of possibility to do fifty-two.

We had two wireless sets, one a perfectly ordinary receiving set, and the other a short-wave sending and receiving set with a morse key. The latter could reach the wireless post at Nottingham Island, and Chesley was able to talk shop with many of his friends in the other posts along the straits, through the medium of morse. I never learnt to master the morse key properly. As regards the listening set, the reception was rarely very good. We got no news of the convulsions into which the world was being thrown. We listened hard on Saturday nights to messages from home, on a programme called the Northern Messenger, by which our families could send a short message to their relations in the far north. Chesley used to try to listen to the big ice hockey matches, but at the critical moment the reception would go dim, and he would be driven wild with frustration. I had no wish to listen to the wireless, and hear news of the outside world, when we had a very much pleasanter world of our own.

Time never hung heavily on our hands, even in the darkest part of the winter. We talked about "outside". It meant little to us, for it was an unimportant place. It was the whole of the globe except Baffin Land. We read peaceably, or talked at length, or played cards together. We sat in our shirts and braces while we rolled cigarettes and luxuriated in the warmth, pleasantly tired. We must have presented a strange picture. We shaved our heads according to the custom of the North. Chesley shaved completely. I wore a beard to keep my chin warm. As we faced each other in the lamplight across the small table, eating our evening meal or playing cards, my skinny arms were a sad contrast to Chesley's ham-like fists and great biceps. I must have looked a long wisp of a man beside his florid, four-square bulk. As the winter wore on the Eskimos began to appear with their furs. They arrived in the darkness, far on in the evening, and one of us would have to go down to the store and trade with them. We put on all our clothes, for the store was unheated, and an Eskimo who has purchasing power loves to linger deliciously over his purchases. How often have I stood behind that counter, the store dimly lit by the radiance of a hurricane lamp, my breath and the breath of my customers rising like thick smoke. The white foxes would be thrown on the counter, sometimes a rare blue fox, perhaps a few ermine weasels, sometimes a polar bear or a beautiful brindled Arctic wolf, the latter rough to the touch as a nutmeg grater.

As the advances that they received in the autumn were gradually covered by the furs that they brought in, so they had more and more to trade. The company has its own coinage in that part of the world, coins stamped with a fox's mask, and of value according to their size. We pushed the coins, to the value of his furs, across to the Eskimo, who was beaming and leaning on both elbows on the far side of the counter. Then we would stamp our cold feet in the frost while he made up his mind. He would certainly want some more cartridges, some more square plugs of tobacco, and some matches, probably some flour, some tea or coffee and some sugar. He might want some needles, some skeins of wool, perhaps a length of duffle or moleskin for clothes, and the last few coins were nearly always a present to his family. Perhaps it was some little thing for his wife to wear, or perhaps some sweets for his children. If we took an electric torch to help us in our trading, we ruined the torch because the frost destroyed the battery. Most of our trading was done within the pool of faint yellow radiance of a hurricane lamp.

The week spent on the trail was a severe one, when the frost was at its worst. It was not until half-way through the winter that we acquired one suit of deer-skin clothes, which are much warmer than any man-made garment. For the first half-dozen trips, we shivered in clothing of two thicknesses of duffle blanket which sounds warm enough, but which is no match for wind sweeping on an inland plateau, many degrees below zero. Our legs were the part that we wrapped up the warmest. We had a thick pair of stockings, and over them a long stocking made of blanket which came up above the knee, then there was a slipper of blanket, and another slipper of deer skin, and then a seal skin boot, but even so I was many times on the verge of freezing my feet.

The start was in the chilly darkness of the early morning. The big sledge had long runners of solid baulks of timber. These were shod with steel, which was in turn covered with mud, boiled up, and applied in layers which froze solid and was then smoothed. Each morning they had water applied which made a skin of ice to make them slide well on the snow crust. The same application of mud remained all winter.

A few hundred yards along the shore lived our single permanent employee, the charming and genial Otoochie. He lived there with his wife and family. He had a small, smiling son who was allowed to go hunting hares with a .22 rifle. His father spoilt him, as all Eskimos spoil their children, and had made for him a miniature sledge which was pulled by a team of husky puppies.

Otoochie would be there with the dogs in harness, a dim outline in the freezing darkness, bending over the lashings of the sledge which carried our two sleeping bags, the sacks of walrus meat for the dogs, all lashed on beneath a polar bear skin which was the covering for our snow house floor. At the front of the sledge was a large box which contained our food, the primus stove and its fuel, and sundries such as mugs and spoons. This was lashed on very securely; and across the top was lashed a bar which we could put our weight against and give direction to the sledge, when we were negotiating a difficult place in the rough ice. The last things to be packed were our rifles in their seal-skin covers, which were poked under the lashings, where we could get at them if we needed them in a hurry.

The dogs would be howling to get off by this time, eighteen of them, each with an independent trace which met a double walrus hide line, called a bridle, some ten feet ahead of the sledge. From the steering bars there hung a long walrus hide whip, sixteen feet in length, which in the hands of an expert would cut through a two inch wooden board.

When we were ready and perched on the sledge, the dogs would be off in a mad gallop into the darkness. The sea ice, where it meets the shore, lies in a great jumble, for the tide was fifteen feet high at Cape Dorset. Great pieces, like part of a giant's jig-saw puzzle, lay unevenly heaped along the shore line. Through this we rocked and swayed and bounded, and then we were on the smooth surface of the snow-covered sea ice. You sit sideways on an Eskimo sledge, and your loads are high enough for your feet to be above the snow.

The dogs, when fresh, would go like the wind down the bay, and out through the entrance, and along the coast till we came to the point of shore where we struck inland. As it got light, the sky would be filling with radiance, and the dog's breath would rise in orange clouds.

The whole of the first day was spent in getting through the coastal range of granite hills. It was a world of purest white, except where the wind had whipped the snow from the edge of a cornice of rock. Moustache and beard and eyelashes would be hoary with the frost. We would glance occasionally at each other's faces, for the small white patches of frostbite. Contrary to the long-established belief, it is the greatest mistake to rub snow on frostbite. We would draw a hand from a seal-skin mitt, and hold it for a matter of a second or two against the patch to thaw it. A second longer and you felt that your hand had been gripped by steel claws as the frost seized hold of it, and you would thrust it back into the warm lining of duffle, surrounded by fur.

When we were travelling in those winter months, it was too cold to halt to make a cup of tea. In fact we only ate one real meal a day, and that was in the evening, when we had camped. We kept going as hard as we could while the light lasted, to get as much of our journey behind us as possible.

It is not easy to remember discomfort in detail, after the passage of years, but I do remember on the inland trail, thinking that my friends of school and university who went daily to offices in London, or stamped about on barrack squares, whose lives I had always previously considered dreary beyond belief, where probably in a more enviable situation than I was.

Darkness brought a close to travelling. But one night there arose, like a great spectral curtain draped across the sky, the Aurora Borealis. Never have I seen it so clear. We travelled for nearly five hours by its light, and then, dogs and men alike, we were so nearly dropping of fatigue that we halted, and built ourselves a snow house for the night by its brilliance. That day we must have covered well over seventy miles.

Making camp on the winter trail is an exacting routine when you are tired, and hungry, and frost-bitten. Very few white men can make a snow house, and that was left to Otoochie. We would seek the right kind of snow with which to build it. And snow is not just snow in the North. It comes in as many different kinds as cheese. First there is the hard, wind-packed snow in which your heavy sledge will often not even leave a track. Then there is that soft, new-fallen, undriven, snow in which the feet of the dogs sink and the sledge runners wallow. It is like going through cotton wool, feet deep. The snow of the snow house must be of a certain, even strength, but soft enough for you to get the blade of your snow knife into it, to cut the blocks. The blocks that go to build a snow house all come from the area of snow it covers, and thus when you are in it you are two feet below the level of the surrounding snow, and out of the wind.

Otoochie used to cut his blocks deftly and surely, in perfect lines. He would set them in a circle, then add tier upon tier until there was a single space at the top in which the last block was driven. In this a hole was cut for ventilation. Such is the tensile strength of the structure, that you can walk to the top of it, and it will bear your weight.

While all this was going forward, I was unharnessing the dogs, unhitching their traces from the bridle and coiling them up, then heaping them on the top of the snow house for the night. Two more blocks would be cut, and the sledge laid across, runners upwards, after all the impedimenta had first been removed. The dogs gathered round while the sledge was being unpacked, an eye on the sacks of walrus meat.

When the snow house was finished, Otoochie would creep inside, and, in the gathering dark, it would suddenly begin to glow like a lighted mushroom with the radiance of the candle that he had lit. The bear skin and the two deer skins would be passed through the entrance to him and laid on the floor, then the box with the food and the fuel, the sleeping bags, and the bags of dog food, which must be kept away from where the dogs could reach them and rip them up. Lastly the foxes from the traps, frozen in the attitudes in which they had died.

The rifles in their seal-skin cases had joined the traces on top of the snow house, for they could not be exposed to the warmth. The final task was the feeding of the dogs. We would open the neck of a big sack of dog food, as heavy a weight as one could lift at that time of the day, and walk backwards showering its contents on the snow in front of us while they leapt at it like wolves. It has never been finally established whether wolves are huskies gone wild, or huskies are tamed wolves. At feeding time our minds came back to this question. Half a bag of food was their ration. You never give a husky dog as much as he can eat. They could have eaten five times that amount with ease, but we should have got no travelling out of them the next day.

Then, at last, I would join Otoochie in the snow house, with one last chore to do, the beating of the snow out of our clothes. The fur of our seal skin trousers and our boots had to be freed of it, or it would melt and soak them once the primus had been lit. That last ritual over, the primus was lit.

I will always associate the hissing of the primus and its claw-like flames with all that luxury means. In a matter of minutes ice had gone from beard and moustache. In a few minutes more we could divest ourselves of our frocks with hood attached, which they call "a dicky" in the North. Then off came our seal-skin pants and seal-skin boots. We sat on a floor carpeted with furs, leaning back against our rolled-up sleeping bags, in stock-inged feet and rolled-up sleeves, basking in the heavenly warmth and rolling a cigarette.

The new-made snow house threw back the light from a myriad pinpoints so that it looked like a fairy palace, and, for the duration of one wonderful cigarette, I lost myself in a luxury which drove out even the recollection of the day's hardship. Then the dixie was produced and some snow shaved from the walls and melted, and the pleasant business of cooking supper would begin. Usually it was deer meat, or perhaps a tin of stew with ship's hard tack biscuits, and a large handful of seedless sultanas as dessert.

Then we would sip our big enamel mugs of black coffee, and smoke and talk until we were drowsy. We talked of everything under the sun that the limits of my knowledge of Eskimo would allow. We talked of everything to do with the land in which we lived. We talked of marriage, of foxes, of the primeval race of Eskimo Picts, of ghosts, and of anything that came into our heads. Occasionally I would try to tell him about the world outside, but generally abandoned the explanation for no con-ceivable basis of comparison existed.

He told me a ghost story that I have never forgotten. It con-cerned a friend of his. This man was riding his dog team on the inland plateau, when he chanced to look up and see a dog team on the white horizon approaching him at right angles. It was a long way off. That was a strange thing, for he knew of no one who would be setting traps in that part of the world. He looked up a few minutes later, and to his consternation saw this other team was almost on him. It was travelling at a speed that was not of this world. At that moment his own dogs stopped, threw themselves down and wallowed in paroxysms of fear on the snow. On came the team like a whirlwind. A man sat on the sledge facing forwards. As it hurtled past him the figure on the sledge turned towards him and threw back his hood. His was a face so terrible that the Eskimo would wake shrieking in the night when he dreamed of it afterwards. Then it passed, and he watched the team disappear into the gathering dusk. There had been no sound from the dogs' feet, although he clearly heard the swish of the snow along the runners. It left no track. This man came home and told his story. He had no doubt but that it portended his own death. Chesley had tried to reason with him, but to no avail.

The following spring that man was hunting seals at the floe edge. He lost his footing and the tide bore him away beneath the ice.

Otoochie was a charming character, always happy with the beaming happiness of a child. His skin was brown and his face Mongolian, like all his race. He wore his hair as they all did— bobbed. It was beautiful hair and would catch the sheen of the light like a raven's wing. He had a natural politeness, which is a quality of nearly all of his race, and which I never saw matched in the world outside. As we conversed, becoming drowsier with warmth, he would carry on his conversation in words that he knew that I knew. He could tell a story well. He would speak of his childhood when the caribou were so plentiful that they came right down to the coast, and they could then be ambushed with arrows.

The predecessors of the present-day Eskimos were a race of Eskimo pigmies, who died out many hundreds of years ago. Otoochie would not talk of them much, he seemed to feel that they belonged to an eerie world and, like ghosts, were not to be lightly discussed.

Chesley heard a strange story from one of the Eskimos who had gone several hundred miles inland after caribou. He had been riding his team when his dogs had bolted towards a little mound. He had laid the whip over them, and stolen up the side of the mound with his rifle at the ready, expecting to find a sleeping bear on the top. He reached the top, and there rose from behind a rock not six feet away, a tiny man, bow in hand, who pulled an arrow to his ear pointed at the Eskimo's heart.

"Why didn't you shoot?" said Chesley. "He drew on you first."

The Eskimo shook his head. His rifle had fallen from nerveless hands, his knocking knees just got him to his dog team and for close on a hundred miles he lashed his dogs to get away from that place. Chesley had cross-examined him very carefully, but could not shake him on any detail of his account. It was a strange story, and probably true, for these Eskimos never tell lies in any circumstances.*

Otoochie was a wonderful language master, for if one ventured into some ambitious sally in the intricacies of Eskimo grammar, he would admit that it was a sage remark, and then, with a most charming smile, say what you had said as it should have been said, under his breath but just audibly.

When tiredness became too much for us both, we would unroll our eiderdown sleeping bags and climb into them. It is a curious scientific fact that the more clothes you take off, the warmer you are, in an eiderdown bag. But you were sobered by the thought of having to put them on again next morning, and so took off as little as possible. Last thing of all we put out the primus and blew out the candle. Then the frost that had been kept at bay came in, but by that time we were asleep.

And thus the winter passed and gradually the light lasted longer, and the sun grew brighter and gilded the snow. There was no warmth in it as yet, but the turn of the year was coming. The northern spring was on its way, all the more precious when it comes, for its footsteps are so laggard in the coming.

* Alas, this is no longer true.

31

Northern Spring

THE Arctic Islands in winter are a land of silence, a silence which is not oppressive, but soothing. It is not the silence of the mere suspension of noise, but of the absence of any means by which noise can be created. Three birds only spend the winter in Baffin Land, as I have mentioned earlier. One is the great snowy owl whose legs are clad in warm white feathers. The second is the ptarmigan which is similarly trousered. The third is the raven, bare-legged and scantily clad, probably the hardiest bird in the world. And these make no noise. The moving dog team makes its own noise; the runners hiss in the soft snow, or clatter and whine across the stretches where the wind packs it to the hardness of ice; there is the thud of the dogs' feet, and the noise of their breathing and an occasional snarling wrangle between them. But when you are out of earshot of the team there is silence, complete and absolute. Sometimes snow falls with a faint tinkle from the over-hanging cornice of a tall drift, many times higher than your head, but otherwise there is only the thud of your seal-skin boots on the snow.

Alone in that waste of snow-covered granite there is no feeling of loneliness. But sometimes a feeling akin to awe will lay hold of you, the feeling of being a tiny spark of human life afoot in this unearthly hyperborean waste, which would require so little to extinguish.

On the grey days, when the lowering snow clouds lie heavily on the land, you are in a world of no shadows.

Gradually, with the New Year, the light lasts longer, and you do not have to build your snow house quite so early in the afternoon. The coming of warmth, with the lengthening light, is a wearily slow process. As the days pass you become aware that you are screwing up your eyes more and more when the sun shines, for its strength is waxing greater. But the moment comes when you realize, with something akin to shock, that a pheno-menon has occurred and that, for a matter of half an hour, the temperature has risen above freezing. You have to attend to the dogs' harness frequently, for they cross and re-cross each other, and plait their traces together, and you suddenly realize, as you labour, that you are sweating in your heavy clothes. Then the frost grips again and you wonder whether you have not imagined it all. Then the time comes round, when, after a day's travel in the sun, you come into the shade and are conscious of seeing strange colours in front of your eyes, and that is the time to put on your sun goggles. That comes some time in the month of March. From then onwards you never move without them.

I crept out of a snow house one morning, on all fours, to see six fat ptarmigan not 100 yards away. I loaded my rifle and made towards them. Then, quite suddenly, my eyes began to stream and I called to Otoochie to lead me back into the comforting darkness again. That was a warning. If you get snow-blinded you suffer the tortures of the damned, and must sit in darkness with streaming eyes, for days on end. The sun striking low, and ever more powerful, turns your face almost black with sunburn. When the skin peels off, a new fresh skin is there beneath, and all the marks and blemishes of the frostbite of the winter trail have disappeared with the skin you have shed.

At the beginning of April I set off with Otoochie and the dogs to visit our neighbours at Lake Harbour. We loaded the sledge with everything we should need for about six nights on the trail, and away we went. The coast of Baffin Land is jagged along its southern shores. Thus for some part of the way we would travel on the sea ice, and then we would take to the shore to cut across the big headlands, and then take to the sea ice again.

The Eskimos, who traded with us, had their little villages of snow houses down beside the shores, and there were many calls to make on the journey.

Pitsulak was a most able, attractive, and energetic man. He was slim, with an alert, intelligent face. He excelled all others as a hunter and a trapper and a sailor of boats.

We spent the first night in Pitsulak's snow house. He had

two baby polar bears which he had captured. One slept in the snow house of another Eskimo, the other had a snow house of his own. The latter had enjoyed the hospitality of Pitsulak's roof, but his snores woke the baby, and so a snow house had been built especially for him.

One Eskimo encampment was very like another. There was the same huddle of snow houses which, when it was dark and the seal oil lamps were lit within, gave the village the look of an encampment of gnomes living in illuminated toadstools. Sledges were laid up athwart two snow blocks. Harpoons, fish spears, and ice lances bristled from the surrounding snow. Politeness dictated that we shook the hand of every man, woman and child in the village. A small largess of sweets and biscuits was made to the children.

It was exciting for the children to see a white man, as most of them had never been to the post. They would stare at me, their eyes dark as grapes. The Eskimos are an exceedingly sociable people. Whoever was our host for the night, would sit us down beside the seal oil lamp, and the Eskimos of the village, as many as could possibly squeeze into the dwelling, would sit round and ask for the news. As we got farther down the coast there was more and more news to give; an old woman had died; a well-known hunter had lost his footing on the edge of the floe and disappeared; a baby had been born; a boy had had an accident with a snow knife and cut off his thumb, and so it went on.

Sometimes on that journey the sky would clear and we could see for miles on the trail. At others the world was so shrouded in snow gloom that we could hardly see 100 yards. At times it got quite hot, and the runners dug deep into the snow as we walked beside the sledge. Sometimes the soft snow was blown around us by a strong wind, and the glancing sun turned it to all the colours of the spectrum.

One night darkness found us far out on the sea ice, and we made a comfortable snow house and settled down for the evening. It was rather strange to reflect that one was lying down to sleep in a little house with six feet of snow below you, eight feet of ice below that, and many fathoms of Arctic sea beneath it all.

We dropped down on Lake Harbour Post, from the high ground behind it, and for two or three days relaxed in the luxury of conversation, and the hospitality of the North was showered on me. Jimmy Bell from Grantown-on-Spey was in charge. He was jovial and elephantine. His brother was a gamekeeper at Balmoral. Herbert Figgures and Jock, the policeman, I already knew. I do not think I ever enjoyed a visit so much.

Going home was a slow business. The temperature had risen, and our progress was painfully slow. The sun when it shone had real warmth, and the dogs went at a foot pace hauling the sledge through snow which seemed as resistant as new bread.

After seven days of slogging we arrived at Cape Dorset. It was just after midday. Chesley was sitting in his chair reading a book. He led me to a looking-glass which was something I had not seen for a week. My beard was bleached nearly white with the power of the spring sun.

I had one other long spring trip, this time to the ice of Foxe Channel. Otoochie and I spent a night with the patriarch of those parts, a splendid, dignified old man called Saila, whose camp was on the distant coast. He had three large snow houses joined together, with windows in the roof made of seals' intestines. The squalor of the interior had to be seen to be believed, but you do not become unduly fussy when you live with the Eskimos. Here was fulfilled a long cherished ambition, for from that group of snow houses the land slipped down to the ice of the Foxe Basin. I had pored over the map of Baffin Land in my Oxford days and had been drawn to this part of it. Here the coast was shown as a dotted line, a mere conjecture of its shape denoting that it was unmapped.

These people do not have an idea of hereditary chieftainship, but Saila had almost the powers of a chief by virtue of the position that his own character had won for him. He was a man who had lived long and seen much, an opinion to be respected, and thus to be obeyed. The object of our journey was to search for some asbestos, of which an Eskimo had shown me a sample. We took a guide with us from Saila's entourage. We had no difficulty in finding the place, but our journey had taken longer than we thought, and we had very little dog feed left when we started home. The sun was warm, the snow was soft, and the dogs were short of food. We did 100 miles at a walking pace, and Otoochie and I had to walk every step of the way. We shot ptarmigan, which fortunately were plentiful, but they did not go far with eighteen gaunt, famished dogs. Eventually, while we were building a snow house, one dog chewed several feet off the walrus hide whip.

We were glad to see home again, for we were weary and hungry. It is pleasant to return from the trail to the comfort of four walls, and move freely again without heavy clothes. It was pleasant to wash, and change, and sit down to a table with a knife and fork, talk your own language again, and sleep in a bed.

But now spring had gathered momentum, and the floe ice, stretching from the shore out into the straits, was breaking up at the edges. The rivers that ran from the lakes in the high ground, and rushed down the little valleys to the sea, had been silent in the grip of frost all winter long. But now patches of rock were showing through the snow, and gradually first one stream and then another began to flow again, and there came the sound of running water, and it was a land of silence no longer.

Driving up from the south, in great wedges, came the geese; the Canada, the greater and lesser snow geese, the blue and the brent, headed for their breeding grounds which lay just inland from us. We had good hunting now. On the trail there were ptarmigan, white as the snow itself, betrayed by their boot-button eyes. They were good eating and we nearly always got one or two in the course of a day's travel. When the geese came we would go inland and, finding them by their clamour, would stalk them on the marshy flats with our big rifles. We seldom got closer than 150 yards. With Otoochie and another Eskimo I spent one glorious sunny day stalking them, and following them to the next pitching place to stalk them again. We got a Canada goose, two blue geese and one greater snow goose.

On the floe edge we would sit and wait for seals to bob up. Often it was warm enough to roll up our sleeves. We sat with a canoe beside us, as the floe was breaking up, and great chunks broke off without warning, sometimes acres in extent. If you float away on an ice pan, you will never float back.

The world was ringing with life now, and sparkling with the newly risen sun. The breeze on our faces no longer seared, but gently caressed. Up the little rivers, now freed from the winter-long burden of ice, the Arctic char ran in their myriads. For some reason I had never brought a fishing rod, and by no means could I improvise one. A three-pronged fish spear is a poor substitute.

The big white falcons returned. Then came flocks of eider ducks, and wading birds which I could not identify. There were gulls again, the big glaucous gull, and sometimes the delicate ivory gull. The air was full of the sound of birds and running water; and a faint smell of moorland was in the air.

This is a busy time for the fur trader, as the packing and baling of the furs, the inventories, and a great deal of book work has to be done. Then there is the painting of the outside wood-work, which must be done before the mosquitoes appear. It is strange that in that far northerly land, mosquitoes should be such a scourge, but for anything up to a fortnight they make life almost unendurable.

The darkness had gone and we could read at midnight. Chesley and I could sleep only by rigging up blinds over our windows. The snow was going and, in the valleys, grasses and boggy herbage were springing up. The granite slopes became studded with plants like pin cushions. Nicholas Polunin, an Oxford friend and now a famous botanist, had given me a flower press. I religiously collected grasses and plants. One turned out to be new to science and is now known as "Tweedsmuir's catspaw".

Soon the ice in the straits was a floating jigsaw puzzle, and in the bay formed a floating sheet that went hither and thither with the tides, daily growing smaller. It was a long time before it was small enough to float out through the narrow entrance. I took the schooner to try to get to the wireless post of Notting-ham Island, which lies next to the island of the walrus hunting grounds. We were unlucky. Pitsulak was with me, and two other Eskimos. As far as the eye could see there were pans of ice, of all sizes, motionless in the straits. A puff of wind would set them moving. A strong wind could set them grinding, and then the schooner would be crushed like an egg-shell between strong fingers. We turned back regretfully.

There was little left in the store with which to trade. The last fur had been brought in. May became June, and June became July. Chesley and I did not talk much of the coming of the ship. We did not want to think of the breaking up of our friendship. How often we had sat and faced each other across the small table at which we ate our meals. I had grown so used to Chesley's outline. His broad shoulder, his strong arms and his huge hands, and his cheerful red face with its odd-shaped nose. We had discussed, at one time or another, almost every subject in the world. We had laughed, we had sorrowed, we had rioted, but we had never quarrelled. Clad in his red duffle coat, he seemed a symbol of leadership in that strange northern land. He loved the Eskimos whom he looked after, and was loved by them in return.

It was sad, too, to leave that simple and delightful people, a people with a civilization appropriate to the strange circumstances of their life. A people intensely friendly, and of wonderfully good manners, which are now becoming so sadly uncommon in the civilized world; and, with all this a childlike simplicity, which is really no more than a lack of that tedious sophistication in which civilization indulges.

July was just ending, and August beginning, when the ship came; looking strangely alien in our little bay from which the ice had now departed. It looked very big and black, and made so much noise with its anchor chain. Chesley and I went out in our best clothes in the dinghy with the outboard motor. Ralph Parsons, the Fur Trade Commissioner, took us to his cabin, and we talked. Now that I had done a year in the Far North, I was to serve the next year in a post in the forest, among the Indians, or such was the company's intention. Then we got down to business, and overboard went all the next year's supplies, and inboard came our catch of last year. The post was inspected, the passengers and the crew wandered round our little group of buildings, which we had painted and furbished to look their best.

T

We said good-bye—at the top of the gangway. It was with a heavy heart that I watched Chesley's broad back go down the steps. Then, in a matter of minutes, we were moving ourselves. Eskimos in their kayaks paddled beside us and waved, the others grouped on the shore, Chesley's sturdy red figure among them. And then we were out of the bay, and into the straits and headed back into the big world, which for a year we had talked of as something vague and unimportant—called "outside".

32

Active Service

IN the distances of Baffin Land, no rumour of war came to disturb the even tenor of life. When the *Nascopie* nosed its way into the harbour of Cape Dorset a flood of disquieting news had been unleashed. As we sailed south and unloaded stores at the posts on our way, one grim item of news was piled upon another.

Hudson's Bay was calm. Early in the morning, of the day that we reached Churchill, we saw a mother polar bear and her two cubs on the floating ice. That evening, in the clear northern dusk, we steamed into Churchill Harbour. Strange seem the works of man after a year alone with the works of nature. There was a great grain elevator. There was the railway spur on which my father's two private coaches were standing. There were buildings of various sorts varying from the large and solid down to the wooden shack. Husky dogs roamed about, hungry and tormented by flies. There were Eskimo and Indian faces. My father and mother and my brother Alastair were waiting on the quay. Nothing in the world is easier than to slip back into comfort. It was strange to see polar bears on the floating ice in the early morning and to dine in a dinner jacket on the same evening, and drink your first glass of wine for a year.

Next day the train pulled out. We rocked our way at a leisurely pace through the barren lands, and then, raggedly at first, the forest began. We halted at little stations whose centre of life is the Hudson's Bay Company post. We had a little time on our hands. We went west from the Pas, the first sizeable town, into the wheat lands and across them and on beyond to the rising country which cradles the Peace River. It was still possible to make out a case that war might be averted, but deep down there could be no question about it.

My father and I had had many golden days fishing together.

They started twenty years before when I caught my first trout in Kilbucho Burn. The last was on Maligne Lake in the Rockies, where the mountains soared upwards from the lake shore, with their sparse covering of tall lean pines thinning away to bare stony summits. The lake was so clear that we could see the bottom anywhere. We caught four trout and those were not large. Much of our time was spent in stalking a bull-moose, who clattered down over the stony beach and stood up to his belly in the lake. He sunk his great bladed horns out of sight, rooting for water lilies. Every now and then he lifted a dripping head to munch the weeds he had pulled up. We got within twenty feet of him before he seemed to notice us. He gave a long stare, tossed his great bladed horns and withdrew his huge bulk, dripping on to the shingle. Then the forest hid him. We took down our rods. Our last day, like all the rest, had been very happy.

As we packed up our belongings a trail rider rode on to the shingle on the far side of the lake. The crunch of pony's hooves on the shingle reached us, as it strode into the waters up to its girths and started drinking. The rider was a small man wearing a wide-brimmed sombrero hat, with his bandy legs encased in leather chaps. A ring widened across the still waters from where the pony stood. The rider sat his beast as if he was one with it. His right arm was extended to ease the reins, while it drank. Four years later that right arm was round my waist, as, utterly disregarding his own safety, he supported me down 200 yards, of sun-baked Sicilian hillside, while a German machine-gunner from not 100 yards away, followed us faithfully with his sights, nearly deafening us as his bullets cracked like whips in our ears.

It was a far cry from that still lake in the cool mountain twilight, to the din of battle when blue skies and bare hillsides rocked before my eyes, and the blood ran and ran and would not be stayed.

That trail rider was Tommy Waitt. He was usually called Rusty, because of his auburn hair. He was widely known in that part of the world as a marksman. He came to me as a batman at Aldershot in February 1940, a week after my father had died in Canada. We parted only when we were demobilized. Among a race of marksmen he was one of the deadliest I have ever seen with rifle or pistol. His companionship made the war bearable.

Without him this book could not have been written.

We spent several pleasant days in the Peace River country among the hospitable folk who live there, many of whom Alastair and I were destined to meet again in the circumstances of war. On the way back the train broke down at a wayside station. According to western custom, most of the inhabitants had come to watch the train come in. A very old man was leaning on a stick, wearing a strange, sombrero-like straw hat, and smoking a pipe with a bent stem. He had a long white moustache, and was enjoying the August sunshine.

"Good morning," I said.

There was no answer. I repeated it louder, and there was no sign of recognition; and yet louder still, but no flicker crossed his brown wrinkled face.

A woman turned to me, middle-aged and going grey. "It is no use talking to him," she said. "He's my dad; he's deaf. He's not heard anything since Bull Run."

It was strange to stand in that clear sunlight and reflect that we were on the brink of a fearful war, and here beside us was a man who had seen smoke rise from very different weapons, on a civil war battlefield that had seen the greatness of Jackson and Lee.

We reached Ottawa at the end of August, and then, at breakfast time one morning, we were at war. Alastair joined a cavalry regiment, and I resigned from the Hudson's Bay Company, and joined the Governor-General's Foot Guards on the same day.

The recollection of a year in northern tranquillity was precious as I pored over a manual on how to become a soldier at short notice, and did arms drill in a blue suit while my uniform was being made. Having risen no higher in the Eton O.T.C. than 2nd Senior Private, there was a lot to learn and a very short time to learn it.

The First Canadian Division sailed in early December of 1939. My regiment was not in the First Division, but I came over as a very junior officer on General MacNaughton's staff. Halifax Harbour was cold, and still, and sparkling with frost, as we pulled out in the big liners painted with funereal drabness. The battleship *Resolution* ploughed steadily along beside us. The crossing was calm and, as often happens, the air was much milder than on either shore.

The snow lay thick on the mountains of Bute as we steamed up the Clyde, and the clammy chill of a Scottish winter made men to whom sub-zero weather was part of life, shiver and wrap their overcoats tighter round them.

At Christmas I was fortunate enough to get some leave, to stay with my sister Alice and her husband Brian Fairfax-Lucy, in the most beautiful and tranquil part of the Cotswolds. It was pleasant, after long gazing on northern distances, to look up the wolds, patterned with neat stone walls and, as evening fell, to see in the stubble fields the silhouette of the cock pheasant, pompous and furtive, and hear the rasp of a partridge calling.

Because we had so much to learn we worked at a furious tempo during that first winter. Troops are not trained in a few weeks, or even in a few months—however great their enthusiasm, and the enthusiasm of the First Canadian Division could not easily have been exceeded. A small stocky man of the Edmonton Regiment was pointed out one day who had travelled some 300 miles on foot to join up, and there were many others like him.

One night at the end of January I was Duty Officer, and making myself as comfortable as I could in our bare and cramped Headquarters, when a telegram arrived for me. It said briefly that my father was mortally ill and was not likely to recover. I stared at it with disbelief. To me, he was something beyond the touch of time or age, too strong a stem for the Reaper's blade. But in the days that followed other telegrams came, and I put through a call on the transatlantic telephone and talked to Alastair, who was still training with his regiment at Ottawa.

That Sunday I went over to Elsfield, where my grandmother, Mrs. Grosvenor, was living. Things seemed slightly better from the last news that we had. There was enough hope on which to lay hold, but that night the nine o'clock news said that his condition was grave.

It was a very cold, frosty night. I got back to Aldershot at about eleven o'clock. I went to my room, and had just started to undress, when one of my brother officers, Darrell Laing, opened the door and told me the news—he was dead. It was a blow which stunned me for six solid months. The only variant to hard military work was the answering of hundreds of letters which poured in, from all sorts and conditions of people. The world will forgive most things, but it finds it very hard to forgive success; but they had undoubtedly forgiven him.

During the rest of that cruel winter I managed to steal one or two short visits to Elsfield. Jack Allam was his old self, and was a stepping-stone to the happy carefree Elsfield of our childhood. The cold was so intense that it was possible to walk up to a flock of pigeons in an open pasture field to within range, but they were not worth eating when we shot them—wretched, thin creatures with breast-bones as sharp as knives.

A friend of mine on leave, at Brechin, took his gun down to the woods to shoot pigeons one frosty evening, and found the woods full, not only of pigeons, but of grouse as well, huddling for shelter. Just as the whole world of man was in torment, so the world of wild life was riven by disaster. My mother and my brother Alastair returned from Canada. She joined my grandmother at Elsfield and took it over once more.

Spring was late in coming that year, and with it came the fall of France. It was serene summer weather, as no one is likely to forget. Without it, the men would never have got off Dunkirk beaches. The First Canadian Division got as far as embarking on paddle boats at Dover to go across, and then the order was cancelled. But we crossed to Brest a week later, and had got quite far inland when the surrender brought us back across the Channel again.

We were withdrawn and concentrated, incredible to relate, within five miles of Elsfield. The Canadian soldiers hobnobbed with the Oxfordshire villagers. Canadian officers carried out reconnaissance of the higher ground and the few natural vantage points. Guns and lorries scattered dust in the narrow lanes that were drowsy with summer. Then we moved south.

We formed a Canadian Corps, and our Headquarters was a big house outside Leatherhead in Surrey. This whole formative period was one of gruelling hard work, for we had still much to learn, and, had at the same time, to be at readiness to fight on our own ground if Hitler landed.

The countryside had come to mean something different. Woods were points of defence, and not the home of birds and beasts. Stretches of water might or might not contain wild fowl; now it was important to know whether or not they would prevent the passage of tanks, and this long drawn period of suspense covered the winter of 1940 and all of 1941, when I spent the summer at the Staff College, and the winter commanding a company of Canadian Seaforth on the high ground above Brighton.

The spring of 1942 was spent in Hampshire, at Odiham aerodrome within a mile of that admirable little trout stream, the White Water. Then back to Leatherhead again for all the summer and all the winter. The spring of 1943 brought me to Oxford to live again in my old college which was now the Senior Officer's School. It was strange poetic justice to have spent four years at Brasenose living high and doing no work, only to return there nine years later to spend four months living austerely and working extremely hard. David Wedderburn and I used to spend the spring evenings at Elsfield and walk back together after dark. My grandmother had died in 1940. My mother was at Elsfield alone.

I got a week's leave there in June. I enjoyed two days of it. Returning late the second evening from the Cherwell, with my dry-fly rod and two good-sized chub, I found a telegram waiting for me. It informed me briefly that I had been made second-in-command of the Hastings and Prince Edward Regiment, and was to proceed at once to join them in Hamilton, in Scotland. They were strangers to me, and I was a stranger to them. But not many weeks were to pass before I felt more completely one of them than of any group of men I have ever known in my life. For they were countrymen, and we saw life through the same eyes.

After two frantic exercises, in which we captured the stretch of beach between Prestwick and Troon in Ayrshire—as most closely resembling the Sicilian beach which was our target—

I got two days' leave and went to Peebles. I borrowed a rod from Mr. Veitch, the tackle-maker, and cast a dry fly in the waters below Neidpath Castle in the clear June sunshine. Four days later we detrained at Glasgow and we went down to the ships. Then on an afternoon of beautiful sunshine, which turned the waters of the Clyde to purest blue, the big convoy set off, on what was at that time, the greatest combined operation in history.

Much had happened since we landed in the Clyde in December 1939, which we were now leaving in June of 1943. Time had passed quickly in the midst of so many and such curious activies. Every leave I had gone back to Elsfield for a precious week, and the hurry and bustle of the Army had been partly forgotten in watching for the shapes of the pigeons through the sprawling branches of the oak trees. Each of those autumns had been crowned by a beautiful Indian summer. The evening sunlight had turned the pastures to gold, as Jack Allam and I had walked down to Noke Wood to await the vanguard of the pigeon flocks.

Periods of leave in winter were always spent in the same way, in old clothes, with a gun under my arm; though often it was a cartridge belt worn over a battledress. Sometimes, stalking the pigeon on the roots when it was very cold, and always a stand in Noke Wood at dusk. It was ineffably peaceful to hear the strike of Beckley Church clock and see the moon climbing through the branches as the few cock pheasants clattered their way up to roost. In the silence of the wood I could momentarily forget the war, but only momentarily. It had become an environment which pervaded everything. Like the nagging remembrance of a debt unpaid. In the stillness of the wood every footfall was magnified on the carpet of dead leaves, brittle with the frost. The heavy lumbering tread of the cock pheasant, the noisy shuffling of the grey squirrel on the ground, or the sound of the blackbird or robin turning over the leaves in search of some bleak fare.

I always stayed on long after it was too dark to shoot, and the last pheasant had crowed and settled down to sleep. My shotgun came to be a symbol of short spells of rest and peace, as it had been a glorious symbol of holiday time as a schoolboy.

Leave in the summer months was always spent fishing for chub. It meant walking to the river, which was more than a mile away. On one occasion a troop of the Sherwood Foresters was quartered in our stables, and they gave me a lift to the river in a Humber armoured car. The War Agricultural Committee were busy dredging the River Cherwell. Fishing was only possible upstream of them, for below they left a fishless and sterile canal. Once Jack Allam and I borrowed a punt from a farmer, and slowly made our way upstream for a matter of two miles, to where the river runs under a little bridge and flows almost like a trout stream.

On one side is the beautiful old manor house of Water Eaton, looking across the line of willows that bordered the river to a big field called Sparsey. Big chub were on the feed, and unimpeded by the willows, one could flick a Red Palmer under every bush and tree root. We got two big chub. The biggest was three and a half pounds, and I saw him gently breaking the water where a hawthorn bush made a pool of shadow on it. We lost two more big ones, and came back well satisfied. This stretch, and a large green field which is an island and is called Mill Meadow, which was the nearest point of the river to Elsfield, was our happy hunting ground. The chub may not be a noble fish, but he is shy and watchful, and you fish for him in all the glory of an English summer early morning, or as the sun goes down, when the air is drenched with luscious scents which no other countryside in the world can boast.

In 1943 the dredger was almost up to Sparsey, leaving only a short fishable stretch, and only now in 1952 has the river begun to recover, and the forest of weed to grow up to provide that verdant under-water world without which fish cannot thrive.

There were odd days of trout fishing thrown in. I had one day in Mayfly week on the upper Colne, in the most ideal conditions. I caught six trout in an afternoon and evening, which is a good basket on that difficult water. Once we had a day in Wychwood Forest, at the two ponds, with the ancient stone coping, which formed part of the domain of the great Lord Clarendon, where he planned to spend his last days in peace. A retirement that was cruelly denied him. On the lower pond there is a little island covered with trees. One tree hung out over the water, and under it a giant trout gently cruised. It was out of reach from the bank, and wading was impossible, and I had perforce to look at him and leave him. In the pond above I had a splendid fight with a one-pound trout, on 4x gut, battling to keep him out of the water lilies and the weeds and the rushes. Such an evening was as good as a whole week of leave spent in any other way. One blazing hot day my mother and I spent beside the Colne at Fairford, while I tried to tempt a highly sophisticated trout to take. I hooked one and lost it, and we were drugged with five hours of brilliant sunlight as we walked home through the buttercups to the car.

Only once did trout fishing come my way in the course of duty. That was when I was doing an air liaison job at Odiham airfield. A kind friend invited me to fish the White Water, and as it was only a mile from the airfield I got down on many an evening in the very early spring. I could not get the fish to touch a dry fly. They were taking nothing but nymphs. I would see a big trout, showing a triangle of slowly moving tail as he nosed about with his head down. I cut down dry flies, to try and make convincing nymphs of them, but without success.

One day I met a brigadier on the bank. He was having an afternoon's fishing at my hostess's invitation. I saw him go up the bank to start fishing, and I met him in the evening when he returned. His net was full. There were four fish in it, and one of them was a pike. I looked at the pike and I looked at the brigadier. No pike ever yet took a dry fly.

The brigadier plainly did not like being looked at reproachfully by captains. He detached his line and held up the fly. It was a two-and-a-half inch salmon fly. "The fish are there to be caught," he said in a voice which did not invite argument from his juniors in the Service. Why they should take a salmon fly in a clear bright spring day, I do not know, but I must confess I followed the brigadier's example and with a salmon fly caught several trout, the biggest being one and a half pounds.

These interludes with the rod and the gun were infinitely refreshing in that long weary waiting period of the early 1940's, when all hopes that the enemy might be internally disrupted had long disappeared, and there was the certainty that he could only be overthrown by a titanic battle, and that battle seemed to come no closer. Those interludes opened one's eyes to that other cycle of life which went on unperturbed by man, where rivers gently gurgled round the weed beds, and big chub lying in the shadow of the hawthorn bushes made slow rings at the evening hatch of fly. The rest of the universe might be torn with strife and hate. But blackbirds nested every year, and fat cock pheasants strutted warily out into the stubble in the gloaming. It was a reminder of that enduring world that was there centuries before the men of strife were born, and would be there centuries after they were dust.

33

Mediterranean War

JUNE of 1943 was very hot. As we sailed south to Gibraltar the heat intensified. The Bay of Biscay was, happily, calm. Nearly everyone was on deck when a submarine attacked the convoy. The destroyers dashed hither and thither like hunting dogs, and the smooth, blue surface erupted in great fountains of foam from the depth charges which made the hulls of the troopships shudder at each explosion.

It was in warm, velvety darkness when we went past Gibraltar, with the lights of the Portuguese fishing boats all round us. Farmers from Ontario, with only England for comparison, stared at the painted blue of the Mediterranean and pointed at the rolling dolphins, until these sights and scenes became too stale to remark.

The afternoon of D-Minus-One found us rolling and pitching in a gale off Malta. As darkness fell the sea began to subside. Slowly we approached the shore of Sicily. A lighthouse was winking from the unseen coastline. The darkness was a deep mauve. Men blackened their faces with cork and fondled their weapons. Then, after seemingly hours of darkness, we came to a halt.

The sun was not full up before that golden strip of sand was crowded with men and anti-aircraft guns; then vehicle after vehicle bumped ashore, and the battle for Sicily had begun.

It is a merciful dispensation that the human mind is so made that one remembers what is pleasant in detail, but what is unpleasant loses its clarity. There were miles and miles of dusty road trodden by feet that became increasingly sore. White dust like flour rose from the boots of marching men and the tracks of tanks, and, added to the burning sun, produced a degree of thirst such as men from well-watered Ontario had never before known. The sun shone down like an inverted blowtorch on

301

that landscape of rock and dusty stubble and bare pastures. Thus the luxury of a halt at evening was something never to be forgotten: the weight taken off tired sore feet, a bar of chocolate, and a drink from a water-bottle which had been lowered into the cool depths of the stone well. For the rest, one vivid scene merges into another in that riverless-country, seemingly devoid of wild life and scorched by the July sun: dust erupting from the shell bursts, and weapons almost too hot to touch; marching up for a night attack, and the moonlight that turned the olive trees to silver, amidst the soothing smell of the night dew on hot dust.

In every Hell there must be the vision of a Heaven. To those sturdy men of Ontario it was the little wooden farmhouse, the smell of rain among the trees, and the buzzing of bees in the quietness of summer. To me it was the smell of wet moorland, and the mist on Peeblesshire hills, and the view from Elsfield.

On a day of rest between battles, we occupied a beautiful house standing among its own grove of olives. On the hillside behind it were two hoopoes, and, from the short grass rose a covey of partridges. They were the first birds that I saw in Sicily. The partridges were a link with a happier world. The steel blue sky and the hilltops shimmering in the heat seemed for the first time to be related to the rest of the globe.

I saw only one more bird—it was five days later, when I was wounded. We were in the hills, and the rising sun found us on a low ridge. The firing seemed to come from all round us. The mortar bombs exploded on the ridge in a steady shattering sequence. Machine-gun bullets came from so many angles it seemed hopeless to find their point of origin and deal with the marksmen who sped them; but everything seems difficult when you have lost a good deal of blood. There was a small olive tree over my head, and suddenly on the lower branch there was a redstart. It did not seem alarmed. It turned round on the twig on which it was perched to get a better look at its surroundings. A small, beautiful spark of innocent life on this ridge that reeked and reverberated with the fury of man. When I recovered consciousness again, the redstart had gone.

It was still and pleasant in the hospital in North Africa after the clamour of battle and the bumping of jeeps and ambulances and the long flight in the hospital 'plane.

The Canadian Convalescent Camp was high on the dunes above the sea east of Philippeville in Algeria. It was wonderful bathing, though we had to take care about the undertow which ran hard when there was a swell. When the day was calm I could look down at my feet on the sandy bottom and see strange fish swim past them. I made a fish spear of a very primitive kind, which was merely a nail on the end of a short pole. It was fun stalking the fish, but I never got one.

Frank Hersey was my chief companion. He was a major in the Signals. Some years before he had taken part in the chase of that strange moronic ruffian in North Western Canada who became known as "The Mad Trapper". The trapper must have been an astonishingly fine shot. They had followed his trail for many hundreds of miles, and he had accounted for several of his pursuers. Then they followed him into the high country, and his trail led up a snowy valley which was a cul-de-sac. There in front of them, with his pack on his back, was the man they sought. He had started to climb the steep, snowy ridge when Frank fired. The bullet hit the pack on his back, and the force of it knocked the trapper from his foothold. He picked himself up and turned on his pursuers, just as Frank started to squeeze his trigger a second time. He never fired. The trapper put his right hand to the rifle on his back, and, as he brought it down on the open palm of his left, it seemed to Frank to go off at the moment of impact. There was no more that Frank could do— he was lying on his back with the trapper's bullet through his chest. Then the trapper fell to the rifles of the others.

Frank and I had many pleasant afternoons together watching the sea beating on that golden beach.

Then came the journey to Italy where our troops had landed and were already fighting. I rejoined my battalion near Canossa. The details of the pilgrimage of the penitent king to the Pope at Canossa, had been one of the few questions I had been able to answer satisfactorily in the history paper at Oxford. But there was not much to see as our Bren-gun carriers rattled past it two days afterwards.

Autumn was in the air now and the nights were cooler. Cold rain fell with cloudburst force and we shivered in our summer kit of khaki drill. The first frost came as we fought our way over the ranges of hills to Campobasso. The sun was warm at midday, but the evenings were chill. Fewer and fewer troops tried to bathe in the pools of the mountain streams. Sometimes it rained for days at a time, and a Scotch mist would close down on the higher tops.

Beyond Campobasso runs the River Biferno. There are trout in it, and good ones. This I know, because four of them floated up after a German 88 mm. shell fell in a pool close to us as we crossed.

The rain fell steadily, and the ragged oak woods dripped round the mountain village which we occupied for a week. Slit trenches filled to the brim, and, in spite of the ceaseless shelling, men preferred the danger of the open ground to crouching in cold water and comparative security. We were relieved at midnight after seven or eight days' vigil in that sordid huddle of hovels. Our last elements were only getting clear as the first beam of pale light showed on the horizon.

Once down at the foot of the hill, we climbed the slope of the next ridge. We were dog weary. In the shelter of a tiny haystack, beside a cottage, a covey of partridges rose at our feet and went away in front of us resting on their wings. The tired, soaking infantrymen cheered up at the sight. A leaden silence gave way to a buzz of cheerful conversation, and a pleasant speculation on the good sleep and the good meals they were going to have in the week of rest which we were being allotted. There is great peace of mind in being a countryman.

The battalion was quartered in a substantial village which we rendered reasonably clean. and after a few days I left them for hospital again.

After that it was a different aspect of war. The Medical Board found me unfit to return to the line and I was posted to the Headquarters of the Eighth Army as a Liaison Officer. The Army commander lived with a very small staff at his Tactical Headquarters. It was a Nissen hut surrounded by caravans. We stayed there until the beginning of April. With Hugh Rose,

who was on a few days' leave from the Scots' Guards, I cast a
fly in the milky waters of the Sangro without result. The next
day an Italian farmer appeared with several trout to sell us. He
said he had caught them in his hat—or that is what we understood him to say.

That was a winter of shivering desolation. The rain and lowering clouds, and mud, stripped that magic country of all its
enchantment. It became again small, dirty and sordid. Only
one thing looked clean and that was the white snow-covered
peak of the mountain of Maiella, rising out of the jumble of
hills on the other side of the valley. The Army was stuck fast,
but spring was approaching and with it the plan for the delayed
offensive. The Eighth Army Headquarters moved quietly and
unobtrusively, and its main Headquarters came to rest in the
valley of the Volturno River. Tactical Headquarters was at the
foot of a steep rocky hill on a little plain of rounded stones,
out of which grew a ragged wood of olive trees. We were ten
miles, as the crow flies, from where the Cassino Monastery,
which had for so many centuries been a beacon of Christianity,
was being ground to rubble by falling bombs and incessant
shelling.

And then quite suddenly winter gave way to spring. In a
week the mud had turned to dust, and a blessed sun warmed
our faces and shone blinding white on the hills that were still
capped with snow. The world came to life again, and a few
birds began to sing.

34

Year of Reckoning

LONG spells in hospital had cured my various specific ailments, but they left me with a slender reserve of strength. While the Plan went forward for a great advance, General Oliver Leese sent me off in his aeroplane for a week's leave in Cairo. Here I had two splendid days of duck-shooting, as the guest of the Killearns. The latter was on that magnificent shoot which belonged to the British Embassy, and which is situated close to the battlefield of Tel-el-Kebir. I was loaned a gun, so short in the stock, that I was in doubt as to whether to put it to my shoulder or use it as a pistol. I compromised by padding my shoulder with a rolled up scarf. But even after I had made every possible adjustment, the little Arab boys could only find twenty duck to pick up when the sun had reached its zenith, and the morning flight was over. My host on the left, who had had rather more shooting, had 171.

That crisp desert sunshine drove out the accumulated chill and depression of an Italian winter. When I returned to Eighth Army Headquarters, the Italian summer had arrived. Our Headquarters had moved and was now in a little olive grove, far enough back from the road to Cassino to avoid the dust of the traffic, and a few miles to the south of Monastery Hill. The preparations went on. The roads were covered with a pall of white dust, and there was the incessant rumble of wheels and tractors, as the day of the great assault came nearer. When the day came there was nothing more to be done, for all the plans had been laid and none of them could be altered.

As dusk fell that evening, our eyes were on our watches as their hands slowly moved on to the time of the barrage. All was perfectly still except for the nightingales who sang almost as a choir. Then came the long awaited moment. Several hundred gun position officers, at the same split second shouted ,"Fire," and the Italian night was rent by winking flashes from sea to sea. The nightingales sang the louder.

All the world knows what happened then. History had never before seen an army made up of twenty-six nations banded together to prevent a tyrant from becoming master of the world. Cassino fell to the second desperate onslaught of the Poles. The French Equatorial Corps broke through on their front. Down the flat Liri Valley which lay dreaming in heat haze, surged the British, the Canadians and the South Africans. To the west the Americans forged forward with Rome as their target.

Day after day the limpid early morning air turned to heat and haze and dust and noise and on the army went. Rome fell on June 4th, and the Eighth Army passing through, crossing the Tiber, sped north to harass the withdrawing enemy before they could reorganize, and then, at Lake Trasimene, two days of thunderstorm slowed the gallop to a walk. The wary and able German commander, Kesselring, reorganized his force and deployed them across the waist of the peninsula.

We were encamped on the edge of an oak wood south of Trasimene when General Smuts appeared. The thundering rain beat on our mess tent, and trickles of water gradually encroached from under the flaps to make a lake on the floor. We sat with our elbows on the table, and listened to the wisdom of that quiet, placid voice. He seemed a being without generation, untrammelled by time or age. Forty-four years before he had fired five shots at a trooper of the Rand Mounted Rifles, from the back of a galloping horse. He was shooting from the saddle at the three British troopers who lay face downwards on their horses grinding them with their spurs, to force the last ounce of effort from them. It had been a long chase, about ten miles, which had ended within shot of the British pickets, and Smuts and his ragged comrades had wheeled and disappeared into the veld again. The trooper whom Smuts had covered five times never forgot an item of that mad adventure. He would sometimes relate it with a curious relish. He was my father.

After General Smuts's visit, the thunder had washed the skies clean and we were forging ahead once more. Trasimene was like a great emerald in front of us. There was the battle for

Arezzo, and the advance which culminated in my old battalion lining the south banks of the Arno in Florence, while the Germans defended the other. Sunburned Ontario farmers lay on their faces, and aligned their sights on anything that moved in the ancient beauty of the streets across the little river.

Then began one of those games of "general post", so intricate in their organization and carrying out. The Canadians moved over to the Adriatic coast to face the Gothic Line. The night of the initial attack, Winston Churchill was our guest. He wore a large topee, the uniform jacket of a Lieutenant-Colonel of the 4th Hussars and a pair of nondescript trousers. The sight of him, to the infantry, was worth reinforcements of several divisions. He was with difficulty prevented from crossing the river with the leading troops, but next day when the battle was at its hottest he drove in a car right up to the firing line, and placidly watched sweating mortarmen assemble their weapons to engage the enemy, fiercely resisting, not many hundred yards away.

Looking at the map we had only to surmount the top of the ridge, and the broken country beyond, to find ourselves on the Lombardy Plain, neatly covered with square grids of road, seemingly a paradise for rapid movement. The first autumn storm came and lashed the country with rain and bent the olive trees with its force. After that, we had many a fine day, but the days of blinding heat were over. Cattolica fell, and Rimini, and we were in sight of the plains.

The rain fell on the victorious army in a steady pitiless deluge, and rained away our hopes. The vineyard soil clung to the feet of the infantry and made each step an effort. The drainage ditches between the vineyards flooded to a depth which a man could cross only by swimming. Tanks were immovable, and so the army settled down for another static winter, with the line pushed forward into the plains. The ancient city of Ravenna, the last home of the dwindling Roman Emperors, was the buttress of our right flank on the sea.

Ravenna had its compensations. The flooded land was the resort of duck. There is a pine wood that runs parallel to the sea for several miles and is a quarter of a mile in width. There are marshes on both sides of it which hold snipe, and it is a good place for woodcock. I got hold of an old Belgian hammer shotgun and acquired 500 cartridges from a gun-maker in Florence, at the cost of about fivepence each. They were dust shot. Several of my brother officers had guns, and we made many sorties into the pinewood or along the edge of the floods. Once, with two friends, I walked into a minefield, inflamed by the sight of vast quantities of duck on the mere beyond. We withdrew, walking like three Agags, and clutching our bag, which was one teal.

We fell in with a band of partisans with whom we had some uproarious expeditions. The war had moved several miles on, when I first visited the farmhouse that acted as their Headquarters. Every man was armed to the teeth, and rifles leaned against the walls, while their owners wore their cartridge belts, to say nothing of knives and pistols as well, and sat round a table in the middle of the kitchen playing an Italian version of Happy Families. A roaring fire in the big kitchen fireplace heated the room like a furnace, and the air was filled with a delectable smell of cooking, as their womenfolk roasted teal and woodcock on spits in front of it. A small girl sat in the corner intent on a book. It was an Italian translation of the *Water Babies*.

We had several expeditions together, and as many as ten partisans would lay aside their rifles and shoulder ancient shotguns. We sometimes walked the pinewood for woodcock, and there were roars of laughter when we missed, as we usually did. Sometimes we would walk the swamp on the landward side, and the snipe would curl back over the pine wood making splendid shots.

They were cheerful people, and their theatrical flamboyance was very lovable. We had many happy days in their company, We generally brought back something for the Mess, if it was only a snipe or two, or a woodcock or a brace of teal. But it was a breath of home to hunt these familiar birds again.

One cold foggy afternoon I spent in a barrel, sunk in the midst of a large mere. The partisan, who had guided me to it, was carrying a sack on his back. He extracted from it a live mallard which he proceeded to anchor beside me. The mallard shook itself and quacked good-humouredly. It did not succeed in attracting any of its kind. Coots flew backwards and forwards in and out of the clammy fog, but of duck there was no sign. They came at last, just after dusk. There must have been thousands, for the steady roar of the wing-beats never slackened for minutes on end. But we could not see them against the night sky, and came home empty-handed.

There was a large marsh where I often wandered alone. It reminded me of Otmoor with its little pools, its forests of reeds, and occasional clumps of tall bulrushes. On a fine evening, the slanting sun would sometimes turn the swamp waters to gold, and it was a pleasant place to wander and muse, trudging through the grass and rushes, until the rasping squeak of a snipe brought my gun to my shoulder, and myself back to my surroundings.

It was dark by the time I would reach the farmhouse, where I had left the jeep. Trudging along, under the night sky, I could hear the whistle of widgeon high above, and smell the smell that all marshes have the world over. By candle light the farmer and I would drink a glass of his own red wine before the long, cold drive back to Headquarters.

The pine wood and those marshes, and my companions of the hunt are the only pleasant memories of an otherwise terrible winter, the last of the war.

Others beside myself have memories of that long dark shapely strip of woodland. A Liberal elder statesman told me that the only day's hunting that he had ever had in his life was in that wood. In the course of a walk there he had sighted, pursued and captured a tortoise, which he had brought back alive to amuse his children in London, which it survived to do for several years and was christened Dante. Let it be said at once that he did not stress the pursuit, or the capture of the tortoise, as a feat of the chase, but rather the sighting of it. Byron too, had walked in that wood, and it had sheltered Garibaldi from his pursuers.

It was a bitter cold winter, and at one time the temperature fell to zero and remained there for days on end. Bombs had burst the embankments of the rivers which drained the plain and had turned much of it into an inland sea. The troops stamped cold feet in the slit trenches, and anything that was warm and dry was high luxury.

The winter months dragged slowly past, and then in February the Canadian Corps was withdrawn, and ordered to Holland. I drove down to Naples, staying the night in Florence, and another night in Rome on the way. Early in the morning I said good-bye to Tommy Waitt, my batman, at the airfield outside Naples. He was to come over with the main body and join me in north-west Europe. That night I was drinking a glass of port in the Travellers' Club in London.

I had a pleasant two weeks' leave at Elsfield. It had been a long absence, and it was peaceful to hear the rooks cawing in the elms, and see the little platforms of twigs appearing as they started to build new nests. My brother Billy was there. He had been serving as a fighter pilot in Ceylon and India. He was still alive by an amazing stroke of good fortune, having fallen, almost unconscious from his fighter plane, from a great height into dense forest in Ceylon.

Together we walked in the fields and woods. In a field at the top of the village was an ugly black smear on the pasture. A Liberator bomber, deserted by its crew and blazing like a torch, had passed low over the roofs of the village to crash in flaming smithereens. It had greatly affrighted our old gardener and his wife, as it swept low over their roof, lighting the whole firmament with its flames. They were very old, and the wife's grandfather had fought at Waterloo, as not a particularly young man. They thought that it was the Day of Judgment.

The reckoning was getting pretty close now. Hitler had lashed out with his massive counter-attack in the Ardennes during the winter but the toils were closing in on him.

It was winter weather everywhere when I joined the Canadian Headquarters at Nimeguen. Italy had taken a powerful hold on us. The neat little Dutch villages, with shiny tiles and modern bricks, were a strange contrast to the sultry Mediterranean sun on ancient walls. The surrender was coming, but we were still to lose many valuable lives before it came. The Rhine was crossed at Arnhem, and we pushed steadily forward down the broad roads lined with tall beeches. Here and there a dwarfish castle or a small manor house, looking like the setting of an old master, reminded us that this country had its history too.

Then came the surrender. What had begun on September 3rd, 1939, came to an end with steady rain pattering down on us in a pine wood near Appledorn. It seemed a curious anti-climax. The war ended for us upon a strangely human note. All the trucks, and all the equipment, and all the thousands of men, who had been gathered together to destroy and destroy until victory was achieved, were now devoted to bringing back life to a starving and gallant people. Day after day the shuttles of transport went backwards and forwards carrying food—not ammunition. Little by little the Dutch administration was rebuilt and gradually the country came to life again. There was the great task of taking the surrender of the German Army, and setting the columns of un-armed men marching to their destinations. Next, the great pile of arms had to be gathered together and destroyed. But as the people of Holland took over more and more of their own affairs so there was less and less to do, and bit by bit our Army was re-patriated.

Children are wont to muse on all the different places in the world that they would like to visit. It is not confined to children. An abiding interest in birds had always given me a special wish to visit two places in Europe. One was the Camargue, and the other Texel, in the Friesian Islands, which were referred to so frequently in all my bird books. I have never had an opportunity of visiting the Camargue, but the tide of war bore me to Texel in the course of duty.

A large number of Russian prisoners had been impressed into the German Army. As the war neared its end, they realized that they must give some striking manifest of their loyalty to their own country's cause. The German force, in which they were serving, was defending Texel Island. In the course of a night they slew all but a few of their German comrades. It was a night as grim as St. Bartholomew's Eve.

The Germans reacted violently. Troops, guns and tanks were landed on Texel, from the mainland. The Russians fought with great heroism, but their numbers were reduced by a half. And now the war was over, and they were still in German uniforms, and faced with return to their native land. The Germans against whom they had been fighting had been removed, and they were left in sole possession of the island. Somebody had to parley with them, and the job fell to me. It was not a very easy parley, for many of them, to show their independence, would fire their rifles up in the air, and not always upwards. But in the end an agreement was worked out by which, if they laid down their arms, they would be conveyed to the nearest Russian authority, who was a Russian liaison officer in Wilhelmshaven, in Germany. I was to go with them, to explain to the Russian authorities that they had been forced into the German Army against their will, but had since struck a valiant blow against their country's enemy. In short, I was to testify that the colour of their uniforms was not their fault, and that they deserved well of their own people.

I went with three other Canadian officers in a motor-boat from Den Helder to Texel. It was going to be a hot day and the morning sun was shining and sparkling on the waves. A good-sized vessel, the Texel ferry-boat, was lying in the little harbour. The Russians were lined up on the quay with their weapons. After a great deal of delay, and further parley, we persuaded them to embark not many minutes before the falling tide would have stranded the ferry. They enlivened the short trip to Den Helder by throwing potato-masher grenades overboard, and occasionally firing their weapons.

On the quay at Den Helder, a trim company of Princess Patricia's Canadian Light Infantry were awaiting us. After the Russians had surrendered their weapons, we conducted an intensive search and removed nine more automatic pistols concealed in various folds of their garments.

The whole of that long summer's day, our convoy of trucks wound along the roads. The guards were relieved at two points, farther on, by companies of other Canadian regiments. It was nearly dark when we reached our destination, and we parleyed with a Russian colonel with one eye and, apparently, the basic minimum of human intellect. I handed over to him a document, signed by our Canadian general, attesting to the feats of arms of these men on the Allied side. The chief of Texel Russians told me that he was perfectly satisfied that everything reasonable had been done, and that his country would receive him and his comrades back to the fold. He thanked me warmly for my help, and I shook hands with his officers. I was told afterwards that these unfortunate people were butchered to a man.

I had had another opportunity of seeing the shores of Texel, from the sea, in the course of a day's trip in a German E-boat with a somewhat sullen German naval crew, from Den Helder to Terschelling, when I had gone with one or two brother officers to look at the German fighter control installation, which was in a series of chambers dug down under the sand dunes on that island.

By now most of the urgent tasks were finished, and a brother officer, Bernard Neary, and I, got a chance to explore Texel. As an island, it is flat with a rampart of sand dunes on the North Sea side. A charming little village is its capital, and there are one or two other small villages. The fields are divided by little walls of turf and dotted with little thatched farmhouses. It is to the eastern end that the great nesting grounds lie.

Bernard and I put up for the night in a small inn in Den Bourg, which is the little capital. Outside the inn was a space where they held their little sheep market once every so often. On the other side was the tall tower of an old church. From the top of the tower we could see all over the island, and back across the straits to the flat lands of the mainland. We found a guide next day, or rather we chose one, from the many who offered their services. We went south first of all, on his advice, and took the jeep to the edge of the rampart of sand dunes. Then we clambered up past the minefields. Camouflage nets were flapping in the sea breeze over the deserted gun positions.

There were Montague's harriers in abundance, floating backwards and forwards athwart the sea breeze. All birds of the hawk family have a hunting territory, and I have never seen so many of that family in so small an area. In the midst of a mine-field we were pointed out a place where the spoonbills nest, and through field-glasses we could see one or two of these tall, white, ungainly birds pottering, occasionally halting to probe for food. It was too hot to do anything strenuous. We returned to the jeep, and drove slowly with our guide towards the north-eastern end of the island.

We stopped and ate our sandwiches beside a small Luftwaffe aerodrome. Peering inside we saw what must have been the Officers' Mess. There were five eighteenth-century Delft tiles set in concrete above the fireplace. They are now in Bernard's house in Canada.

We meandered on with our guide, and left the car beside a little farm, just short of a tall grassy sea wall. Already we were conscious of the distant clamour of birds. We clambered up on to the grassy ridge of the dyke, and saw stretching out on the seaward side a salient of sand and shingle, covered in patches with the rough growth of such herbage as likes salt water. It was a big salient covering many acres, and over it wheeled and flashed sea birds beyond counting. Their cries made a continuous accompaniment. Our guide pointed to the seaward edge and there we could just discern a tiny little cube, planted close to the edge of the tide, which he informed us was a tent. We made our way along the top of the dyke. An avocet flew past us slowly against the breeze, not twenty yards away, its strange shaped beak opening and shutting as it called.

Once down off the dyke we found the going muddy; we took off our boots and hung them round our necks, and rolled up our battledress trousers to our knees. We were headed for the tent. At every step we took, more birds seemed to rise and wheel and scream at us. We had to put our feet down with care to avoid treading on the eggs of gulls and terns. Occasionally a fluffy, ungainly, young bird would waddle away in front of us. We neared the edge of the rippling tide. Standing 100 yards from the tent on the edge of the water were six spoonbills, tall and gauche, and they took flight and moved out beyond our vision, looking like herons of purest white.

There was a convulsion in the tent as we neared it and a man emerged. He looked at us and smiled. He had a pleasant, brown, wrinkled face, but though he smiled he looked old and worn. This was the climax of our good fortune, for it was none other than Nols Binsbergen, the great Dutch ornithologist, whose home was on Texel and who had recently returned after suffering cruelly at the hands of the Germans. There were the rarest birds in my bird books, wheeling before us, and we had a master of his art to interpret them. He spoke little English, but our guide helped us to converse. He had been photographing an Arctic tern at its nest, and motioned Bernard and me to get into his little tent while he and our guide withdrew. The tent was not made to accommodate two large men. We had to compromise in the end by putting our feet outside. Although we were hunched like monkeys, we bulged the canvas sides.

The terns' nest was perhaps four feet from the openings through which we looked. In half a minute the mother bird was back, and seemed quite unconcerned by our toes which looked like twenty grubby pebbles protruding from beneath the tent. We sat for a while and watched her fascinated. Then the afternoon began to draw on, and we emerged by the simple process of lifting the tent over our heads, and joined our guide and the great naturalist.

I have a bird book which has a chapter, and only too sadly long a chapter, on "rare, vanishing and lost British birds". And here in this sunlit island we were seeing so many of those birds which were common enough in Britain in our grandfathers' time. There was the spoonbill and the avocet, the Montague's harrier, the marsh harrier, and the hen harrier as well. This was the land of the bittern and the black-necked sclavonian grebe, the ruff and the black-winged stilt, and the rare small birds of the marsh; birds whose appearance in England would be kept a close secret if seen by a discreet observer, and whose whereabouts would be trumpeted to the newspapers by an indiscreet one. We wandered back, as evening fell, to the farmhouse where we had left our jeep. The farmer's wife told us that an American bomber had crashed near there, a year or so before, and she had hidden two of the crew. The Germans had found them and led them away. She gave me a piece of paper with their names scrawled on it. I put it in my pocket. Unfortunately it got wet and the names became indecipherable.

We accompanied Nols Binsbergen to his little house. He lived very poorly, but plainly very happily, surrounded by his birds, perhaps unconscious that he had an international reputation. He showed us box after box of the finest bird photographs on which I ever set eyes. He asked us if we would like to take some as a present. I took six of them which I greatly treasure. Four of them I have never seen equalled in bird photography, one is of an avocet and another of a black-winged stilt, each with its chicks, the third is of a black tern alighting on its nest, and the fourth is of a ruff in all his glory.

We left him when night fell and returned to the little inn, and next day sailed away to Den Helder and the easy routine of post-war soldiering. Nols Binsbergen died not long afterwards, worn out by the hardships he had endured at the hands of the Nazis. But he died among his beloved birds.

Texel is a strange little island, and much history attaches to it. It is the only place where a fleet has ever been captured by a charge of cavalry, as happened when the Dutch fleet were frozen in the ice between Den Helder and Texel in the wars of long ago. In the beautiful church of the hamlet of Den Hoorn, the villagers assembled to pray for the fortune of the Dutch expedition up the Medway, whose marked success seriously embarrassed King Charles' Government. It has heard the crash of the British cannon when we sparred with Holland for pre-eminence in the sea power in the world. And it had seen war by land, and air, in plenty, over the previous five years.

If you go there now you can see such a paradise of birds as the northern hemisphere can show you in few other places. You see the birds that the marshes of Lincolnshire and Norfolk must have held two generations ago, before the egg collector and the collector who slays rare birds for the money, and, worst of all, the oaf who kills the unfamiliar bird to get a better look at it, had had a chance of annihilating them.

Epilogue

IN August I presented myself with the necessary documents at a camp in Surrey, strangely enough called Tweedsmuir Camp. A sergeant clerk, behind a deal table, handed me a piece of grey paper, which stated that I had served in the Canadian Army and had been honourably discharged. I spent the night in the pleasant Victorian quietness of the Travellers' Club, realizing that I had no more right, and that there was no more reason, to wear my uniform with the neat brass shoulder badges which spelt the word—Canada.

It wasn't easy to say exactly to what one did belong now. I pondered on that as I hung up my uniform and changed into old clothes at Elsfield, in the afternoon of the following day. They were very old clothes, for I had worn them as an undergraduate. I went outside. Oxfordshire was in its August torpor. It was hot and sultry, but the sky was overcast. It was an afternoon of absolute stillness. Somewhere a wood pigeon murmured, and rooks cawed, unseen. I halted in an aimless walk to look down over the view. The sloping lawn, once so trim, was a riot of grass, knee high, and most of the paths were overgrown. The whole world seemed to be a jungle of untidy green though the field, at the bottom of the lawn, that had been cut for hay, was as a kempt and shaven rectangle. It was twenty-six years almost to the day since we had come to Elsfield. We had made something of a mark on it. For there on the right hand of the lawn was the tall yew hedge that my father had planted the year before the great drought of 1921, and replanted, the year after, because of it. In the Crow Wood on the left, the curtains of green leaf on the tall chestnuts and elms rose up to foreshorten the sky. They contrasted with the copper beech that he had planted in the year that I went to Oxford. Now his tree was nearly twenty feet high, and looked like a russet ballet dancer, its head nearly level with where the century old stems around it disappeared behind their billows of foliage. Trees take their time. Generations of humans come and go during their lives.

The little rounded grove of oaks at the bottom of the hay field was planted for Queen Victoria's Diamond Jubilee. The oaks in the leafy oblongs of Long Wood and Little Wood, away and beyond on the right, would have been growing at the time of Waterloo. The tall trees in the Crow Wood were there when Prince Charlie turned back at Derby. Over in Pond Close was a stubby giant of an oak. Cromwell's soldiers may well have sheltered beneath it, when Pond Close was his gun park for the siege of Oxford. I wandered on with aimless steps. There seemed to be no future, only a past. The stable yard seemed very quiet, and there were weeds growing among the cobbles. It was hard to open most of the doors. They creaked and resisted from disuse. There was a rank smell of dust and cobwebs within. It was a long time since there had been hawks or horses there. It was a long time since we had set off on hawking and shooting parties, I and all my friends. So many of those friends had gone. They had ridden their fast horses on into the gathering autumn mists, too far ahead to hear their laughter. It was left to us to plod after them on foot. How lucky we were to have known them. Already the stonemasons and engravers were at work, cutting out their names in college chapels and village halls. Glib men had told us that for the last six years we had been fighting to make it a better world. We had not. We had been fighting to prevent it from becoming a far worse one. That is a struggle as old as time. It is the never-ending fighting for freedom.

There were steps on the cobbles of the yard. It was Jack Allam, with his black dogs at his heels. His weather-beaten face lit up, and his dog beamed. Although it was a sultry day he was, as always, wearing his thickest clothes. Although it was not the shooting season, he had his gun in the crook of his left arm. "Been a long time," he said, for he has always economized in the use of words. "Yes, it's been a long time, Jack." "Good job it's all over." He alone in the village had been bereaved by the war. Then he pondered for a while and, sentence by sentence, gave me the news. As he talked there came again the feeling that there was a future. The dredger had spoiled the fishing in the Cherwell, but the chub would come back when the weeds came back in a few years time. The Italian prisoners-of-war had snared all the rabbits and most of the pheasants, but that would get better when they went away. The squirrels were threatening to eat all the hazel nuts, and he patted his gun to explain its purpose. It looked as if there were going to be a lot of acorns this year. Now that was interesting as it only happens once in every decade or so, in that part of the world. For the rest of the time the blight strips the bloom off the oaks, and you will hardly find an acorn anywhere. It was good news about the acorns. Here was something of the future. Oaks do not grow big in these clay woodlands, but they grow extremely fast and are ripe for the axe in as short a time as eighty years. In two months time the acorns would shower down. The few pheasants would gobble them pompously. The wood pigeons would be at them, and the squirrels. But many would take root and struggle up, in spite of the blackthorn and the rabbits, and become timber. "Got to be getting along now," said Jack. "Going to be a fine day to-morrow." And he was off with his dog padding at his heels, not noticeably more bent than when we had come to Elsfield twenty-six years ago. We had called him "Old Jack" even then. That brought the world back to life. Jack had to be getting along. A countryman cannot live in the past, it takes him all his time to keep up with the seasons, for nothing grows that hasn't been planted. I had to stir myself and be getting along too.

Jack was right. It would be a fine day to-morrow. Whenever to-morrow was going to be.